The History of the Port of London

The History of the Port of London

A Vast Emporium of All Nations

Peter Stone

Maps created by Nick Buxey

PEN & SWORD
HISTORY

First published in Great Britain in 2017 by
Pen & Sword History
an imprint of
Pen & Sword Books Ltd
47 Church Street
Barnsley
South Yorkshire
S70 2AS

Some parts of this book first appeared on the website
www.thehistoryoflondon.co.uk

ISBN 978 1 47386 037 7

The right of Peter Stone to be identified as the Author of this Work has
been asserted by him in accordance with the Copyright, Designs and
Patents Act 1988.

A CIP catalogue record for this book is available from the British Library

Typeset in Ehrhardt by Mac Style Ltd, Bridlington, East Yorkshire

Printed and bound in Malta by Gutenberg Press Ltd.

Pen & Sword Books Ltd incorporates the imprints of Pen & Sword
Archaeology, Atlas, Aviation, Battleground, Discovery, Family History,
History, Maritime, Military, Naval, Politics, Railways, Select, Transport,
True Crime, Fiction, Frontline Books, Leo Cooper, Praetorian Press,
Seaforth Publishing and Wharncliffe.

For a complete list of Pen & Sword titles please contact
PEN & SWORD BOOKS LIMITED
47 Church Street, Barnsley, South Yorkshire, S70 2AS, England
E-mail: enquiries@pen-and-sword.co.uk
Website: www.pen-and-sword.co.uk

Contents

Acknowledgements

With special thanks to Olwen Maynard and Ursula Jeffries who have done sterling work in reading through drafts of this book and challenging my facts, grammar and spelling. Mike Paterson of London Historians, Roger Williams (author of *London's Lost Global Giant* amongst other books), Stephen Freeth (archivist at the Vintners' Company and formerly Keeper of Manuscripts at the Guildhall Library), Geoff Marshall (author of *London's Docklands – An Illustrated Guide*) and Chris Ellmers (President of the Docklands History Group, author of several books on the Port of London and a founder of the Museum of London Docklands) all read through and commented on certain chapters. Without these people this book would have contained numerous bloopers that have since been eradicated. Thanks also to Kate Bohdanowicz, whose idea it was that I should write a book and who introduced me to the publisher. During the course of researching, my knowledge of the Port of London has been greatly enhanced by the many talks I have attended at the Museum of Docklands, organized by the Docklands History Group. Chris Ellmers and Edward Sargent of the DHG have been particularly helpful. Numerous members of the aforementioned London Historians group have also encouraged me and spurred me on. Others who have contributed in their own way include Martin Garside and Samantha Broome at the Port of London Authority, who provided much useful information; Perry Glading, COO of the Port of Tilbury, who kindly answered my many questions with enthusiasm and obvious expertise, and his assistant Joanne Stroud for making arrangements and sourcing materials; and the helpful staff at: the British Library; the Guildhall Library; Tower Hamlets Local History Library at Bancroft Road, Mile End; the Museum of London; and the People's History Museum, Manchester.

Finally, I salute the many authors and historians who have gone before and thus provided me with invaluable source-material. Without their efforts my volume would not have been possible. You will find their work listed in the bibliography at the end of the book.

The quotation from Flora Tristan's *Promenades dans Londres* was kindly translated from French to English by Ursula Jeffries.

The quotation from Julius Caesar was kindly translated from the Latin by Leonardo de Arrizabalaga y Prado.

The quotation by Gustav Milne is taken from his book *The Port of Medieval London* and used with his permission.

The quotation by L. Granade is taken from the book *The Singularities of London, 1578*, published by the London Topographical Society and used with the permission of the Society.

The quotation from Edward Sargent is taken from a talk he gave to the Docklands History Group, April 2016, and used with his permission.

All photographs and illustrations within the book are from the author's collection unless otherwise stated.

I sincerely apologise if I have unknowingly used any material without permission that is still within copyright.

This book is dedicated to my father, William 'Doug' Stone, who unwittingly first introduced me to London's docks, but passed away during the writing and is greatly missed. Also to my mother, Lily Stone, whose stories about growing up in wartime Stepney and Limehouse have inspired me to study London's history, particularly the East End.

Preface

The ancient London Bridge had stood on the same foundations since the end of the thirteenth century. After years of patching, making-do and deliberation, in July 1823 an Act of Parliament was finally passed for the City of London Corporation to replace it with a completely new crossing. On 15 June 1825 a ceremony was held in which John Garratt, Lord Mayor of London, laid the foundation stone for the new structure. In the stone's cavity was carved an inscription that explained why the old bridge was being replaced. It was a time of 'universal peace', claimed the text's author, with 'the British Empire flourishing in glory, wealth, population, and domestic union'. The 'Metropolis has been daily advancing in elegance and splendour.' Echoing an eighth century description of London, it described the city as a 'vast emporium of all nations'.

The nation's wealth was being driven by a major empire and trading network that spanned the globe, while at home the Industrial Revolution created new methods of production. London was the Empire's economic capital, the 'workshop of the world' as it was described during the Great Exhibition of 1851, and at the heart of the vast emporium was the Port of London. Raw materials and foodstuffs arrived and manufactured goods were dispatched. The docks and wharves were also a hub – an entrepôt – through which cargoes passed on their journey from one part of the world to another. London became a rare example of being both a port and capital city.

Since Roman times the city's raison d'être had been the Thames. The town had been founded where Roman troops could most easily cross the river, but the small settlement soon grew into a trading port where seagoing ships would arrive from Gaul and beyond. The port became so busy and congested that in the early eighteenth century the writer Daniel Defoe claimed to have counted two thousand sailing ships at one time. For centuries, goods were loaded and unloaded at riverside wharves, but twenty years before Lord Mayor Garratt was laying the foundation stone, a series of major new docks had been created on the east side of the metropolis, the first step to expanding the port into what would become the largest in the world.

London became a trading place and finance centre because it was a port. And because it was all of those things it was, until the Second World War, Britain's greatest manufacturing base. Without the port, London could never have developed into the great city it became. In the latter part of the nineteenth century the writer Walter Thornbury gave the opinion: 'In no single spot of London, not even at the Bank, could so vivid an impression of the vast wealth of England be obtained as at the Docks.'

Until the nineteenth century Londoners and visitors to the city would, like Defoe, witness a sea of sailing masts all along the river, from London Bridge down to Woolwich and beyond. The French social activist Flora Tristan made four visits to London between 1826 and 1839, following which she published her observations in *Promenades dans Londres*. Of the river and docks she wrote: '... these countless boats, ships and vessels of every size and type which mile after mile cover the surface of the river and reduce it to the slender width of a canal ... the docks, huge warehouses and stores take up 28 acres of land; these domes, bell-towers, buildings strangely transformed by clouds of vapour and these monumental chimneys which hurl their black smoke into the sky and proclaim the presence of the great factories.' The protagonist of George Borrow's *Lavengro*, published in 1851, looked downriver from London Bridge.

There I stood, just above the principal arch, looking through the balustrade at the scene that presented itself – and such a scene! Towards the left bank of the river, a forest of masts, thick and close, as far as the eye could reach; spacious wharfs, surmounted with gigantic edifices; and, far away, Caesar's Castle, with its White Tower. To the right, another forest of masts, and a maze of buildings, from which, here and there, shot up to the sky chimneys taller than Cleopatra's Needle, vomiting forth huge wreaths of that black smoke which forms the canopy – occasionally a gorgeous one – of the more than Babel city.

From the first decade of that century those masts were increasingly hidden behind the high walls and guarded gates of the enclosed docks. The walls were deliberately high to cut the basins off from the outside world and protect the valuable contents within. Thereafter few people other than dockers, merchants, seamen, lightermen, customs officials and those with business within were aware of the great docks on which the city's economy depended, despite their vast size. As the travel writer Robert Byron wrote in London Transport's guide *Imperial Pilgrimage*, published in 1937 for visitors who flocked to the capital for the coronation of George VI, the port 'engage[s] one-third of the whole trade of the United Kingdom … Yet many visitors to London, and many Londoners too, are unaware that London has a port at all.'

There was another good reason why Londoners were unaware of the great maritime commerce on their doorstep: the riverscape may have had character but it was grimy, and industrial, so not somewhere for the casual visitor or tourist to linger. Virginia Woolf wrote of the riverside warehouses below Greenwich in the 1930s: 'They huddle on land that has become flat and slimy mud. The same air of decrepitude and of being run up provisionally stamps them all.' Some of the older Georgian and Victorian buildings had a functional attractiveness and dignity about them yet over the years had become blackened by London's sooty atmosphere, some of which belched out from the stacks of the coal-fired Thames-side electricity-generating stations. The docks and wharves were each created for their individual commercial benefit, often with little thought for aesthetic beauty. Before the upper port closed, the river itself was given over to mercantile purpose: muddy and oily and unattractive.

Of course, beauty could be found, or at least imagined. The American-born artist James McNeill Abbott Whistler, a contemporary and friend of that other great painter of the Thames, Claude Monet, had an affinity with London's Victorian riverside. His etchings of Rotherhithe, Limehouse and the Pool of London, drawn in 1871, are a fascinating and evocative record of the busy working port in the days when many of the vessels were still under sail. His most famous Thames work, *Wapping*, is a vibrant and colourful oil-painting from a decade earlier, when he was not yet 30 years of age. It was actually set at the *Angel* pub at Bermondsey, on the south bank of the river as it loops from the Upper Pool downstream to Limehouse. Its main focus seems to be the three characters at a table in the foreground, appearing very much as two sailors and a prostitute (although in fact Whistler's lover, a fellow artist and a sailor) in an ambiguous pose. Yet what really catches the eye, and gives the painting its title, is the hectic scene behind them, of ships' masts and rigging, of Thames sailing barges, lighters, a steam boat, men unloading coal, and the Wapping warehouses on the opposite bank. 'You can see the whole Thames!' he wrote enthusiastically of the painting to his friend Henri Fantin-Latour in Paris.

At the beginning of the twentieth century London was the greatest port in the world. The docks and wharves reached their maximum size and volume of goods in the 1930s and, despite severe difficulties due to enemy bombing during the Second World War, reached another peak in the early 1960s. At its height the Port comprised seven major dock groups, with enclosed water space of 700 acres, 36 miles of quays, and hundreds of acres of warehouse and transit areas, together with large numbers of independently-owned riverside wharves.

We are fortunate that in the same year that London Transport published its *Imperial Pilgrimage*, the Port of London Authority had the idea of commissioning a photographer, whose name is sadly lost in the mists of time, to capture the entire length of both banks of the river, from the Upper Pool at London Bridge down to Greenwich and the Isle of Dogs. That magnificent panoramic set of photographs, now in the care of the Museum of London, shows the true higgledy-piggledy nature of the pre-war river just before it was bombed to near-extinction. In some frames we see great and majestic warehouses rising up from the river; while, in another, humble and Lilliputian workers' dwellings stand beside the entrance to Millwall Dock. Over the years the PLA commissioned a number of films that promoted the Port, not least of which is the magnificent *City of Ships*, a half-hour documentary filmed in 1939. It was the first of two films about the Port made by the acclaimed documentary director Basil Wright. The film can be viewed online and I recommend watching when you reach the 'Port of London Authority' chapter of this book. Sadly, a year after the film was shot, much of the Port would be destroyed in the Blitz. So vital was the Port to the nation that if Hitler had achieved his aim of destroying it there may have been a different outcome to the Second World War.

During the Great War of 1914–18, the dock union leader John Burns, speaking to a Canadian and an American, exclaimed: 'Your St Lawrence is just *water* and your Mississippi plain *mud*, but the Thames is *liquid history*!' In 1960, at a time when it was reaching its peak of cargo-handling, the writer Arthur Bryant, in his celebration of the Port, *Liquid History*, wrote: 'What Venice was to the commerce of the medieval Mediterranean, grey, smoky London and her river are to the ocean trade of our age.' Describing the 211 dockside cranes of the Royal Docks at North Woolwich he gave the opinion that 'the sight of them at work is one of the wonders of the modern world'.

So rapid were the changes to the methods by which cargo moved around the world that Bryant could not have imagined that just a decade later some of the historic docks of his modern Venice were being demolished and filled in. Ships became too large to navigate as far as the upper docks and wharves and air travel had replaced journeys by passenger liner. Cargo-handling in the twenty-first century has moved downstream and liners have been replaced by cruise ships, which regularly bring tourists to the city. It remains a busy port but, located in unpopulated sections of the river to the east, continues to remain unknown to almost all Londoners.

My own personal connection with the docks is slight, I must admit. Some of my ancestors, going back generations, worked as watermen on the river, one of whom in the early nineteenth century was a winner of the Doggett's Coat & Badge Race, in which apprentice watermen have competed every year since 1715. As a child I often visited my maternal grandmother at her home at Limehouse in the East End, unaware of the still busy docks close by and of the rich maritime history of the area. My grandfather spent his whole working life based at Hermitage Wharf at Wapping. My mother was a young girl when she would spend the day in the cab of her father's truck during the war years, collecting wine that had been unloaded from Spanish or Portuguese ships and making deliveries into the City or further afield. For some years my father's business was based in the centre of the Isle of Dogs until it relocated to make way for the new Docklands development. As a young teenager, I made a number of trips around the dock areas, earning pocket money as a van-boy delivering groceries to workers' cafés that must have once bustled with dockers but by then were rather quiet and forlorn. Little did I know in my youthful ignorance that those vast docks were under sentence of death and about to be closed, ending a century and a half of London's history.

I have vague memories – or is it a trick of my imagination? – of waiting for swing-bridges to close as a vessel passed through between docks, of ships' funnels dotted around the landscape, and of the occasional blast from a ship's horn. But without doubt I can recall arriving for the first time at Wapping High Street. What a strange place it then seemed, consisting of only tall, imposing Victorian riverside warehouses linked by overhead walkways, and a few pubs. Where were all the retail stores, bustling with shoppers, that you would find on any other high street in Britain at that time?

A favourite film of mine is the British movie *The Long Good Friday*. Set in the late 1970s it catapulted the actor Bob Hoskins to fame as the East End gangster Harold Shand. His crime headquarters is a luxury motor cruiser moored amongst the transit sheds of the derelict West India Docks from where he plans, in partnership with the American mafia, the redevelopment of Dockland as London's answer to Manhattan. The scheme ultimately falls apart but life imitated art and forty years later Shand's celluloid vision is there for all to see.

In July 1763 James Boswell took a boat from London to Greenwich together with his mentor, Dr Samuel Johnson; '… to Billingsgate, where we took oars, and moved slowly along the silver Thames,' he later wrote. 'It was a very fine day. We were entertained by the immense number and variety of ships that were lying at anchor and with the beautiful country on each side of the river.' The great London working docks and wharves have come and gone since then, transformed and replaced by shining offices, houses and modern apartments, a large exhibition centre and even an airport. Gone too are the big cargo ships that lined the miles of quays. The bustle of the lighters and tugboats that constantly moved up and down the river has been replaced with river cruisers, tourist launches and party boats. Whereas the bascules of Tower Bridge once lifted regularly for merchant ships, they now rise only for tall-masted yachts and a few other visiting vessels. London is a city that has evolved and transformed itself over many centuries. Its commerce is now largely based on service industries. The busy, mercantile port has reinvented itself accordingly, to provide a vibrant vista, with booming finance and tourism industries. According to the Port of London Authority in their 2016 Annual Report, the tidal Thames accounts for 140,000 river-related jobs. It is a different world since Virginia Woolf, describing the commercial Thames in 1931, stated: 'there are no pleasure boats on the river.' Today Old Father Thames is once again a scenic part of London's landscape.

Author Millicent Rose wrote of her studies of the East End: 'The material discovered has proved so rich that a book begun with confidence is finished with a feeling of inadequacy.' I echo her statement with regard to this book I lay before you. There are so many facets and complexities to the Port of London – its history, topography, the finances, the people, its working practices and the continuous change – that it is simply impossible to incorporate everything into one volume. Over the centuries vast numbers of men – though only a few women – carried out myriad tasks, many perhaps spending their whole working life in a particular job or for one company. To do justice to that aspect of the port would in itself require an entire book. Here I have attempted to include, within the space available, what I consider to be the key topics regarding the development of the commercial port but there is much, much more that can be written (and has been written) on this boundless subject.

Peter Stone,
London 2016

Chapter One

The Romans and Early Saxons

At the end of the last Ice Age the world warmed and the glaciers melted. Large volumes of water flowed from Britain, south and east, through what is now the London area, which at times would have been completely submerged by a very wide river. The rising water level formed the English Channel, separating Britain from the Continent. The wide, slow-moving Thames deposited gravel at its edges. As it narrowed and became smaller over thousands of years, its gravel-depositing edges moved inwards in an ever-lower series of terraced banks, and thus the youngest layers lie closest to the current banks of the river and the oldest further away on the valley sides. Many rivers and streams flow into the Thames from the higher ground to the north and south and erosion from those during the past 50,000 years created the many valleys around which London was later built.

In 54 BC Julius Caesar led his army across the Channel to Britain to subdue the native Catuvellaunian tribe. Yet having beaten them back he decided there were more pressing issues and swiftly returned to Gaul. Back in Rome, he later recorded his campaign against the British 'whose territories a river called the Thames separates from the maritime states at about eighty miles from the sea'. We therefore have the earliest record of the river, written long before the establishment of the city through which it now flows.

Tiberius, a strong military leader, secured the Roman Empire's northern Continental borders. After his death the nobles who controlled the Senate in Rome became tired of their new young Emperor Caligula's pleasure-seeking and longed for imperial glories such as the legendary exploits of Julius Caesar ninety years earlier. Caligula thus attempted an invasion of Britain in 40 AD but his troops, assembled at Boulogne, had other ideas, and it seems they threatened to mutiny. Britain, to the ordinary soldier, was a mysterious place at the far edge of the world, where boats carried the souls of their dead crews. The British were to be left alone for another three years.

Following the assassination of Caligula, his uncle, Emperor Claudius, felt the need to spread and reduce the power of the armed forces by sending 40,000 soldiers to the mysterious island, so the Romans finally arrived and conquered Britain. It took Commander Aulus Plautius and his troops a short while to actually find any Britons with which to engage but once located they were pursued across the Thames. Having taken the south-east corner of Britain, Plautius set up a 'marching camp', probably on the north bank of the river at Cornhill, waiting for the Emperor to arrive with reinforcements. Claudius came with a large reserve force, together with elephants (according to a later Roman account) that no doubt gave the natives a huge fright. The imperial army moved on to the main Catuvellaunian stronghold at Colchester, which the Romans took without too much difficulty. Claudius received oaths of loyalty there from eleven tribal kings and then returned home after just sixteen days, leaving his troops to set up the capital of the new Province of Britannia.

For the Emperor and so many troops to reach Colchester, as well as maintain supply lines back to Gaul, a bridge was required across the Thames. The first crossing was most likely a temporary pontoon structure put in place by army engineers. The Romans found the best location was just downriver from where the Thames was joined by the River Fleet. The banks of the Thames were quite marshy and the chosen site probably the most easterly, or downriver, point at which the river was sufficiently narrow, with solid land on either side.

When the Romans arrived, what is now central London was an area of small hills surrounded by marshy land that was often flooded by the incoming tides. The Thames was then the border between different warring tribes. The wider London hinterland, with its poor clay soil, remained forested and largely unpopulated, being far from each of the main tribal capitals. The thick forests and marshes on each bank made the river a natural barrier between the different groups of people that lived to its north and south but also a better means of transport and trade than overland.

Despite there being surprisingly little contemporary written evidence of the Roman city of Londinium, much has been pieced together by historians. There was a great deal of uniformity across the Empire, which allows an understanding of Londinium through discoveries made elsewhere. More locally, the remains of a Roman ship were discovered on the Thames in 1910 and two more in 1958 and 1962. After the Second World War many of the buildings in the City of London, particularly along the riverfront, were redeveloped and this gave the opportunity to delve below, before the replacement buildings were constructed. In the early 1970s a systematic programme of archaeology started and discoveries began to be made. Gradually, piece by piece, an understanding of the Roman Port of London emerged. Similarly, the existence of the Saxon town of Lundenwic was only revealed following excavations at Jubilee Market at Covent Garden in 1985.

The foundation and growth of Londinium

As the Romans established a new provincial capital at Colchester their forces moved northwards to continue the advance through Britain. In order to hold the areas they had conquered, one of their first priorities was to build well-engineered roads so that troops could move swiftly and have a means of supply. By the time they arrived in Britain the Romans were masters of rapidly building good roads and in the first years of occupation they constructed a network in the south east of Britain, partly based on native tracks that existed before their arrival.

A number of those roads connected at points to the north and south of the Thames bridge. The original temporary military crossing was probably soon replaced by a more permanent structure, thought to be located in line with the modern Fish Street Hill, slightly downstream of the current bridge. Such an important point required a military guard and a certain amount of management to supervise traffic and make repairs, so a small settlement was established on Cornhill. It soon became clear that a larger presence, formally constituted, was required on the site. The decision to build the new town of Londinium on the north side of the bridge was taken in around 47 AD and building works started the following year. A commercial district of shops and workshops evolved along the *Via Decumana*, the modern-day Cheapside. It quickly grew into a busy conurbation, home to people from all parts of the Empire but probably mostly from Gaul. The population increased rapidly and by 60 AD it is estimated to have been in the region of ten to twenty thousand people.

Londinium enjoyed a favourable location. A long navigable tideway brought vessels fifty miles from the North Sea, providing relatively easy access from Continental Europe. There was fresh water, fish stocks, and rich agricultural land further upriver. The first town lasted for little more than a decade before being destroyed and reduced to ash during Queen Boudicca's rebellion. It had by then become an important and strategic place so had to be restored. Its destruction gave the Romans the opportunity to rebuild on a grander scale. During that same period a decision was taken that Londinium should become the capital of Britannia in place of Colchester. In the latter first century a vast basilica, the administrative centre, was constructed. Various government and public buildings were established, many in Kentish ragstone brought up the Thames by boat from a quarry near the River Medway. By the end of the century Londinium was beginning to look like the type of Roman town we would usually imagine. At some time between 85 and 90 AD a new bridge was built over the Thames, constructed of wood. The city continued to evolve and expand in the second century, particularly at the time of the visit of Emperor Hadrian in 122. Many public buildings were rebuilt for the occasion, including the amphitheatre, and a forum (marketplace) was created adjoining the basilica.

At some point during the period between 190 and 210 a semi-circular wall was constructed around the land-facing sides of Londinium. It was a massive undertaking, requiring around 1,300 barge-loads of ragstone from the Medway. It was not put up in haste, probably taking around two years to construct, and did not protect the vulnerable riverside, indicating that the city was not under immediate threat of attack. The existence of the wall thereafter created a barrier to further outward expansion of Londinium, which remained the case until the Middle Ages.

Initially many of the town's daily requirements were imported but as time went on workshops were established to produce goods for the resident population. The remains of mills, slaughter houses, and a glassworks have been discovered as well as many tools for metal-working, carpentry, engineering, building and shipping. Britain was a major source of wool and it is most likely that the city was a centre of textile and leather industries.

The staple food of Roman times was cereals and bread, which depended on the seasonal harvests. Occasionally riots occurred in various parts of the Empire when availability was scarce and prices high, so each town arranged warehouses where grain could be stored in plentiful years. Londinium had the disadvantage of being surrounded by poor farmland so grain had to be transported lengthy distances, much of it arriving at the Thames quays by boat from Buckinghamshire, Oxfordshire and along the River Lea.

Fish was plentiful and could be caught in the river and estuary. Varieties included herring, cod, sprat, eel, carp and bass. Oysters were a staple diet of both the wealthy and working people. The largest oyster beds in Britain were in the Thames Estuary and the shellfish were either brought upriver live in barrels of sea-water or pickled and stored. Fish and shellfish were usually eaten with *garum*, a sauce made by boiling down whole fish until it became a paste, after which it could be stored in jars and sold in shops. A factory where it was made seems to have operated close to the Londinium waterfront. British oysters were exported to other parts of the Empire and their shells have been found in excavations of Rome. Salt was brought to Londinium from inland mines or by boat from around the coast, particularly from Essex where it was extracted from water using pans.

By the third century the population of Londinium is estimated to have been at least 50,000 and perhaps as much as a 100,000 people, a number that would not be achieved again until the fourteenth century.

The port of Londinium

Even before Londinium had been established, the invading army created a supply base at Richborough in Kent, north of modern-day Sandwich, which in those days was a natural harbour. Its closeness to the coast of Gaul ensured that Richborough continued as a port throughout the Roman period, particularly for larger vessels from southern Europe. From the first until the late third centuries it was, along with Dover and Boulogne, a base of the *Classis Britannica*, the division of the Roman navy entrusted with the security of the English Channel.

Roman ships generally only sailed to Britain in the calmer weather of the summer months. The open sea was avoided whenever possible, with ships hugging the Continental coast until able to take the shortest possible route across the Channel. Goods from the Mediterranean were generally shipped to Britain via the inland Rhône-Rhine route, rather than around the more exposed Iberian Peninsula, and transhipped at Domburg in the Netherlands. From there the sea journey from the Rhine estuary to Londinium was around thirty-six hours so, with turn-around time, a ship could make three or more voyages each fortnight. An alternative route, particularly for goods originating in central Gaul, was along the Rhône and Loire rivers and up the west coast of Gaul.

Navigating up the Thames from the North Sea was always slow and difficult for sailing ships. First they had to negotiate the many sandbanks along the north and south shores of the Estuary, then wait for incoming tides to sweep them up to Londinium. The prevailing wind is more often westerly than from the east and thus the going could be slow as the crew tacked their way upstream along the winding river. It was therefore more convenient for goods arriving on larger vessels to be reloaded onto smaller vessels at

Richborough. From there they were brought up the Thames to Londinium or transported by road.

In the first decade or two of the settlement of Londinium boats, were most likely berthed on a sloping prepared beach. The first attempts at establishing a harbour were probably not made until the rebuilding of the town following the Boudicca rebellion. In around 62 AD new timber quays and warehouses were constructed, perhaps at the same time as a new bridge. They included a landing stage for small vessels, parallel to the bank. The work was almost certainly a public, not private, initiative and probably undertaken or supervised by military engineers. To the west of the bridge the waterfront buildings seem to have been residential whereas those to the east formed commercial wharves. Quayside warehouses of timber may have been constructed in the first century and later replaced by others built in stone.

By the end of the first century the original quays and landing stage had been replaced. In those times the Thames was much wider than today, possibly as much as one kilometre across at Londinium, with marshy islands on the south bank that became submerged by high tides. The quays were built out into the river, gradually advancing the waterfront terrace by around fifty metres in various stages of development between the first and third centuries. This advancement would have provided berthing in deeper water for larger vessels.

Initially Londinium probably acted as a supply hub for Roman Britannia, with goods and equipment passing through for the military campaign and the first wave of Roman occupiers. As Londinium grew, other towns were also established, with over forty Roman coastal harbours known to have existed to which goods could be shipped. Food, manufactured goods and luxury items continued to be imported into the capital from all parts of the Empire but by the early second century produce arriving was simply to meet the daily needs of the city and its immediate hinterland. The harbour was to remain relatively small compared with the great ports of Portus and Ostia that served Rome.

Many goods landed at Londinium came from northern and central Gaul, the Rhine ports and Bordeaux, but there were also some from Spain and Mediterranean harbours and North Africa. Certainly sculptures, bronzes, household goods and foodstuffs that have been unearthed in Londinium were of Italian, Spanish or Mediterranean origin. Olive oil for cooking and lighting came from Spain, wine from Gaul, the Rhine and Moselle areas, Italy and Spain. Other imports included textiles, silk, linen, quernstones (millstones),

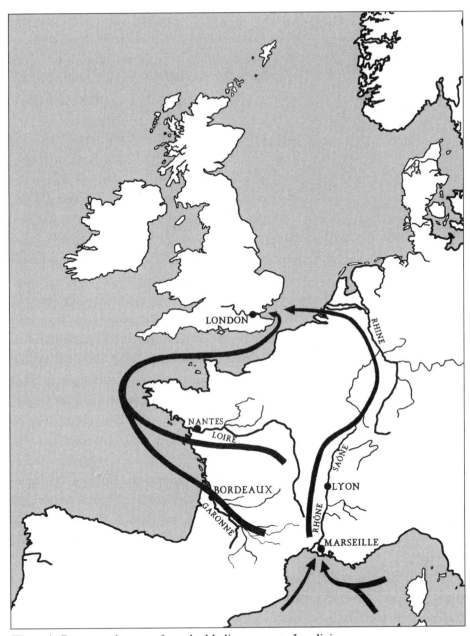

The main Roman trade routes from the Mediterranean to Londinium.

timber, pottery, samian crockery, glassware, lamps, jewellery, fish, fruit, honey, grape-syrup and salt. *Garum* came from Gaul and Spain, at least until it was manufactured in Londinium. Most cargoes arriving from long distances would have been transhipped several times through the extensive Roman entrepôt network on their journey. Ragstone and other kinds of stone were quarried locally in Britain and shipped to Londinium by river or around the coast, as were locally produced ceramics and roofing slates in the second and third centuries. There is less information regarding exports from Londinium but they are known to include capes, rugs and lead ingots. Most likely other exports were wool, grain and slaves.

As is known from other parts of the Empire, goods were carried in sacks and barrels. Liquids, such as olive oil, were transported and stored in pottery storage vessels known as *amphoras* that could be stacked upright or horizontally. Unloading a Roman vessel was labour-intensive and, as it was seasonal work, probably required a casual workforce. It is possible that lifting mechanisms were used to unload larger items but there is so far little evidence. As boats arrived, some goods were probably sold directly to the public on the quayside while others were put into transit buildings or stored in warehouses.

Sea levels in the first century were about three to four metres lower than today. There is evidence that the Thames was then tidal perhaps as far upriver as Westminster, but may have gradually receded during the Roman period in one of the world's slow cycles of climate change. If that is the case, vessels could no longer be swept up as far as Londinium on an incoming tide. That would be a significant factor in the decline of the city in the late Roman period.

Roman ships

When Julius Caesar's fleet took part in a battle against the ships of the Veneti tribe of Brittany in 56 BC he noted how their vessels were better than his own for the conditions of the Atlantic coast. The Veneti ships had shallower keels that were more suited to tidal waters, solidly-built of oak, seams between planks caulked with moss, reeds or hazel shavings, with higher prows and sterns, and sails of leather that could withstand Atlantic storms. Thereafter Roman-era ships generally divided into either those of the Grecian/Roman tradition, suited to tideless Mediterranean conditions, or those for northern European seas based on Celtic designs. Goods arriving from the Mediterranean were generally transhipped several times throughout their journey, those ships arriving at Londinium would normally have been of the latter type.

Some Roman cargo ships are known to have carried loads of over 1,000 tons but it is unlikely that such large long-distance vessels ventured up the Thames. Those to be found in Londinium were more likely to be either smaller round-bottomed river and coastal boats, which were unable to beach at low tide and therefore anchored in mid-stream to load and unload, or flat-bottomed barges.

Importation and exportation was a precarious business, with large investment in the vessel and its cargo, financial risk and high reward. Much of the cost was raised in the form of syndicates of wealthy men who would not be ruined in the event of a ship being lost at sea. At first, cargo ships arriving were owned by traders from other parts of the Empire but there is evidence of later shipbuilding at Londinium, which indicates ownership by locally-based traders.

A typical Roman ship or barge was propelled by a single sail, mounted towards the front of the vessel. The centralized sternpost rudder had not yet been invented and thus direction was achieved by a large oar protruding from the right-hand side of the stern – the steer-board or 'starboard' side of the boat – or oar rudders on each side.

The decline of the Roman Empire

Roman civilisation reached its zenith during the mid-first century, at around the same time that Londinium was being established. While the city matured and grew on the western extremity of the Empire through the second and third centuries it was protected, and occasionally prospered, from troubles in Rome and elsewhere.

During the 170s victorious troops arriving back from battles in the east carried with them a plague that had a devastating effect on the Roman people. It wiped out about 5 million people, perhaps between 10 and 25 per cent of the entire population of the Empire. Garrison towns were particularly affected by the plague, leaving the Empire's border vulnerable. At around the same time, the Langobardians invaded from Northern Germany, causing a war that lasted for seventeen years, during which they captured areas as far south as northern Italy; the first time Italian soil had been occupied for three centuries. A peace treaty was signed in 181 and the border was restored along the line of the River Danube but it was clear to the northern barbarians from that time on that Rome was not invincible.

To the north of the Continental Empire new nations formed, with the Goths, Franks and Alamanni becoming a major threat in the third century. The Franks, based in the lower Rhineland areas, began making raids on the wealthy and vulnerable east coast of Britain and the Thames estuary, while inland agricultural areas prospered and large mansions were built. People of wealth abandoned the coasts of East Anglia, the Thames Estuary, Kent, the south and the Severn Estuary, where they were vulnerable from raids by the Franks or Irish. A significant factor was the disbanding of the *Classis Britannica* fleet in the late third century. Long-distance voyages in and out of Londinium were unlikely to have been affected but coastal shipping was probably in greater danger. By the mid-third century the population of Londinium had reduced, as had the amount of imports arriving. As Londinium declined in importance and fewer ships arrived and departed, the timber quays and jetties along the river began to decay, probably from around 250 AD. Riverside warehouses were converted for residential use as trade diminished.

Londinium went into a long, slow decline during the fourth century. It had become successful partly because it was the most convenient port from which to trade with the Rhineland and near Continent. As the Roman armies lost control of the northern Continental areas it became safer to ship goods to and from Boulogne to the ports on the south coast of Britain. By the end of the fourth century Venta Belgarum (Winchester) overtook Londinium as Britain's leading commercial centre.

When the east coast of Britannia came under attack from Germanic raiders a riverside wall was built to complete the enclosure of Londinium. Unlike the first three sides, the riverside section was certainly erected in haste and with far less care taken in its construction, using whatever materials were to hand. We can therefore be sure that it was constructed when the city was under immediate threat of attack. With the town almost cut off from the river by the wall, the timber quays had largely been dismantled by the fourth century. Despite its defensive wall, Londinium was overrun in 367 by an alliance of Picts, Irish, Franks and Saxons and had to be retaken by Roman forces.

In the early fifth century Visigoths invaded the Italian peninsula. Rome no longer had the ability to defend Britannia and the province became independent from what remained of the Empire. The population of southern England had been shifting more to the West Country and Londinium gradually dwindled until, at the end of the fifth century, it was most probably largely deserted. For a period of time life continued in Britain as it had done previously, with the Romano-British choosing their own leaders and prospering. In order to repel attacks by Picts from the north they enlisted Saxon men from the area around the mouth of the River Elbe in what is now northern Germany, as well as Jutes and Angles. The Romano-British began to squabble amongst themselves, however. During the first half of the fifth century the immigrant fighters rebelled against their Romano-British paymasters, slaughtering many of their leaders in about 459. In the following decades England was gradually divided into a number of tribal kingdoms.

The Saxon port of Lundenwic

When Londinium was abandoned, the Thames and its tributaries continued to be used for carrying and communication. The early Saxons were seafarers and did not possess the knowledge of how to maintain roads to a Roman standard. Yet they also initially lacked the skills to build sophisticated ships, and even their largest vessels were designed to be pulled up onto a beach.

Saxons began to berth their boats at low tide on the sloping foreshore two miles to the west of the deserted Londinium, where the river suddenly swings southwards in a large curve near the modern-day Charing Cross station. A new community known as Lundenwic began to grow there from the mid-seventh century. From a simple start of pulling boats onto the sloping bank, a market and trading port developed in the area of modern-day Covent Garden. 'Wic' was the Saxon word for market, indicating that Lundenwic developed for the purpose of trading, and is still remembered in the modern street name of Aldwych ('old market'). At the early stages in the life of the community there was no need for shops, stalls, warehouses or quays. Traders could arrive from along the river or around the coast, moor up and, as the tide went out, allow the boat to berth on the muddy bank, selling goods directly from the vessel. Evidence indicates that a planned town grew rapidly in the 670s, which would be during the reign of the Mercian king Wulfhere. From the late seventh century a wooden embankment was constructed along and out into the river, perhaps with jetties.

Many artefacts of the time have been discovered around Covent Garden and therefore the limits of the settlement of Lundenwic can be defined. The line of the north shore was about 100 metres south of, and roughly parallel to, the old Roman road that was still in use. (By the late twelfth century the road was known as the Strand, Germanic for bank or shore). Lundenwic stretched from there northwards to around where the street Shorts Gardens now runs. The east side was approximately along Kingsway, stretching westwards to Trafalgar Square, a distance of over a kilometre. Its centre is now the site of the Royal Opera House. Within that area a permanent community developed,

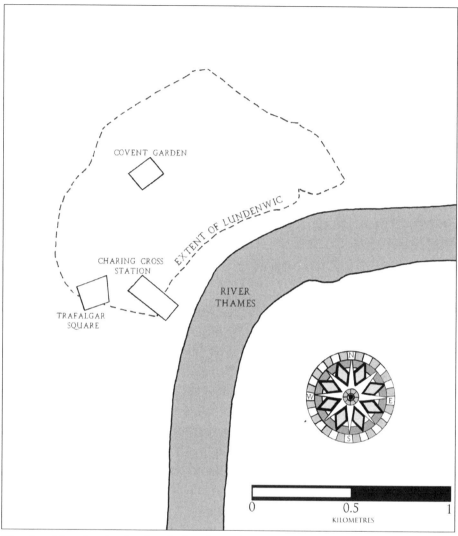

The site of Lundenwic, showing the locations of the modern-day Covent Garden, Trafalgar Square and Charing Cross Station.

living in small wooden homes. The population consisted of farmers and smallholders, fishermen, traders and craftsmen dealing in bone, antler, metal and cloth. On the town's fringes were gravel pits and horticulture, with some farms between Lundenwic and Thorney Island (modern Westminster) further along the river, including one at modern-day Downing Street. Northwards, towards the Roman road of Holborn/New Oxford Street, there was boggy ground.

The early Saxon period was an age when any form of transport other than boats was rare, with very few people owning a horse and cart. As a result, beach markets developed at locations along the river at Woolwich, Greenwich, Twickenham and Hampton Wick. Other port markets that developed around the same time included Sandwich, Hamwich (Southampton) and Gipeswic (Ipswich).

There is a written reference from around 672, in a grant by Frithuwold, sub-king of Surrey: 'by the port of London, where ships come to land, on the same river [the Thames] on the southern side of the public way [the Strand].' The historian Bede wrote in the early eighth century of a Frisian trader buying a Northumbrian slave at Lundenwic back in 679. In 731 he described London as 'an emporium of many nations who come to it by land and sea'.

Saxon period trading markets existed by royal charter, with revenue collected by port-reeves on behalf of the king or landowner in the form of tolls on boats that berthed to trade. Extant documents from around 680 state the trade regulations to be observed by the men of Kent when they bartered at Lundenwic. At that time King Hlothere of Kent appointed a royal official, or reeve, to administer local wics and by at least the 730s the kingdom of Kent was levying tolls on boats using the market of Lundenwic. A document dated 734 refers to 'the remission of all dues … which are exacted by the tax-gatherers in the port of London' and from that time the king gave the bishops of Rochester and Worcester and the abbess of Minster in Thanet the right to levy tolls on certain ships at the port.

The lack of exotic items found in excavations shows that during the early stages of the development of Lundenwic, from around 630 until the mid-eighth century, trade was quite local in its nature. Most goods brought to the beach market were perhaps produce from further along the river or nearby coastal villages. The inhabitants probably survived mainly on grain, meat, hay, timber and wool from the immediate hinterland. Local farmers visited the market from up and down the river to buy and sell produce, arriving in small punts that were dug out from the trunk of a tree, between two and four metres in length. They were sufficient to carry up to about four people or several animal carcasses and were propelled by a pole or paddle. Long distance traders arrived in ships made from oak planks of between 20 and 30 metres in length, powered by a sail and steered by an oar, probably of clinker construction. Excavated fishbones and shells include freshwater species, as well as marine varieties such as cod, haddock, herring, whiting, bass, plaice, flounder, whale and oysters.

Money was required in order to easily buy and sell goods. Seventh century gold coins known as *thrymsas* have been found at other places bearing the name 'LONDVNIV', showing that a mint had already been established. During the late eighth century silver penny coins were being minted for the Mercian kings bearing the name 'LUNDINIA'.

By the eighth century the population of Lundenwic had grown in size and goods were being traded with ports such as Gipeswic, Eorforwic (York) and Hamwic. The greatest international trade was with settlements around the mouth of the Rhine and the north-west coast of what is now France, and Lundenwic was frequented by Frisian and Frankish traders. Ships sailed to and from the ports of Dorestad (Wijk-bii-Duurstede in the Netherlands), Sliaswich (Schleswig in Germany), Quentovic (near Boulogne), and even as far as Norway. Wine, quernstones, pottery and luxury goods were imported

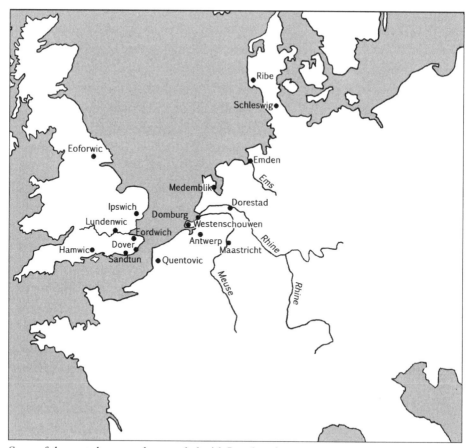

Some of the ports known to have traded with Lundenwic.

and ships returned with wool or cloth. Dried figs and grapes indicate trade with places even further afield.

Lundenwic was a relatively large community of perhaps six to seven thousand people by its heyday in the mid–eighth century, by then within the kingdom of Mercia on the border with Essex. Excavations show a settlement at that time of around sixty hectares, laid out in a grid pattern, similar to earlier Roman towns. Although never as large as the old Roman city, it was nevertheless probably the largest Saxon settlement in England. On several occasions, between 764 and 801, the town suffered from fires from which it may never have fully recovered. It went into decline during a period of unrest in the Carolingian kingdoms in France and Germany in the late eighth century, suffered from rivalry between the Saxon kingdoms of Wessex and Mercia, and the added threat of attack from Vikings from the early ninth century. Lundenwic, like its Roman predecessor, was thereafter abandoned by the Saxons, having flourished for less than a century.

Chapter Two

The Medieval Port

Alfred was already a battle-hardened young man when he succeeded his father to the throne of Wessex in 871 at the age of 21, having spent much of his teenage years fighting the Vikings on land and sea. Following his victory at the Battle of Edington in 878, the Viking forces, under their leader Guthrum, retreated eastwards. King Alfred began a policy of creating defensive 'burghs' (fortified towns) in the areas he controlled, which is the origin of the word 'borough' and of town names ending 'bury'. The following year Alfred and Guthrum reached an agreement that created a border between Wessex (in the south and south-west) and the Viking territory (to the north, north-east and east). It formally recognized the area west of the River Lea as belonging to Alfred and to the east as Guthrum's territory of Danelaw. Alfred re-founded the former Roman capital as 'Lundenburg', now a strategic border town. In constant danger of attack, it needed to be more defensible than the early-Saxon settlement of Lundenwic so the old walls and riverside quays of the former Londinium were rebuilt and repaired and, despite occasional Viking attacks during the following century, it once again began to thrive as a port.

The early-medieval Port

In order to revitalize London, Alfred granted sections of land – yokes – to important allies. Two charters dated 889 and 898 provided a yoke each to two of his closest advisors, Plegmund, Archbishop of Canterbury and Waerferth, Bishop of Worcester:

> Alfred, king, and others to Plegmund, archbishop, and to Christ Church, and to Wærferth, bishop, and the church of Worcester; grant of 2 yokes of land at Ætheredes hyd on the Thames. One to each.

The purpose was to create a point on the river within Lundenburg where vessels could land and a market could be held for goods to be bought and sold. The King collected tolls for boats arriving on the 'ripa emptoralis' (trading shore). By the time the Saxons once again began to populate the old walled city in the ninth century the former Roman timber quays and jetties would have long ago rotted away and they reverted to berthing their boats on sloping beaches. The location of Aethelredshithe (named after Alfred's son-in-law) was probably dictated by the lie of the Roman wall at that point and provided a convenient foreshore up onto which vessels could be pulled. Thus Aethelredshithe (renamed Queenhithe in later times) became the first part of the late-Saxon port of London.

By the tenth century two more 'common quays' had joined Aethelredshithe on the waterfront. The newly rebuilt London Bridge formed a barrier through which larger vessels coming upriver had difficulty passing and the response was the creation of new landing places at St Botolph's Wharf and Billingsgate. They probably each began as small, prepared beaches on which a boat could be berthed.

To travel downriver to the sea in the late ninth and early tenth centuries involved passing Viking Danelaw territory so trade tended to be with villages upriver rather than the east coast or overseas, but international trade gradually increased. The fourth law code of Ethelred II ('the Unready'), issued around 1000 AD, details the various berthing tolls at Billingsgate due to the monarch. A small boat was to pay a half penny and a larger 'keel' four pence. Tolls were payable on certain days of the week for those carrying cloth; a ship carrying planks paid one plank and tolls were set for boats arriving with fish. By then ships were arriving from the Continent and they are dealt with in the law code. Those from Rouen, Flanders, Ponthieu in Normandy, Huy, Liège and Nivelles in Flanders had specified tolls, whereas men of the Emperor – Germans – were to be treated as locals, except to additionally supply specified provisions to the king.

The town's importance as an international port continued to grow because of its proximity to the Continent and, in particular, being directly opposite the mouth of the Rhine, the gateway to the heart of Europe. Pottery, jewellery and other items of the late-Saxon period from the Continent have been found in London. There is further evidence in the form of coins of that period from Belgium, Normandy and Norway found along the Thames. In 1016 the Danish leader Cnut inherited the throne, uniting Wessex and Mercia as well as bringing an end to Viking hostility. During his reign England became part of a kingdom that included Denmark and Norway, thus stimulating trade with

Scandinavia and the Baltic. English coins unearthed in Continental towns during the eleventh and twelfth centuries indicate the spread of London's trade during those times. Many from the early part of that period have been found in Scandinavia. Later coins have been discovered throughout the Baltic coast, Germany, Normandy and Flanders.

The Walbrook stream flowed southwards through the centre of the city and in London's early history was possibly navigable for a short distance upstream from its confluence with the Thames. On the eastern side of that junction, a short distance above the bridge, foreign merchants set up their base, perhaps as early as the reign of King Edgar in the mid-tenth century. A landing place was created some time before the mid-eleventh century when the 'port of Duuegate' was referred to in a charter from Edward the Confessor. (In the late sixteenth century John Stow names it as 'Downgate' and in more recent times it has become known as 'Dowgate').

There is archaeological evidence, dating from the late tenth or early eleventh century, of a jetty extending into the river slightly downriver of London Bridge (the modern-day New Fresh Wharf). This would indicate the earliest example in medieval London of the development away from hauling vessels up onto a beach.

The Normans could be more confident in their safety and the ancient Roman riverside wall was not replaced as it was gradually undermined by the river. For them the greater priority was trade along the waterfront and the wall was an obstacle to the construction of warehouses and wharves. Where the wall had previously stood, a new street was created running parallel with the river, known today as Upper and Lower Thames Street. The sloping beaches used by the Saxons were gradually replaced by timber jetties and wharves at which ships could berth. The stretch downriver of the bridge where larger ships moored was already then known as 'the Pool of London'.

Roads throughout Europe deteriorated throughout the Middle Ages whereas water transport gradually developed. Former established major towns such as St Albans and Colchester, without a major river, would never again compete in importance with London. By the middle of the twelfth century the city, abandoned after the Roman occupation and re-established by Alfred the Great, was once again one of England's major towns, although not yet its capital. The rebuilt bridge formed a barrier past which the largest seagoing ships could not easily pass, creating an additional need to unload at London. The creation of new wharves by the Norman riverside landowners, as well as the ever-increasing size of ships arriving to unload, was turning London into a major port. Foreign merchants had established riverside bases for the importing and exporting of goods and London merchants had obtained charters from the monarchy that put them in a favourable position relative to other ports in England.

London Bridge

London Bridge, which was the only crossing over the Thames in the immediate London area until the construction of Westminster Bridge in 1750, was, and remains, the limit of navigation for larger vessels. At some point in time the last Roman bridge must have collapsed and for around 600 years thereafter the river could only be traversed by boat. It was during the late tenth century that a new wooden structure was built. Its purpose was probably as much to do with creating a barrier preventing the passage of invading Vikings as to provide a crossing. Perhaps it had a drawbridge to allow boats to pass upstream to the dock at Aethelredshithe.

The tenth century bridge was severely damaged by a flood in 1097, and again in the great fire of 1136, and was probably repaired enough that it could continue to be used. Between 1176 and 1209 a replacement was built slightly upstream to the west, in line with Fish Street Hill, in the position it occupied for the following 700 years. It was built under the supervision of a parish priest, Peter of St Mary Colechurch.

The foundations of the new stone bridge were constructed by ramming wooden stakes into the river bed and infilling with rubble. With 19 broad-pointed arches, ranging from 14 feet to 32 feet in width, it was for many years the longest stone bridge in England. It was 926 feet in length, 40 feet in width, and stood 60 feet above the water level. London Bridge became an impressive sight, the most magnificent such structure in Britain.

The bridge was erected on piers that in turn stood on starlings that protected the piers from the flow of the water. Set close together, the starlings formed a barrier to the incoming and outgoing tides, creating a weir effect that was a continuous force against the fabric of the bridge. Taking a boat through while the tide was flowing was described as 'shooting the bridge' and could be very dangerous. In his *Chronicle of London*, William Gregory describes an incident in about 1428:

The vij [7th] day of Novembyr the Duke of Northefolke wolde have rowed thoroughe the brygge of London, and hys barge was rentte agayne the arche of the sayde brygge, and there were drowned many men, the nombyr of xxx [30] personys and moo of gentylmen and goode yemen [yeomen].

A drawbridge between the sixth and seventh piers from the southern end could be raised twice each day, when the tide was high, to allow for the passage of ships. It was operated from a stone tower on its northern side, variously known as the 'Great Gate' or 'Traitor's Gate'. The drawbridge could also be raised as a defensive measure on the occasions that London came under attack by road from the south.

In the centre of the bridge was a chapel dedicated to Thomas Becket, a twelfth century parishioner of St Mary Colechurch, who had been canonized only three years before construction began. It was soon joined by shops with accommodation, something that was not unusual across medieval Europe. The bridge became an extension of the city and a busy and colourful commercial street as much as a river crossing. In 1460 the bridge wardens were receiving rents from around 130 properties. Over the centuries these structures were rebuilt as they decayed.

Since the Norman period, London Bridge (and then later other public bridges connecting to the City) has been maintained on behalf of the Corporation of London by the Bridge House Trust, which throughout the Middle Ages was located adjacent to the Southwark end of the bridge. Bridge House was headed by wardens who were initially appointed by the king, but later chosen annually by the City's Common Council. They were citizens of substance, often with interests in waterborne trade or riverside parishes. The Trust employed a full staff to maintain the bridge and collect rents and tolls and the senior officers comprised the Clerk of Works, Renter and (from 1496) the Comptroller. Others included the clerk of the drawbridge, numerous carpenters, masons and various labourers and servants. The bridge also owned several 'shoutes' (barges) in order to transport materials, with 'shutemen' to operate them. A substantial part of the income for maintaining the bridge came in the form of rents derived from numerous properties in the City and elsewhere, as well as the City's Stocks market.

In 1460 the toll for a ship to pass through the drawbridge was between one and two pennies. Three years later it had increased substantially to six pence.

Fewer vessels therefore passed through to dock there and the drawbridge seems to have been raised less frequently. It began to fall into decay and after 1476 no income was being received for the passage of boats because it was in such a poor state and dangerous to lift. In 1500 workmen were required to work night and day for the repairing of the 'full rynous drawbridge and thereof making sure to be drawen alle redye for the Kinges berkis [barques] to have hadde passage'. That seems to have been an exceptional occasion however, and thereafter any contemplation of raising the bridge was for defence rather than the passage of ships.

The twelfth and thirteenth centuries

In the eleventh century the size of seagoing ships increased so that boats were too large to beach, with loads too big to sell directly from the riverside. By the end of the twelfth century merchants in Northern Europe operated 'cogs', a high-sided, flat-bottomed vessel of around eighty-five tons. Thus wharves and warehouses began to be constructed on the riverside, owned and operated by land-based shipowners or middlemen. Many rules were introduced during the early twelfth century to regulate trade, merchants and ships' captains.

In Saxon times London's riverbank was a beach along which the town's population could access the water but during the Middle Ages it became a series of private wharves. The old Saxon streets continued to slope down to the river between each property, or were truncated by riverside steps or jetties, allowing the population to reach the water for their animals to drink, to draw water, make use of the public latrines, or hire a ferry.

Aethelredshithe was renamed 'Queenhithe' during the early twelfth century in honour of Queen Matilda, wife of Henry I, the name it still retains today. Later in the century King John gave it to his mother, Eleanor of Aquitaine, who made herself unpopular with those using it by the way she collected tolls. The Constable of the Tower was commanded by Henry III in 1224 to arrest ships from the Cinque Ports and compel them to land their corn only at Queenhithe. Two years later the constable was to confiscate all fish not landed there. Richard, Earl of Cornwall, leased it to the City Corporation in 1246 and they developed a market selling salt, fish and corn, collecting tolls from ships docking there. Other quays handled wine, hay, oysters, coal and wool.

The main docks and wharves were on the north bank of the river either side of the Walbrook, at Queenhithe, Vintry and from Dowgate downstream to Billingsgate. During the thirteenth century the axis of the port moved to below the bridge as Queenhithe diminished in importance. New wharves were constructed at Billingsgate, with large undercrofts for storage. The wharves and their successors on the north bank of the Pool of London below the bridge would continue as the heart of the port for the next 500 years, until the end of the eighteenth century. Imports were unloaded and exports loaded there and, when it became too congested, ships would moor in the middle of the river, with cargoes ferried to and from the shore by barge or lighter.

Tides and the general river level had begun to increase from around 700, and still continue to do so in modern times. River walls of the thirteenth century were about a metre higher than those of the Roman period. As early as the tenth century wharf owners began to expand their properties into the Thames by constructing new embankments. During the twelfth century the technology of revetments developed. Stout vertical planks were slotted into a timber base-plate with internal and external braces to form a vertical wall of between two and three metres high, infilled behind with stable muck and materials from London's rubbish dumps. Sections found in modern times by archaeologists show that it was common to reuse timber from broken-up ships to construct revetments and mooring posts.

As loads increased, ships were required to have higher sides, round bottoms and greater depth of water for berthing and therefore quays were built ever further into the river. Encroachment by individual property owners continued step by step, particularly between the twelfth century and the end of the fifteenth century, until a strip of land measuring between 25 and 150 metres had been reclaimed, greatly enlarging the size of the city. This reclamation, with lack of uniformity or alignment between properties, often had the effect of elongating properties southwards. Upstream of the bridge some were industrial operations, with one example at Swan Lane being a large dye-house, a factory for colouring textiles, which was possibly one of a group of cloth-finishing establishments.

During the reign of King Stephen, Robert FitzRichard, constable of the riverside Baynard's Castle and guardian of the City of London, claimed overlordship of the Thames from London to Staines. A council of all England was held in St Paul's Cathedral to settle the matter. Navigation of the river and the estuary, with its strong tides and numerous sandbanks and other hazards, held considerable danger for shipping and required a degree of supervision. There was the threat of piracy and the possibility of smuggling to avoid tolls and duties. In 1197 the City authorities made an agreement with Richard I whereby, in return for a cash payment (which he desperately needed to fund his Crusade), they gained authority over the Thames from Staines to the River Medway, allowing them to introduce unified policies. Their responsibility for the river down to Yantlet Creek at the mouth of the Medway, including part of the Medway itself, was reconfirmed in 1606 during the reign of James I and continued until the nineteenth century.

Regulations stipulated that ships were obliged to sell their cargoes at the legally-approved markets in London. This was to prevent 'regrating', whereby a merchant could buy in one market and sell at higher price in another nearby market, or 'forestalling' when an entire cargo was purchased by a trader thereby creating a monopoly in a product. These were considered 'unjust' practices, what we would call in modern terms 'anti-competitive' or 'price-fixing'. It was something that was frowned on by both the authorities and the Church, with the earliest such laws dating from the second half of the thirteenth century. For a ship's captain however, it was more convenient to sell the entire contents to one 'engrosser', so illegal transactions continued to take place. When caught, offenders could expect to have their goods seized by officials and given a fine or even banished from trading. A charter to London from Henry III laid down the law:

No merchant or other person shall meet merchants coming, by land or by water, with their merchandise and provisions towards such city, for the purpose of buying or selling again, until the same shall have been duly exposed for sale, under forfeiture of the thing bought and pain of imprisonment.

As merchants bought and sold from each other they needed a way to keep track of how much money was owed. From the thirteenth century a system was introduced using tally sticks. Each stick, made from alder or hazelwood, recorded a particular transaction. Notches of varying sizes were cut to indicate amounts of money, with the largest notches having the greatest values and small nicks for the smallest denominations. The stick was then cut along its length into two parts of different widths. The thicker part, known as the 'stock' was retained by the party to whom money was owed and the narrower section, called the 'foil', by the debtor. The longer the stick the more complex the transaction, with the longest on record measuring almost forty centimetres. When the debt was settled the stick was destroyed and discarded.

As with all of London, the various wards were responsible for the security, good order and maintenance of the public areas along the riverbank. The bridge came under the jurisdiction of Bridge and Candlewickstreet wards; upstream were Vintry, Queenhithe and Castle Baynard; and downstream Billingsgate and Dowgate.

Having been re-established by Alfred in the late ninth century, London had grown into one of the major towns of England. By 1203 one eighth of the entire national revenue was being collected in London and its merchants had become powerful enough to ensure their interests were represented in *Magna Carta*, sealed by King John twelve years later. As medieval sailors approached London from the Thames estuary they must have been faced by a wondrous sight which we can only imagine today. First they passed the formidable Tower of London. Beyond that was London Bridge, filled with houses and its church, teeming with activity and stretching across the river. The city itself – large by the standards of the day – was a mass of church spires and dominated by the vast St Paul's Cathedral in the west.

Imports and exports through the medieval Port

When King Cnut ascended the thrones of Denmark, England and Norway, hostilities between Anglo-Saxons and Vikings had ended, providing an opportunity for trade to take place between the parts of Cnut's kingdom. Thirty years after his death England had become part of the Anglo-Norman Empire, with little hindrance or threat to cross-Channel shipping. Furthermore, from 1154 the country was part of the Angevin Empire that included south-west France.

Almost all the ruling class in England were by this time French and they expected the same domestic luxuries as they enjoyed at home in France. As many of the country's royalty, nobles, and clergy grew in wealth (creating houses and palaces around London, Westminster and Southwark) they looked for supplies of wine from Bordeaux and Poitou, fine cloth, jewellery, exotic furs, furniture and other materials and there were a number of merchants on hand to import them. By the end of the thirteenth century London had established itself as the principal supplier of such goods within England, all of which passed through the capital's port. In the late twelfth century, William FitzStephen had already written about the exotic merchandise arriving at the Port of London:

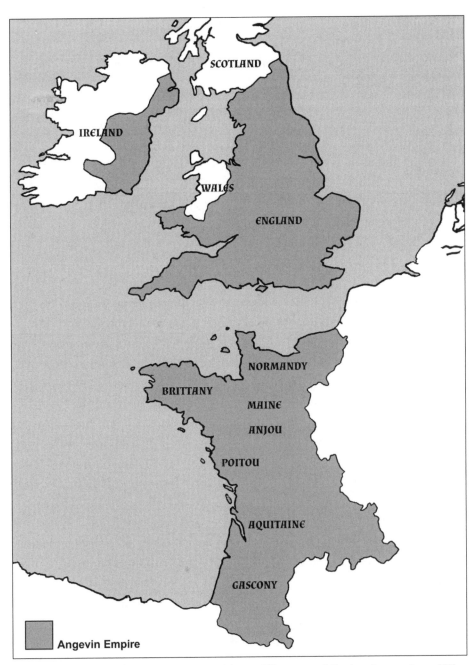

The Angevin Empire in the latter decades of the twelfth century following the marriage of King Henry II of England, Count of Anjou and Duke of Normandy, to Eleanor of Aquitaine.

The Arab proffers gold, the Sabaean spice and incense … Thy rich soil,
O Babylon, gives oil from the fertile palm trees, and the Nile precious
stones; the Chinese send garments of purple silk, the French their wines;
the Norse and Russians vair, gris and sable.

Sabaeans were people who lived in the south of the Arabian Peninsula. Babylon
was then often used to refer to Cairo. Vair and gris are furs from different types
of squirrel and sable is from weasels. These were only a selection of the more
luxurious items then being imported by ship.

Most cargoes from up- or downriver, around the coast, or from overseas
were of a more everyday nature. The greatest export was wool, with the major
import being wine from France. Other imports included salt, grain and bulk
cargoes such as firewood, timber for construction, chalk, coal and millstones.

There was also a great increase in internal trade during the early medieval
period and this brought better standards of living to many as could be seen
by the new fashions and quality of clothing, pottery, metalwork, and timber-
framed buildings of the city. London was supplied by boat from around the
south-east with bulk goods like grain that were too cumbersome to be moved
by road. During the twelfth and thirteenth centuries smaller inland ports such
as Henley and Maidenhead came into being on the Thames, on the River Lea
at Ware, and downriver at Maidstone and Faversham. Coastal boats brought
goods from around the rivers of the Essex coast while distribution centres grew
at Kingston and Ham to supply the city with firewood from around Middlesex
and Surrey. Coal was shipped around the coast from Newcastle by the early
thirteenth century and a Sea Coal Lane existed in London in the 1220s.

Large amounts of grain such as rye, barley and oats were needed in London
for the baking of bread, brewing of beer and feeding of horses and other
animals. These were transported into the city from distances of up to 20 miles
by cart but as far away as 60 miles by water. London was supplied by markets
upriver at Henley, the coastal towns of Rye, Sandwich, New Romney and even
as far as Great Yarmouth, as well as Maidstone and Faversham. By the latter
thirteenth century there were four grain markets in London: at Cheapside,
Gracechurch Street, Billingsgate and Queenhithe. Authorized merchants
at Queenhithe held a monopoly on the landing of salt that extended as far
downstream as the River Medway, for which they were each required to pay the
Bailiff of Queenhithe five shillings.

During the twelfth century London also became a leading international financial centre from where the royal mint was organized. Despite the Christian rule that forbade usury, a number of the town's more prosperous citizens were involved in providing finance in one form or another. These included William Cade, a Flemish cloth-merchant who became the leading Christian financier during the early years of the reign of Henry II. He provided funds for a broad spectrum of individuals and institutions, including the king, barons, monasteries, clergy and sheriffs as well as other traders. There was also a small population of Jews who lent money; and a further source of finance were the Knights Templar. After the Jews were expelled from England in 1290 and the Knights Templar supressed at the start of the fourteenth century, their places in the London finance market were taken by Italians and merchants of Cahors.

Despite wars and plagues, overall trade in and out of London gradually increased and spread over a wider geographical area. During the mid-fourteenth century the greatest traffic was with the Low Countries and the Rhineland but goods manufactured in London were finding their way as far as sub-Saharan Africa, probably via Portuguese traders. From the late thirteenth century merchant ships known as 'carracks' from the Mediterranean ports of Venice and Genoa were arriving in England. By the early fourteenth century they were regularly carrying goods to and from London, including the importing of alum, used in dying cloth. The Mediterranean trade continued until the 1530s.

During the third period of mayoralty of Richard Whittington, London's regulations of the time were, in 1419, recorded by John Carpenter, common clerk of London, in the *Libor Albus* (the White Book). Amongst many others, contemporary and past, were included those regarding fees due on imports into London, including 'pesage', 'scavage' and 'tronage'.

Pesage was a tax on imported bulk goods:

Unto Pesage it pertaineth, that all articles of merchandise that are sold by weight, when brought into the City by merchant-strangers, and sold in gross by the hundredweight or half hundredweight, ought to be weighed by the King's beam; in which case, the buyer shall pay unto the Sheriffs [followed by various weights and costs]. And be it known, that the buyer at his own cost cause the King's beam and weights to be brought to the house where the vendor is staying; so that the vendor shall pay nothing to any one by reason thereof.

Two hundred years earlier, *Magna Carta* had standardized weights and measures throughout the kingdom according to those used in London. During the reign of Henry III it was established that imported goods be weighed at the 'King's beam', a set of scales controlled by a London citizen who was usually a grocer. In 1319 a royal charter gave control of the beam to the City Corporation and it was thereafter administered by Livery Companies. A 'great beam' was used for heavy goods and a 'small beam' for lighter goods. A set of standard weights and measurements was kept at the Guildhall.

Scavage was a fee paid to officials and hosts:

> Here is set forth of what merchandise coming into London Scavage ought to be taken on behalf of his lordship the King; and how much ought to be taken for each kind. Of which custom one half belongs to the Sheriffs, and the other half to the hosts in whose houses the merchants are harboured, who bring the merchandise from which such Scavage arises; provided always that such hosts be of the freedom of the city.

In the regulations there followed a long list of goods varying from sugar and pepper to turpentine, glass, whalebone and the exotic-sounding 'pyoine', on which twelve pence per kark (probably a variable amount meaning simply 'load') was due. Other goods listed were squirrel-skins, silk, felt, canvas and other types of materials. Pesage at the rate of a half-penny per hundredweight was due on all merchandise brought into the city. On other goods taken out of the city, such as wool or woad, tronage was due at a rate of eleven pence per sack, and two pence per tun of wine.

With the establishment of a major cloth-making industry in the country, large amounts of dye were required. The main component of dye throughout the Middle Ages was woad, producing anything from a mid-blue, to a deeper blue or black. It had been grown in England during Saxon times but by the twelfth and thirteenth centuries seems to have only been imported. It was arriving in London from Picardy by the end of the twelfth century, brought by merchants from Amiens and Flanders, and (after wine) was the second most important import from France throughout the Middle Ages. Sources other than Picardy were Normandy, Gascony, Spain and Lombardy. *Liber Albus* records:

> It should also be known, that in ancient times no woad used to be harboured in the city, but all was sold in the vessel. In times that are [lately] past,

the merchants harboured their woad, renting the warehouses by leave of the Sheriffs. After this, in the time when Andrew Bokerelle was Mayor, by assent of the greatest persons in the City, the merchants of Amias, of Nele, and of Corby, obtained a letter sealed with the Common Seal of the City, by which it was granted unto them that they might at all times, and whenever they might please, harbour their woad.

The French woad trade was regularly interrupted during the Hundred Years' War, allowing other merchants, such as the German Hanse, to encroach on the business. It was able to resume uninterrupted again following the signing of the Treaty of Picquigny in 1475, although by then the primary source in France was Toulouse rather than Picardy.

Christians abstained from eating meat on Fridays and certain holy days and therefore fish was an important part of the medieval diet. A variety of fish and shellfish caught at sea or in rivers was landed in London according to the seasons. Preserved seafood known as 'stockfish' was brought from Scandinavia. Fees were to be paid to London Bridge for fish being brought into London:

> For every boat that brings sprats, if the boat is not of the franchise of London, the bailiff [of the bridge] shall have one tandel [a basket measurement] of sprats, and for the boat one farthing. The vessel that brings dabs [similar to plaice], shall give six-and-twenty dabs for each hundred; and if it brings less, it shall give nothing, and if it brings more it shall give no more than one hundred dabs. A porpoise owes one penny, and if it is cut up for selling at retail, the bailiff shall have the chawdron [entrails] and the tail, and the three fins.

Until the early part of the fifteenth century there was a great variety of manufactured items being exported but by its end the situation had reversed and the only goods leaving in significant quantities, other than cloth, were tin and lead, pewter pots and brassware, and rabbit-skins. As a result of standards set by Livery Companies, products manufactured in London were of a high standard but expensive to produce. A large range of cheaper products ranging from metal goods to spectacles were imported, as were raw materials such as iron, steel, copper, resin, wax and dyestuffs. In order to protect local manufacturers, laws were passed in 1464 and again in 1484 banning the import of a range of goods by denizens (those foreign-born but with English rights) or aliens, probably with little effect. William Caxton set up the first printing press in England at Westminster in 1476 but books were also arriving from the Continent, for sale by two London booksellers. Portuguese ships brought oranges, sugar and cork, Venetians carried luxury cloths, carpets and spices.

The wool and cloth trade

England's greatest exports by far throughout the Middle Ages were wool and woollen cloth. So important were these goods that they were often the subject of political and trade wars between the English and Continental monarchs. In the earlier part of the period it was almost entirely wool that was sold overseas but England gradually became Europe's leading supplier of woollen cloth.

A flourishing weaving industry was established in Flanders in the twelfth and thirteenth centuries, producing cloth that the Flemish sold in their local fairs. As the industry expanded and began to produce high-quality cloth for export, Flemish merchants, along with others from France, came to England seeking supplies of wool. Such was the demand for English wool that buyers were willing to pay long in advance, effectively lending money to the suppliers. The finished Flemish cloth was reimported, named after their individual towns of origin, such as 'Arras cloth', 'Ypres cloth' and so on, and sold at England's fairs. This trade was no doubt increased after a grant of safe conduct between Henry III and Flemish merchants in 1236 and followed in subsequent years by charters of privilege for individual Flemish towns.

London was far from the major producing regions yet by the later thirteenth century it was the most pre-eminent port for wool, handling around forty per cent of the country's trade, mostly brought to the city by middlemen or shipped by provincial suppliers. During wars between England, Flanders and France in the 1270s and 1290s a large part of the trade was captured by German merchants, mostly from Lübeck and Dortmund, who were neutral in the conflicts. Flemish merchants largely withdrew from trading with England, buying English wool from others and concentrating their energies instead on cloth production.

From at least the twelfth century much of the wool that was exported was produced by English monasteries, notably of the Cistercian order. Such was their selling-power they also acted as middlemen for local lay manors and the estates of the senior clergy. Italians, mostly from Florence, Lucca and Piacenza, were touring the country, collecting taxes due to the Pope from religious houses, and as they did so they began to also buy wool to be sold in both Flanders and for their own cloth industry in Italy. Italian ships rarely ventured up the Thames however, and those merchants shipping from London tended to send their wool by barge down to Sandwich where it was transferred to galleys.

Following violent disagreements between English and Flemish merchants that made it dangerous for either side to trade, Edward II agreed in 1313 to the creation of a staple through which all exports of wool to the Low Countries should pass and where customs duty was to be paid. English merchants fixed the location in the neutral town of St Omer in the province of Artois, but in subsequent years the staple transferred variously to Antwerp and Bruges. The Hundred Years' War began in the latter part of the 1330s. To finance the conflict Edward III attempted, with mixed results, to nationalize the export of wool. It was collected on behalf of the Crown, shipped to the staple at either Antwerp or Bruges, and sold on the King's behalf by English merchants. Towards the end of Edward's reign Parliament demanded that it should henceforth regulate and control the taxes on wool.

Between 1326 and 1335 the staple moved away from the Continent to various locations in London and other English, Welsh and Irish ports but this caused inconvenience and additional cost to wool producers who were no longer able to ship from their closest harbour. This created issues that ultimately increased the cost of wool arriving in Flanders. Cloth produced by the Flemish became more expensive, giving English weavers a price advantage.

Production of long, heavy English broadcloth was stimulated during the thirteenth century by new methods that allowed manufacturing on an industrial scale. Fulling by foot was gradually replaced by a mechanical water-driven method powered by fast-running water. Production moved from urban homes to mills located in rural valleys in areas such as Yorkshire and the Lake District. Further impetus was provided from the time when war closed the English market for Flemish cloth and the Flemish market for English wool during the 1270s. Trade embargoes were followed by a burdensome customs duty on the export of wool, while English weavers enjoyed the advantage of cheap, plentiful and high-quality local supplies. Thus in the 1330s imports of Flemish cloth virtually ceased. Annual export of English cloth increased steadily, from less than 5,000 cloths in the 1350s to 40,000 each year by the end of the century. The main market was then Gascony, the reason for which we will understand when we later look at the wine trade. English cloth had taken so much of the European market that by the 1360s the Flemish industry was in a state of crisis, as was that of Florence in the following decade. The Flemish industry was dealt a further blow by civil war between 1379 and 1385 and that of Florence by their war against the Pope that began in 1375 resulting in a wide ban on Florentine cloth across Europe.

For the following century English wool was woven into unfinished cloth before being exported to the Low Countries to be made into clothing. It was however at the finishing stage where the highest profit was made. Henry VII, during exile in his teens before taking the throne, had witnessed for himself the Flemish cloth-finishing industry and the prosperity it created. Like Edward III before him, he encouraged skilled Flemish cloth-workers to migrate to England and in 1486 banned the export of most types of unfinished English cloth. As the Flemish and Florentine weaving industries declined and English cloth increased, exports of English wool steadily decreased, from an annual peak of almost 40,000 sacks in the first decade of the fourteenth century to less than 20,000 a century later and under 5,000 by the sixteenth century.

It was largely English merchants who developed the export of cloth and they initially controlled about eighty per cent of the business in the early fourteenth century when volume was low. By the end of the century German Hanse merchants were also buying cloth, much of it destined for the Baltic, and Italians were shipping it to Mediterranean countries. Yet alien merchants only ever controlled about half of the cloth export trade. In the thirty-year period from the 1360s shipments from London rose ten-fold, mainly to the Baltic, North Sea and Low Countries with most cloth destined for the Mediterranean leaving from Southampton. In the mid-sixteenth century London's share of a still growing market had risen to eighty-five per cent.

In the middle of the fourteenth century the staple for wool finally settled at Calais, an English possession from 1346, and the merchants formed themselves into a fellowship. It remained there until the town was lost to France in 1558 during the reign of Queen Mary. The Calais staplers, dominated by an increasingly restricted number of London capitalists, were primarily members of the Grocers', Fishmongers' and Mercers' companies but dealt in a wide range of goods at wholesale. In the fifteenth century the majority of large shipments were sent from London, with smaller amounts from Hull, Boston and other ports. Most wool destined for areas north of the Alps was obliged to pass through Calais, with Italians sending their goods to the Mediterranean being the main exception. This ensured a near-monopoly for English staplers. The inconvenience of the staple to the German Hanseatics led them to virtually abandon the trade in favour of English cloth and the diminishing export of wool was thereafter left to English and Italian merchants. Customs duties effectively funded Calais's garrison and were therefore of benefit to the Crown. As trade declined however, funding the garrison became increasingly difficult and on several occasions its standing army mutinied, seizing the wool stock in lieu of unpaid wages.

So strong had been the demand for English wool that during the fourteenth century Edward III had regularly withheld supply to Flanders for political leverage. By the end of the fifteenth century sales had dwindled to the point where it had become a buyer's market. In 1493 Henry VII, in a dispute with the Duke of Burgundy, ruler of Flanders, was able to impose a boycott on sales of cloth and other goods but not for wool. In the early sixteenth century the numbers of Calais staplers dwindled, many being simply small investors who traded through agents. Buyers were no longer paying in advance, becoming more selective and choosing only the best wools. By then the finest quality supplies were produced in the Cotswolds and thus most likely to be exported from London or Southampton.

In the mid-fourteenth century only four per cent of England's wool exports left as cloth but by the mid-sixteenth century that had risen to around eighty-six per cent. The total volume, raw or manufactured, had not greatly changed but the value had doubled due to the change from wool to cloth.

The wine trade

During the Middle Ages wine was the largest foreign import into England. It made up between a quarter and a third of all imports by value in the first half of the fourteenth century when trade reached its peak, with the business increasingly concentrated on London, Bristol, Southampton and Hull.

Wine was transported in casks, the largest of which was a 'tun' (containing 252 gallons), the equivalent of 1,500 modern bottles, which became the standard measurement for cargo-carrying during the thirteenth century. The commodity was difficult and expensive to transport by road – a tun-sized cask requiring a cart pulled by six horses – and was therefore primarily shipped by sea and along rivers. Ships were measured according to the number of tuns they could carry, or 'tonnage', and the word (but not the same measurement) continues into modern times. More typically wine was sold by the half-tun, a cask known as a 'pipe' or 'butt'.

In the early medieval period wine mainly arrived from the Seine basin and Burgundy via the port of Rouen in Northern France and from along the Moselle and Rhine. During the mid-twelfth century England had strong links with central and southern France; Henry II was also Duke of Anjou, which included the Loire wine-growing area. Furthermore, his marriage to Eleanor, Duchess of Aquitaine, brought with it the red wine region of Gascony around Bordeaux. After King John's loss of territory in northern France, including Anjou and its popular white wines, the privileges of the men of Rouen were abolished. Gascony then became the primary source for England's wine supplies and for the following 300 years the overseas trade of England and that region became interdependent upon each other. German merchants continued to bring 'Rhenish' wine from around the Rhine area; it would arrive in small quantities on ships together with general merchandise, but it was never as popular as the French varieties. Loire wines arrived from La Rochelle but only in limited quantities, shipped by Hanseatics, Italians and other aliens. From further south came a small volume of sweet wines from the Mediterranean, 'sack' (or what today we call sherry) from Spain, and port from Portugal.

The main purchasers of wine were the kings and barons and their households and the great religious houses, all of which consumed considerable amounts. They also had the resources to be able to buy in bulk, either at the port of arrival or even directly from Bordeaux, and store the wine. Until the late fifteenth century, at which time the monarchs began buying directly from France, royal purchases were mostly made in London and stored in the cellars at Westminster. The common people drank their wine in taverns, of which there were already over 350 in London by the start of the fourteenth century.

Kings enjoyed the privilege of 'prise' (or 'butlerage'), by which they were allowed wine as a form of tax, and to purchase some casks at below the market rate. It was a task managed by the king's butler, a high-ranking official, who sourced wine for not only the royal family but also the various royal households, parliament and military expeditions. The regulation as recorded during the reign of Henry V stated:

If nine tuns of wine, or less than nine, come in a ship or boat, the King's Chamberlain ought to take nothing, as of right for the King's Prisage. And if ten tuns come, he shall take one tun; and if there are nineteen tuns he ought to take nothing on account of Prisage beyond one tun; and upon twenty tuns he shall take two. And if one hundred or two hundred tuns come together in one ship, the Chamberlain shall take for the King's Prisage only two tuns.

It was in the interest of the English kings to stimulate the economy of their lands in Gascony. To maintain the allegiance of the Gascons, particularly during times of war when their large ships could be requisitioned into the navy, they were given favourable terms. They were, however, resented by the citizens of London who attempted to enforce long-standing restraints on aliens. Edward I, who was no friend of Londoners, settled in favour of the Gascons in 1302. In return for a custom of two shillings per tun of wine he granted them, amongst other privileges, relief from their previous obligation to lodge with London citizens, the right to sell at wholesale to anyone they pleased, and dispensation from the royal prise. The rights of the Gascons continued to be contested by Londoners so Edward merely extended the privileges. The city levied a tax on every cask of wine passing under London Bridge, with the revenue used for its upkeep, which created further friction between the King and the native citizens. London vintners were prominent amongst seventeen ordered to be arrested by Edward II in 1309. In 1327, during the reign of Edward III, London's citizens finally joined the Gascons in gaining exemption from prise.

The Gascons formed the Merchant Wine-Tonners confederation to look after their mutual interests. A number of them had permanent dwellings in London, with twenty-four living in Vintry ward in the first decade of the fourteenth century. Citizenship of both Bordeaux and London provided them with valuable privileges of the two towns in the form of exemptions from customs. Permanent premises in London also made it unnecessary to hire cellars in which to store wine after it had been unloaded.

From early medieval times wine merchants – 'lawful merchants of London' as they were described in regulations during the reign of Henry II – were associated with the churches of St Martin and St James Garlickhithe adjacent to the wharves where wine was landed. The area, around what is now the northern approach to Southwark Bridge, became known as 'Vintry', 'so called of vintners … a part of the river of Thames, where the merchants of Bordeaux craned their wines out of lighters and other vessels and there landed and made sale of them'. By the early thirteenth century the London vintners, many of them with French ancestry, had organized themselves into an influential body. In 1363 they received from Edward III their first royal charter, formalizing in law what was already happening in practice, which was a monopoly on buying and selling wines from Gascony (but not sweet wines) at retail. Gascons and others were only allowed to sell it at wholesale, with the obligation to land it at Vintry. The Vintners' Company was formally incorporated in 1437 and held a monopoly on landing wine in London until the creation of the docks in the early nineteenth century.

Trading in wine was a complex and risky business, requiring trusted connections and partnerships at the source, and a good network of customers in London and beyond. It helped to be wealthy and have wine expertise. London's vintners were some of the richest and most powerful of the city's citizens. Several held the position of mayor and in the early- to mid-thirteenth century at least a third of aldermen were dealing in wine. London's merchants sent supplies far and wide, along the Thames in both directions and all the way up the east coast as far as Newcastle. Yet, with only two arrivals per year, it was a seasonal affair and few dealt with wine as their sole business. The Gascons had given over their forests and fields to the planting of vines for wine production and therefore relied on grain and dairy-produce from England for their needs, as well as becoming the main importer of English cloth in the fourteenth century. English vintners therefore spent much of their time sourcing all types of merchandise from England and beyond, to be sent to Bordeaux on ships that returned with the wine.

In the thirteenth and fourteenth centuries some of the merchants were also owners or part-owners of the ships that carried the wine. During the Hundred Years' War many were sunk or requisitioned by the Crown, so much of the carrying then passed into the hands of foreign shipowners, increasing the landed cost of wine in England. In the mid-fourteenth century, when around half of England's Gascon wine imports came through London, between 150 and 200 ships were arriving annually laden with Gascon wine. It was shipped from Bordeaux twice each year: the season's new vintage was sold and drunk by Christmas, followed after Candlemas in February by the mature 'reek' wine that was sold until the end of April when its quality began to deteriorate.

Mariners bound from London to Bordeaux had largely to sail against the prevailing south-westerly wind, making it a difficult journey. They tended to hug the south coast of England in order to be near a safe haven and able to revictual if the weather deteriorated. It was not unknown for them to wait for up to a month for a favourable wind and on occasions have to turn back. Assembling into groups at the Isle of Wight, they waited until weather conditions appeared suitable before striking out across the open sea to France

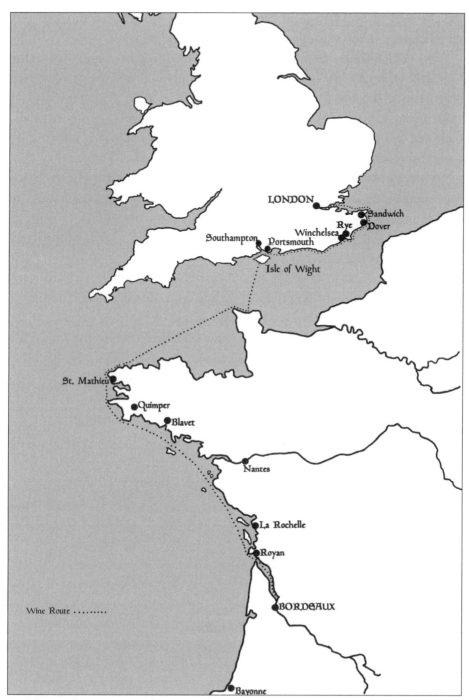

The typical wine route from Bordeaux to London. The outward journey often varied depending from where outbound cargoes were collected en-route.

and the port of St Mathieu at the western tip of Brittany. From there they stayed close to the western French coast down to Bordeaux.

Wine was landed by the wine porters – or 'tackle porters' – employed by the Vintners' Company. Master porters were identified by wearing the company insignia in silver, and junior porters ('servants') in brass. The movement of casks from ship to quayside storage was labour intensive. Ships normally anchored in mid-stream, so casks had to be hoisted overboard into smaller boats that ferried them to the quayside and from there to wherever they were to be stored. At least twelve porters were employed, with a charge levied depending on the distance that the cask had to be moved from the quayside. In 1301 the charge was three pence from ship to Thames Street or four pence to the lanes north of Thames Street. There are records from 1500 of wine porters operating from both Vintry Wharf and Botolph Wharf.

The wine harvest in Gascony was affected by intermittent setbacks such as the Black Death of 1348 and 1373, famine, as well as occasional pestilence and adverse weather. For much of a period of 130 years, from the start of the Hundred Years' War in 1337, there was sporadic disruption to the wine trade between Gascony and England. During times of conflict ships were forced to sail in escorted convoy to England in order to avoid capture.

In the 1440s three million gallons of wine was being brought into England each year, nearly one-third of all imports, of which up to ninety per cent was from Gascony. The final loss of the duchy of Gascony to France in 1453, and the effective suspension of trade with England, forced the merchants of Bordeaux to seek new markets elsewhere. That stimulated imports of wines from other regions, such as Spain, Portugal, Crete and the Canary Islands. At around the same time beer made with hops, which was stronger and longer-lasting than English ale, was introduced into the country from Holland and it became an alternative to wine. Nevertheless, imports of wine continued to increase, reaching a peak in the mid-sixteenth century.

Foreign merchants in medieval London

London's position as the leading town of England, with its many wealthy citizens and institutions, created a desire for imported luxury goods, foods and wine. At the same time English wool and other goods were required around Europe and these trades attracted foreign merchants and ships to London.

The existence and rights of foreign traders in London depended on various factors such as territories held by English monarchs, international wars and alliances, local politics between the citizens of London, and the need of royal finance as much as commercial opportunity. They were encouraged by the monarchs, who needed their support in the territorial disputes in France and elsewhere, as well as the goods, finance and services they could provide. To a large extent the Angevin monarchs – Henry II, Richard I and John – were more suspicious of their English subjects than of aliens. The foreign merchants, meanwhile, were resented by Londoners who saw them as a threat to their rights and livelihoods and continually pressed for restrictions to be placed on their activities. Privileges were given to or taken away from both the foreigners and local citizens in a number of charters throughout the Middle Ages.

The favoured location for foreign traders was Dowgate, where the Walbrook flowed into the Thames. One of the earliest solid pieces of evidence of French merchants in London is the confirmation in 1150 of the earlier privileges granted by Duke Henry of Normandy (later Henry II of England) to the members of the Rouen merchant guild. They were given freedom from all duties in London, except on wine and porpoises, the right to attend markets throughout England, and the possession of Dowgate wharf 'as they have had from the time of King Edward'. The privileges were confirmed again in 1174 and by both Kings Richard I and John. The early twelfth century historian William of Malmesbury wrote in 1125 that London's wharves were filled with goods from merchants coming from all countries, especially from Germany. Merchants from Cologne had a hall in Upper Thames Street from 1157.

The historian E.M. Carus-Wilson has described the latter thirteenth century as the golden age of free trade, when alien merchants were encouraged to do business in England. Various groups from areas of northern Europe had negotiated trade agreements in England and a charter of 1237 states

All these things we have granted unto the merchants aforesaid, that they may the more willingly and the more often come into the city with their merchandise, for the advantage of the kingdom and of the city …

In that year Henry III granted safe-conduct and privileges to traders of Gotland, and the City of London granted privileges to the merchants of Amiens, Corbie and Nesle, three towns in close proximity within Picardy. The latter group were permitted to sell their goods from the quayside shortly after landing but only to citizens of London. They could store goods, except wine and corn, and sell woad, garlic and onions to anyone free of duties and tax. After the start of the Anglo-French War that began in 1294 however, French people in England (excluding subjects of the king, such as Gascons) were declared enemy aliens, arrested and their goods confiscated.

Two of the largest groups of foreign merchants in London were the Flemings who exported wool, and the wine-importers of Gascony. Henry II issued a writ to the sheriffs and bailiffs of London not to molest the men of Cologne and to allow them to sell wine on the same terms as those from France. Spaniards were also active traders in the thirteenth century, importing furs, skins and leather, but their activities were ended until the fifteenth century by the French alliance with Castille against England from 1337. Italians from Florence, Lucca, Siena, Piacenza, Pistoia and Genoa (and later also from Milan, Padua, Pisa, Asti and Venice) became ever more prominent as merchants and then also as bankers to the king after Edward I expelled the Jews in 1290. During the Middle Ages they each formed into firms known as a 'compagnia' (from the Latin phrase 'cum panis', meaning to share bread), usually comprised of relatives. In the early Middle Ages silks, spices and other commodities from the Far East had arrived in London via Persia, Russia and Germany but the Italians began to transport them from the Mediterranean. They gradually took over much of the wool export trade from the Flemish. Normans in the thirteenth and fourteenth centuries mainly dealt in hemp cloth. German merchants, who formed the Hanse trading fellowship, monopolized trade between England, northern Europe and the Baltic region.

Particular berthing tolls were payable to the monarch by aliens – and in some cases they also paid dues to the king at Christmas and Easter – in return for the same protection of their possessions as were enjoyed by natives. Tolls for them differed depending on whether their goods were sold directly from their ship or taken and sold in the town. The surviving document *The law of the merchants of Lower Lotharingia* (traders from Germany) from the early twelfth century details the regulations governing alien merchants arriving in London. It tells of how they should approach London Bridge, the crew singing *Kyrie eleison* (and thus giving evidence they were not pagan pirates); that they must wait for two ebb tides before commencing business, during which time the king's chamberlain and sheriff should take from them a toll of wine and other luxury items; who they could sell to and in what order; the procedures for unloading goods; and how long they may stay in London.

During the twelfth and thirteenth centuries London's artisans and tradesmen formed themselves into guilds, known later as 'Livery Companies', gaining the rights to monopolies. During the turbulent reign of King John London gained certain privileges and right of self-government – a 'commune' – in return for its support of the monarch. The local administration evolved into a 'Court of Aldermen', headed by a mayor, consisting of the city's leading tradesmen. They, naturally, created regulations to protect their business interests, including control of outsiders doing business within London.

In 1285 attacks on foreigners led Edward I to suspend London's charter and privileges for a period of thirteen years, during which time the city was governed by a sheriff appointed by the King. In 1303, following negotiations with foreign traders such as the German Hanse, Edward published the *Carta Mercatoria* (merchants' charter), the most important piece of legislation up to that time regarding foreign merchants. It gave aliens trading throughout the kingdom extensive privileges but they were to pay additional customs duties. Edward II confirmed the *Carta Mercatoria* when he inherited the throne in 1307 but he came under pressure from English merchants. In 1311 he published a set of ordinances that cancelled the charter. Edward III was in his minority when he succeeded his father and made no pronouncement on foreigners, so individual groups of alien merchants were obliged to renew their liberties. Royal charters continued to be in conflict with local privileges however, so in 1335 Parliament, assembled in York, passed a statute that declared that all local charters conflicting with *Magna Carta* were null and void. Aliens could trade in all commodities and sell at both retail and wholesale, although wine continued to require a royal licence.

The situation changed dramatically following the death of Edward III. London introduced a number of severe restrictions on aliens. Thereafter strangers were only allowed to board with freemen, the Exchequer imposed new duties on cloth exports, and they were henceforth forbidden to trade amongst themselves. A charter to London from Richard II stated:

No merchant foreign to the freedom [of London] shall sell or buy of another stranger within the liberties of the said city any merchandise under forefeiture, etc.

The first parliament of Henry IV's reign in 1399 confirmed the right to sell victuals at retail but subsequent parliaments were hostile to aliens. Bullion laws, first introduced in the 1340s, requiring aliens and denizens to import certain amounts of coin or plate to pay for exports, were more forcibly enacted. All proceeds from importing goods were required henceforth to be used to buy English goods. Later laws stipulated that imports must be sold within forty days, restricted even further from 1425.

In the fifteenth century Londoners tended to disapprove and be suspicious of Italians. They were considered profiteers and parasites for selling expensive luxury goods and illegally circumventing laws regarding the export of wool and cloth. The Hanse, in comparison, traded in everyday merchandise. Despite efforts by the mayor, anti-Italian violence broke out on several occasions in 1456 and 1457, orchestrated it would seem by mercers. Venetians, Florentines, Lucchese and Genoese resided openly on Lombard Street and Bread Street but the Hanse largely kept themselves protected by the high walls of their base at the Steelyard. The latter were also safe in the knowledge that any harm caused to them would result in reprisals on English merchants trading in their towns, whereas few Englishmen were doing business in Italy during that period. For a time all Mediterranean merchants decamped to Southampton.

London was an important international port by the beginning of the thirteenth century, yet in the early medieval period, when England was primarily an exporter of raw materials, a third or less of the importing and exporting was handled by English traders. The tide began to turn in the 1330s at the outbreak of the Hundred Years' War and by the end of that century the wool and cloth business was largely in the hands of English, and particularly London-based merchants.

The German Hanse and the Steelyard

The ability to trade internationally in medieval Europe was highly dependent on politics, customs duties and local privileges. It was therefore not unusual for merchants from a particular town to form a fellowship or 'hanse' in order to negotiate with foreign monarchs and ports and to provide mutual protection in times of danger.

The largest trading confederation in northern Europe was the German Hanse, often referred to as the 'Hanseatic League'. It began as an association of individual merchants trading overseas. During the second half of the fourteenth century membership became restricted to merchants of particular towns and it was the towns themselves that were thereafter the members. The emphasis of their interest remained solely commercial; it was never a sovereign or political body, and the individual towns owed allegiance to different kingdoms. There were generally about seventy member towns, and at its height ninety, mostly, but not restricted to, German-speaking areas. It had no permanent officials but matters were debated by a central 'diet' or assembly of members that met when necessary, usually at the inland port of Lübeck close to the modern border of Germany and Denmark.

Regulations dating from around 1000 state the berthing tolls and payments in kind that Germanic merchants should pay in order to trade in London. Such an arrangement indicates that some form of mutual organization already existed amongst the merchants and in 1157 they purchased a hall at Dowgate. Henry II gave protection to men of Cologne, Richard I granted them a charter of privileges and King John issued letters of protection. During the famines of the mid-thirteenth century the Cologners were able to import grain and this led to additional privileges being granted by Henry III. He renewed their charter in 1235, possibly at the request of the Cologners due to aggressive behaviour towards them by Londoners.

Groups of merchants from Lübeck and Hamburg were also trading with east coast ports in the first half of the thirteenth century and in the 1260s Henry III confirmed privileges to match those of the Cologners. During the second half of the century all three groups, plus merchants of Gotland, merged into one community in London, probably based at the Cologne guildhall. It was perhaps demands by Londoners in return for liberties that united the different groups. A disagreement that lasted several years was settled by the Exchequer in July 1282, whereby the Hanse were required to pay 210 marks to maintain Bishopsgate, the entrance to London from the north, for then and into the future, and contribute to the cost of its watch (in the sense of policing). A legal case brought by a London merchant led the Hanse to seek further protection for themselves. In December 1317 they paid the large sum of £1,000 to purchase a confirmation from Edward II of previous rights granted, immunity from arrest, and that neither he nor future monarchs could place impositions on them without their consent. Thus a solid legal foundation was created for the Hanse in England, although political and commercial circumstances would often lead to it being disregarded by monarchs and Parliament in later times.

By the beginning of the fourteenth century some members of the Hanse had been permanent residents in London for enough time for them to gain the rights of denizens. Their proximity to the seat of government at Westminster led them to represent the interests of the Hanse throughout England despite greater trade with the east coast ports. An increasingly hostile Parliament during the reign of Edward III prompted them to ensure their privileges were renewed by each succeeding monarch.

In the early part of the fifteenth century over ninety per cent of Hanse exports from England were of cloth. Their incoming ships brought a great variety of goods from across the Continent and beyond, including Skania herrings from the Baltic, Russian squirrel skins, Baltic fur, copper, iron, laton (a mixed metal resembling brass), wax, timber from southern Sweden, stockfish, corn, tar, quernstones, glass, mirrors, linen, silk, thread, north German beer and much more.

Individual Hanse towns and merchants, who had previously traded with a variety of individual ports in England, were by the end of the fourteenth century restricting themselves exclusively to one destination, such as Lübeckers at Boston and Prussians at Hull. London, at which a number of Hanse towns were trading, was the exception. It had by then overtaken Boston as the leading Hanse 'Kontor' (or base) in England, with at least twenty-eight merchants permanently based at their London guildhall in 1381.

The Hanse guildhall was located upriver of London Bridge, where the Walbrook flowed into the Thames. From the latter part of the fourteenth century it was being referred to as the 'Steelyard'. The nineteenth century German historian J.M. Lappenberg considered it an anglicization of the German or Dutch word *Stalhof*, meaning an emporium of imported goods. Between the twelfth and sixteenth centuries the Steelyard expanded considerably in size, growing to three acres. The historian John Stow, writing at the end of the sixteenth century, described it as:

… large, built of stone, with three arched gates towards the street, the middlemost whereof is far bigger than the other, and is seldom opened, the other two be mured [closed] up. The same is now called the old hall. In the 6th [year] of Richard II they hired one house next adjoining to their old hall, which sometime belonged to Richard Lions, a famous lapidary [gem-cutter], one of the sheriffs of London in the 49th [year] of Edward III … This was also a great house with a large wharf on the Thames, and the way thereunto … which is now called Windgoose Alley, for that the same alley is for the most part built on by the steelyard merchants.

The Steelyard was a walled community with its own warehouses, accommodation and offices, currency and system of measurements. Women were forbidden from entering and the 20 or 30 merchants living there led an almost monastic life, avoiding as much as possible contact with the local population and the pleasures of London and Southwark. Any members breaking the rules were required to pay a fine in the form of candlewax at the neighbouring All Hallows the Great church. It was there on Upper Thames Street that the Hanse merchants worshiped and during the fourteenth century they endowed it with a chapel, altars and a stained-glass window. The church, rebuilt by Wren after the Great Fire, was finally demolished in 1895.

Henry IV confirmed the Hanse franchise in England in October 1399 after he succeeded Richard II but it was by then dependent upon reciprocal rights for English merchants in Hanse towns. That stipulation became an increasingly problematic issue in the following century and a half. The fifteenth century was a difficult time for the Hanse merchants, with various wars and trade disputes as obstacles to their business. There were prolonged disputes with England and instability on the Continent, causing a fall in demand for the cloth that made up the bulk of their business with England. Their trade with the east coast ports declined dramatically, in some cases ceasing altogether. At the beginning of the century around half of all Hanse trade with England took place in London but by the end of the 1430s London's share had risen to over eighty per cent, despite not actually increasing in volume. While exports declined, imports fared even worse.

There were poor harvests across Western Europe for three successive seasons starting from 1437. In December 1437 Henry VI wrote to the Grand Master of the Teutonic Order in Prussia requesting up to twenty shiploads of grain, with a further request the following year. Naturally, the Grand Master and the German Hanse at the Steelyard in London took political and financial advantage of England's needs.

By the fifteenth century English cloth merchants had formed their own trade alliance, known as the 'Merchant Adventurers', who competed with the Hanse in the Baltic and at Antwerp. At every opportunity they put pressure on Parliament to limit the Hanse privileges or revoke them entirely. Queen Elizabeth's Secretary of State William Cecil and the Privy Council worked in close cooperation with the Merchant Adventurers and at the beginning of her reign the Hanse were reduced to the status of aliens. Failing to agree reciprocal rights between the Merchant Adventurers and the Hanse, in 1580

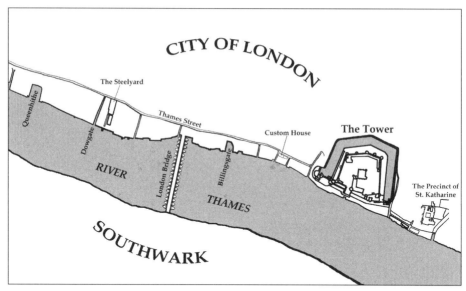

The area of the Port along the riverside as it was throughout much of the Middle Ages. The individual quays (not marked) lay between Queenhithe and the Tower of London on the north bank.

the Privy Council notified the Steelyard that their privileges in England were terminated. In 1598 the Lord Mayor of London was instructed to repossess the Steelyard, although it was given back to German merchants in 1606.

There was no one single event that finally brought the German Hanse to an end; it simply disintegrated in stages. Other groups of European merchants grew in strength, particularly in England, often supported by their own nations, and rulers became reluctant to provide aliens with greater privileges than their own subjects. Individual Hanse towns or regions with their own interests began to make separate treaties, to the detriment of the other parts of the fellowship. Finally, the Hanse could not survive the conflicts of the Thirty Years' War that raged throughout central and northern Europe in the early decades of the seventeenth century.

Ships in the medieval Port

A variety of vessels came and went from the medieval port, ranging from the smallest river and estuary boats bringing produce from nearby farms, to freshwater and sea fishing boats, up to the largest long-distance ocean-going vessels.

Archaeology has provided information regarding the types of boats that would have been arriving at London from abroad during the tenth century. All ships throughout Europe during the Middle Ages were clinker-built, constructed of planks that overlapped each other. Most were similar to the late-ninth century Anglo-Saxon cargo vessel found in 1970 on the north coast of Kent at Graveney, near Faversham. Its size was 14 by 4 metres, with hull planking held together by iron fastenings. It was capable of carrying loads of around seven tons and contained traces of Kentish hops and millstones from the Rhine, indicating that it worked in the Thames Estuary and across the North Sea. At that time these types of vessel were simply beached on London's waterfront.

Remains of early-medieval boats uncovered from the river in modern times were locally built in a very similar style to those around northern Europe, using either iron rivet fastenings, hooked nails or wooden pegs, and caulking of moss and hair. They were likely to have a sharp fore-end and stern, similar to those associated with Viking boats. It seems that ships of the late-Saxon and Norman period were of shallow draught and flat-bottomed for berthing in shallow water.

By the start of the twelfth century the largest cargoes had risen to sixty tons and such boats needed to be unloaded against a wharf, jetty or onto a smaller barge. The greater loads created a difference in methods of trading. It was no longer possible for merchants to sell directly from their vessel. Medieval captains became bulk-carrying wholesale merchants who needed to unload their goods into warehouses for retail sale by others.

Fragments of what appears to be a locally-built, flat-bottomed, broad-beamed boat were found at Custom House in 1973. Its design is in the Scandinavian Saxon or Viking style, with pointed fore-end and stern and it has been dated from the late twelfth century. It probably had a single square sail, with steering from a side-rudder, and worked along the river. Locally-constructed vessels of that period were made of oak, whereas those from Scandinavia were primarily of pine.

In the reign of Edward I in the thirteenth century the loads of ships carrying wine to London varied from 10 tons to 200 tons, the latter being quite a large vessel. In the early fifteenth century two-masted ships were sailing in the seas of northern Europe. As ships grew even bigger it became more common for them to moor in midstream, loading and unloading their cargoes onto smaller craft that ferried back and forth to the shore.

From surviving records we know that by the late thirteenth century a wide range of size and types of boat were landing at London: 'great vessels' and 'vessels with bulwarks' (both seagoing ships); 'coasters with bails'; and vessels with 'oarports' (large boats powered by a number of oars). All those types were recorded above or below the bridge but there were several classes recorded only upstream of the bridge: vessels powered by 'tholes' (a rowing boat); 'shouts' (broad, flat-bottomed inland boats suitable for shallow water) and a 'waterman's boat' (such as a smaller ferry). There was a type of seagoing ship referred to as a 'hulk' and another was a 'barge'. German traders from Lübeck gained an advantage when they developed 'cogs', a superior vessel to the older Scandinavian and Slav style and they became the most common type of vessel in international trade around northern Europe. A thirteenth century version of this was shown on the seal of the Priory of St Bartholomew. Other descriptions in the records of the Corporation of London and Bridge House are of a 'bark', 'flune', 'galley', 'keel' and various others, some of which will have been fishing boats, but their shape or usage is now unknown.

During Saxon and Norman times small ships and boats were constructed and repaired on the London riverfront, mainly in the Queenhithe and Vintry area. After the new bridge was constructed in the tenth century that activity began to move further downstream to the eastern end of the port, along Thames Street in the adjoining parishes of All Hallows and St Dunstan in the East, close to the Tower of London. There are records of fifty shipwrights constructing two warships there for the Crown in 1295. They were probably quite small enterprises because references to them in the accounts of London Bridge indicate that the shipwrights were also employed in more general carpentry work. Perhaps boat-building yards were first established at St Dunstan's when it was still an underdeveloped area with a gently-sloping foreshore and vessels were small. By the late fourteenth century some of them occupied premises on both the north and south of Thames Street.

Although it was necessary for major construction and repairs to be undertaken on the water side there were no doubt several workshops within the city producing ships' equipment. Certainly a rope-making industry grew during the second half of the thirteenth century just to the north of the riverfront in the west of the city. Long lengths of hemp were laid out and turned into rope along what is now Upper Thames Street but known as Roper Street until at least 1456. No doubt over time London became too congested for that activity and it moved out to the east, probably in the fifteenth century.

A shipbuilding and repair industry had grown around the villages of Ratcliff, Wapping, Shadwell, Limehouse, Poplar and Blackwall by the mid-fourteenth century, on the bend of the Thames as it suddenly sweeps south around the Isle of Dogs to the east of the Tower of London. Boats could be pulled on to mud berths there along the river. Work on naval vessels was supervised by the Clerk of the King's Ships who was based close by at the Tower of London. A Company of Shipwrights was established by the fifteenth century with their own meeting hall at Ratcliff. During the Hundred Years' War between 1337 and 1453 ships were required to transport troops, military stores and weapons between England and France and in 1340 a large naval fleet was fitted out at Rotherhithe, on the south bank downstream of Southwark. The shipbuilding industry was further stimulated when Richard II passed laws obliging merchants to carry goods on English ships.

As ships increased in size, better maintenance facilities were required. Maritime industries started to relocate to, and grow in, small riverside towns and villages downstream of London where there was more space. In the sixteenth century Deptford, Woolwich and Chatham became major shipbuilding, repairing and chandlery centres.

The Port during the later Middle Ages

Following the introduction of two-masted ships in the fifteenth century, trade was restricted to ports such as London that could be reached by these larger, deeper vessels. Other formerly busy harbours such as Bruges, York and Boston became less significant. Not all vessels found it convenient to progress up the Thames however, and the town of Sandwich on the Kent coast and its harbour at Dover were used as an outport and transhipment point, primarily by Italians, for goods arriving on large ships. Customs duty was paid there before loading onto smaller vessels to be brought up the river to the London markets. For goods going in the opposite direction customs duty was paid in London rather than Sandwich in order to prevent smuggling.

Water-borne trade in and out of London was not only by seagoing ships. Small barges carried goods up and down the Thames to the riverside towns of Kingston-upon-Thames, Staines, Windsor, Maidenhead, Marlow, and Henley-upon-Thames. They had previously travelled as far as Oxford but the river became obstructed by locks and dams by the fourteenth century and it was by then quicker to travel by road between Henley and Oxford. As a result, Henley grew into an important transhipment point during that period.

Wharves in London continued to be expanded into the river by their owners, either to extend their properties or to repair the former riverbank. Most river walls were constructed of wood, made with increasingly sophisticated joints, but more expensive masonry embankments such as at the Tower of London became more common from the late fourteenth century. They were more durable and needed repair or replacement less often. That had the effect of halting the previous property expansion, which had largely come to an end by the sixteenth century.

As adjacent properties moved forward into the river, Queenhithe and Billingsgate remained where they were and became basins. In the thirteenth century Queenhithe became a public wharf and in 1400 the city also acquired Billingsgate, which, being downriver of the bridge, was more convenient for seagoing ships. A regulation stated:

That no ship or boat shall anchor at night, or moor, between sunset and sunrise, except at Queen-Hythe and Byllynggesgate; nor shall at night remain upon the bank-side of Suthewerk, under pain of loss of vessel and imprisonment of body.

In the middle of the fifteenth century the City purchased land adjacent to Billingsgate to extend the wharf.

Since Saxon times many small lanes had led down to the Thames, giving access to the river to fetch water, allow animals to drink, or to catch a ferry. As the waterfront moved ever forwards some lanes continued to slope down to the river as inlets and those became known as 'watergates'. Others were built up on the same level as the new wharves, ending in stairs and perhaps a jetty at water level, no longer allowing the possibility of animals being able to drink there. Until the middle of the fourteenth century certain bulk goods were landed at particular points and gave rise to the naming of adjacent streets. Rothersgate (where cattle were landed) was named by the early twelfth century; Oystergate was so-called from the mid-thirteenth century. Another was Seacoal Lane. As time moved on the many small buildings along the waterfront were amalgamated into larger properties by new owners, particularly following the Black Death, giving the riverfront a more uniform look than in the previous centuries. Entry points to the river became fewer. Complaints and disputes about access to the river being blocked by building work, goods or rubbish and lack of maintenance of stairs and jetties were common by the fifteenth century.

The increasing level of trade from the twelfth through to the fourteenth century drastically changed the economy and social make-up of both London and England in general. In the eleventh century power was in the hands of barons who held and gained their income from farming lands. By the fourteenth century merchants in London and other ports were often equals of the aristocracy, sometimes exceeding them in wealth and influence. Likewise, whereas the Crown had previously received its incomes from nobles it was by the latter period obtaining the major portion of its revenue from commercial taxes and tolls. The cost of the various wars of the fourteenth century required the monarchy to borrow money from London merchants and it was those businessmen, rather than civil servants, who were often authorized to oversee the collection of customs duties as repayment of the loans. For the kings this had the advantage of ensuring they were collected efficiently by men with a vested interest in their payment. In 1377, for example, the regents of the young Richard II borrowed £10,000 from two London businessmen. They were authorized to reclaim the debt by collecting taxes on wool, exports that were by then producing an income of £18,000 each year.

An increasing share of the nation's imports and exports were passing through London's port. It reached over sixty per cent of volume measured in taxes by the latter fifteenth century, more than the next fourteen ports combined. In most ports two people were employed to collect taxes. Such was the scope, volume and complexity of London's trade that there were no less than forty-two officials working in three completely separate groups: firstly the 'Wool Custom' for wool and hide exports; secondly the 'Petty Custom' for goods imported and exported by aliens and 'Cloth Custom' for imports and exports of cloth; and lastly the 'Tonnage' for wine imports and 'Poundage' for all other goods.

The main focus of overseas imports and exports was by then through Zeeland and the Duchy of Brabant (roughly speaking, the modern southern Netherlands and Belgium). Antwerp and Bergen-op-Zoom had opened up as inland ports for large ships, following tidal surges along the River Scheldt. They eclipsed Bruges after access to the latter town from the sea was cut off by the silting up of the Zwin waterway. Trade mainly took place at the great fairs held twice annually at each of Antwerp and Bergen, where English cloth was exchanged for local products and goods from across Europe.

The fifteenth century saw periods of boom and bust, primarily influenced by wars and harvests. As the political situation changed, recession gave way to a period of boom in around 1440 that lasted for a decade and between 1420 and 1460 there was a trade surplus in England – that is to say, more was exported than imported. That was in turn followed by another slump, with various causes including disputes with the Hanse and hostilities with Denmark. Business rose once again with the signing of the Treaty of Utrecht in 1474 that ended the conflict with the Hanse. The following year the Treaty of Picquigny between Edward IV and Louis XI created a free-trade agreement that abolished certain duties paid by English merchants trading with France, stimulating the wine trade. There were poor harvests in England, and famine in Flanders and Brabant, supressing trade in the mid- to late-1480s, followed by civil unrest in Flanders that prevented merchants trading at Antwerp and Bergen. European dynastic rivalries in which Henry VII and Philip IV, Duke of Burgundy, ruler of Brabant and Flanders, were embroiled led to trade embargoes in the 1490s. That forced the English merchants to relocate from Antwerp to Calais. With continuing harm to the economy on both sides, the embargo was ended by conclusion of the *Intercursus Magnus* treaty in 1496, with favourable terms for England's Merchant Adventurers. Thereafter, into the sixteenth century, London's overseas commerce began to rise again.

The Merchant Adventurers

It was a new class of English trader who exported cloth. Wool exporters were legally bound to be members of the Company of the Staple and in the late fourteenth century to channel their goods through the newly-conquered port of Calais under protection of the English garrison. Cloth merchants on the other hand were bound by no such restrictions. They boldly sought new markets wherever they could sell English cloth and other goods, competing against foreign merchants and risking all. By the mid-fifteenth century the cloth exporters at various ports around England were known as 'Merchant Adventurers' of which there were about 150 at any one time. The spectacular growth in their business made them some of the most substantial men of affairs in the country.

English cloth was sold by the exporters at the great international fairs of Holland, Zeeland, Brabant, Flanders and particularly Antwerp, much of it eventually finding its way to Cologne. The most numerous and influential of the traders at those markets were those of London who each belonged to one of the City's guilds such as the Grocers', Haberdashers' or Skinners' Companies. The majority however were of the Mercers' Company. Thus, it was they who in 1462 procured a patent from Edward IV allowing the Merchant Adventurers to appoint their own Governor in the Low Countries. (The first elected Governor was William Caxton who is better remembered for introducing printing into England). It was a Mercers' clerk who generally dealt with administrative matters on behalf of the Adventurers and it was in their hall in London that the fellowship met for assemblies. In 1486 the Common Council of the City passed an Act that formally recognized the Merchant Adventurers of London. The ordinances of the fellowship were thereafter subject to the approval of the mayor, but whose support they would receive, as with the Livery Companies. The Act stipulated that every year the mayor and aldermen would choose from amongst the Adventurers two lieutenants to the overseas governor, one of whom should be a Mercer and the other from another Livery Company. By then the Merchant Adventurers had for some time already been managing their affairs by way of a general council. As the Low Countries became the predominant market for English cloth, London merchants were increasingly joined there by the Adventurers of other ports around England. Henry VII no doubt preferred to have just one body with which to discuss matters and he decreed that the newcomers should join with the London merchants into one body. Letters Patent of 1505 brought Merchant Adventurers from all parts of England together as one company.

Although individual Merchant Adventurers may have also been members of Livery Companies and investors in Joint Stock Companies, as a body they differed from both the latter. Merchant Adventurers not only regulated their trade and negotiated collectively for favourable conditions but were also concerned with carrying out business, such as chartering ships, determining where and when ships sailed, and levying a charge on shipments, known as 'conduit money', to finance expenditure. Yet, as members traded individually, they were a fellowship or regulated company rather than a Joint Stock Company.

The greatest rivals of the Merchant Adventurers were the Staplers and the German Hanse. The more the Adventurers expanded their cloth business the smaller became the market for the Staplers' wool. In the early sixteenth century between 40 and 50 per cent of cloth was handled by alien merchants, particularly the Hanse, but Henry VII imposed restrictions on the latter group. During the reigns of the profligate Henry VIII, and his son Edward VI, the

English currency was debased, making English cloth less competitive in Continental markets. Merchant Adventurers were forced to adapt, exporting cheaper, lightweight kersey instead of the more luxurious long and short cloths, as well as diversifying away from cloth.

As part of moves to persuade Elizabeth to marry King Phillip II of Spain, his government banned the import of English wool and cloth into the Spanish Netherlands in 1563. The Merchant Adventurers were thereby excluded from their main market at Antwerp and they persuaded the government to ban the export of those goods to ensure their rivals could not gain an advantage. The town of Hamburg, gateway to German markets via the River Elbe, was at that time in a poor financial state and they, along with the other members of the Hanse, suffered from the English ban. They therefore wrote to the Queen in 1564 proposing that the Merchant Adventurers create a new staple at Hamburg through which cloth exports should pass. The Queen gave practical support to the shipments there from England but the staple at Hamburg created a decade-long division within the Hanse. Finally, under pressure, Hamburg refused to renew its ten-year agreement with the English, which expired in 1577, informing Elizabeth that continuation of trade was conditional upon the Hanse regaining its full privileges in England. As we have already seen, this created a stalemate, leading to the termination of the Hanse's rights in England in 1580.

Chapter Three

At the Centre of the World

Throughout the Middle Ages the world's greatest volume of trade took place in Asia and the Mediterranean. England, in comparison, was a small island on the periphery of Continental Europe. In the early period, foreign merchants came to buy wool and to sell their wine and luxury goods. The export of wool by English merchants was supplanted by that of cloth. England thus began to evolve from being simply a supplier of raw material into an industrialized nation. The value of cloth was far greater than that of raw wool and this brought increased wealth to the country.

During the mid-fifteenth century the English merchant fleet had been in decline and much of the import and export trade was carried on foreign ships, putting the country at a disadvantage. Henry VII understood the importance of international commerce and how it would increase the nation's wealth. 'Henry kept out of war, both on the Continent and in his own country. He set himself to make the land of England more productive and the foreign trade more extensive,' wrote Sir Joseph Broodbank in his *History of the Port of London*. In the 1480s Henry resolved to increase the fleet by introducing Navigation Acts stipulating that goods should be carried on English ships with English crews. His son, Henry VIII, was rather indifferent to commerce, instead concentrating on strengthening his naval forces, which at least brought shipbuilding to the Thames. It was events that took place during the reign of his daughter, Elizabeth I, that set the scene for England to become one of the world's financial and commercial superpowers.

By 1500 about 45 per cent of the country's wool and 70 per cent of cloth exports were passing through London, much of it to Antwerp and England's outpost at Calais. Yet the economy of the country was still heavily dependent on those products and on exports to nearby countries, stimulated by successive debasement of the coinage. By mid-century the Continental market was saturated, England lost its outposts at Calais in 1558 during the reign of Queen Mary, and Antwerp was closed as a market during a period of religious conflict and never fully recovered. Revaluation of the coinage in the 1560s depressed exports; England needed new markets and more diverse products to stimulate its economy and began to look further afield.

Pepper from the Far East had long been an essential ingredient for cooking and Western Europe was at the far end of a long supply chain that passed through the Islamic world and middlemen such as the Venetians. The vulnerability of this state of affairs was highlighted when supply was cut off following the Ottoman capture of Constantinople in 1453. The Portuguese went around Africa, successfully discovering a new route of their own. In the meantime, the Spanish headed west across the Atlantic looking for new supplies but instead discovered South America and silver. Thus the Spanish were able to pay in silver for spices, brought to Europe by the Portuguese who violently enforced their monopoly on the trade. For a century the spice trade between Asia and Europe was dominated by the state-owned Portuguese Estado do India from their base at Goa.

Throughout the sixteenth century much of Northern Europe turned towards Protestant beliefs and the Netherlands revolted against their Spanish Catholic rulers. The newly-independent Dutch created a strong navy to defend themselves but they also used it to plunder Spanish and Portuguese maritime trade and established their own spice trade with Asia. Protestant England became reliant on the Dutch for their pepper but in 1599, when the price tripled, English merchants resolved to create their own spice route to the Far East.

Trinity House

The Thames, and in particular its estuary and approaches, holds numerous dangers for navigation. Many vessels have run aground over the centuries, particularly in the days of sail, before reliable charts, when ships tended to stay within sight of the shore in order to navigate by landmarks such as church spires. The Maplin Sands and many other long, shifting, tongues of sand lie up to forty miles off the Essex coast where the Thames meets the North Sea, to be avoided by ships passing into and out of the estuary on the way to east coast ports and beyond. Some are in a Y-shape, where an apparently deep channel ends in a fatal cul-de-sac. Ships en route from London and east coast ports down to France and southern Europe must pass the Goodwin Sands off the Kent coast, described by Shakespeare in *The Merchant of Venice* as 'where the carcasses of many a tall ship lie buried'. Well over a thousand vessels have been recorded as having been lost there since the late fifteenth century, and parts of unrecorded, more ancient, vessels still occasionally snag the nets of fishing boats.

It was vitally important for mariners to understand the underwater dangers, the ever-changing times of the tides according to the moon and location along the river, the effect of the wind, and to know local landmarks in poor visibility. During the thirteenth century the monks of St Albans had compiled tables of the high tides at London Bridge. Local experts, known as 'lodemen' in the Middle Ages, could be hired to advise on the best channels along which to navigate. The term dates back to at least the 1380s and is referenced in the *Shipman's Tale* of the *Canterbury Tales.* Chaucer wrote:

His stremes, and his daungers hym bisides, His herberwe, and his moone, his lodemenage

(His current and the dangerous watersides, His harbours, and his moon, his pilotage)

The ancient nautical medieval Law of Oleron stated that if a ship was lost by default of the lodeman it was a mariner's right to have him executed by cutting off his head, providing it was the majority decision of the crew.

In 1513 a group of eminent masters and mariners petitioned Henry VIII that the standard of pilotage on the river had declined in recent times and regulation of pilots was required. The King may or may not have had an interest in the safety of merchant ships but Henry was at that time at war with France. The mariners pointed out that the scarcity of English pilots caused Scots, Flemings and Frenchmen to learn the secrets of the river, thus jeopardizing English security. From its foundation by letters patent in May 1514 responsibility for safety on the river was given to 'The Master, Wardens and Assistants of the Guild or Fraternitie of the most glorious and blessed Trinitie and Saint Clement in the parish Church of Deptford Stronde in the County of Kent', otherwise known as Trinity House, Deptford. The organization was to provide pilotage – the safe guiding of ships by experienced English pilots – along the Thames, particularly through its shifting sandbanks in the estuary.

The membership of Trinity House consisted of those with various nautical interests and over time they gradually became involved in a range of maritime safety measures. They were distinct from the Fellowship of Lodemanage of the

Cinque Ports, based at Dover and formally incorporated in 1527, which was concerned solely with pilotage. The two organizations between them provided authorized pilots for ships navigating the Thames. After the Fellowship was discontinued in 1854 Trinity House took over complete control of pilotage on the Thames.

An Act of Parliament of 1566 under Queen Elizabeth extended the responsibility of Trinity House to ensure the upkeep and continuation of seamarks around the coast, those being landmarks such as church steeples and trees used by mariners to fix their position. In 1594 the provision of beacons and buoys was similarly transferred from the Lord High Admiral, and the Corporation gradually began providing lighthouses, their first probably being at Lowestoft in the early years of the seventeenth century. The cost to the Corporation regarding all these works was funded by dues paid by ships arriving at London, where they were collected by the officials of Custom House, and at other ports.

The 1594 Act also transferred the right to provide ballast to ships on the Thames, which was particularly necessary for colliers returning empty to Newcastle. Using wet ballast also reduced the cost of the important dredging of the Thames to prevent silting. The Corporation's rights and responsibilities were further extended in 1604 under James I, including the supervision of apprenticeships of seamen, and to hold a court dealing with disputes, such as those between masters and seamen or regarding damage to ships.

Trinity House was governed by a court of eighteen Elder Brethren, some of whom were leading mariners, navigators and naval men of their day, who met at least once each week. At some point in its early years a lower class of Younger Brethren came into being, numbering 254 by 1629, mostly living around Stepney or Rotherhithe. The expansion of the membership effectively created a guild consisting largely of shipmasters, limited to natural-born Englishmen who could afford the subscription. The Brethren were headed by a Master, the first of whom was Thomas Spert, an experienced and eminent seaman from Stepney who rose through the ranks to captain the great *Henri Grace à Dieu*. He was knighted in 1529 and held the post until his death in 1541.

After Spert, a new Master was elected at Trinity House every three years and the naval administrator and diarist Samuel Pepys held the position of Master on two occasions. It gradually became an honorary role, held by the Duke of Wellington between 1837 and 1852, with the management undertaken by the Deputy Master. Since 1866 it has been bestowed on a member of the royal family. For forty-two years it was held by the Duke of Edinburgh until his retirement in 2011 when it was conferred on the Princess Royal. Elder brethren have included Winston Churchill.

In order to achieve their aims, it was necessary for the Elder Brethren to be both supporters of, and have the support of, the monarchs. During the Interregnum in the mid-seventeenth century the powers of Trinity House were transferred to a Parliamentary Committee, although they continued as advisors. At the Restoration in 1660 the responsibilities of Trinity House were reinstated.

In 1618 the working headquarters of Trinity House moved to Ratcliff, the area where many of London's merchant seaman resided. Following the Restoration a move was made to Water Lane, close to the Tower of London. That building was destroyed in the Great Fire, as was its successor in 1714. After extensive repairs in the 1790s the headquarters moved for the final time into a grand building facing the Tower of London across Tower Hill, designed by the architect Samuel Wyatt and completed in 1796. It was largely destroyed during an air raid in December 1940 but restored with much Georgian detail in 1953 and is Grade 1 listed. Many of the historical records and artworks were destroyed in the fires and bombing although some records from as early as the seventeenth century are still in existence. The building now contains a magnificent collection connected to its history, including a contemporary portrait of Elizabeth I.

From the beginning, Trinity House was involved in charitable work. Almshouses for elderly seamen and their widows were created at Deptford. In 1695 Captain Henry Mudd, an Elder Brother, provided an estate of houses and a chapel on his land at Whitechapel north of Ratcliff. Much of it still remains at Mile End Road although no longer for its original purpose. Pensions were also paid to elderly or injured seamen, and by 1618 they were providing for 160 people, which had risen to over 1,100 in 1681.

As part of its responsibility for buoys and lighthouses, at the beginning of the nineteenth century Trinity House established riverside workshops near Blackwall, where the River Lea joins the Thames. From there maintenance work could be carried out and experiments undertaken, for which two lighthouses were built at the yard. The electrical scientist Michael Faraday was appointed Scientific Advisor in 1836 and undertook experiments that led to advancements in lighthouses around the coast. Trinity Buoy Wharf continued in operation until 1988 and the main buildings and one lighthouse still exist.

Trinity House continued as the sole authority for pilotage on the Thames and around the coast until 1986, by which time it managed around 500 self-employed pilots. At that time responsibility for pilotage on the river was transferred to the Port of London Authority. Trinity House today works as a licensed authority for deep sea pilotage in Northern European waters, as well as for navigation aids, including lighthouses, lightships and buoys, around England, Wales, the Channel Islands and Gibraltar. It continues to carry out charitable as well as educational work including a cadet training scheme. In modern times the Elder Brethren are supported by around 300 Younger Brethren.

The shipbuilding and maritime industries

Ships had over the centuries been gradually increasing in size and by the early fifteenth century the largest were 1,000 tons. The general trend for larger ships thereafter reversed and the size of seagoing cargo vessels became smaller throughout Europe, with the majority between 100 and 150 tons and rarely exceeding 200 tons. Advantages of smaller ships are that they require less crew, can enter smaller harbours, are quicker to load and unload, and their loss easier to bear if sunk. The English merchant navy remained modest by European standards at the beginning of Elizabeth's reign, with only 250 vessels above eighty tons. Navigational aids remained rudimentary, forcing crews to stay within sight of land as much as possible.

At the end of the fifteenth century new methods of ship construction were introduced in England and around Europe. Until then wooden ships had been made in the 'clinker' style where each plank of the hull overlapped the one below, with the shell constructed first and the frames added later. From at least 1465 the new 'carvel' method began to be used, where each plank butts edge-to-edge with the next. Construction began with the skeleton to which the planks were fastened. The new method made the vessel much stronger and allowed for gun-ports in naval ships, such as the *Mary Rose*, launched in 1511. The type of timber changed from oak to elm in the sixteenth century, sawn instead of split. With larger ships also came the introduction of more sails, with more than one mast to support them. These new ships were more robust, more easily manoeuvrable, of larger capacity, faster and cheaper to build.

The changes, and local shipbuilding, were stimulated in England by the creation by Henry VII of the first permanent navy. When Henry VIII was at war with France he found it inconvenient that the navy was based at Portsmouth, far from his palaces and the Royal Armoury at the Tower of London. He decided that the ideal locations were close to his palace at Greenwich, at the Kent fishing villages of Deptford, Woolwich and Erith, which were not only more convenient but also easier to defend than Portsmouth. Initially there was a lack of skilled workmen and they had to be conscripted from as far as Newcastle and Cornwall. Over time however, these yards enlisted men with shipbuilding and repairing skills and there was a need for local suppliers and administrators with suitable knowledge. All these factors eventually created an industry that was not only useful for merchant shipping but for the wider Port of London. Initially the facilities on the Thames were rather small but during his reign Henry invested heavily in the navy and they expanded and became better-organized. The King's Yard at Deptford expanded to thirty acres, including two wet-docks, three slips large enough for warships, and with forges, rope-making and other facilities. The area to the east of London grew to become the shipbuilding capital of England by the end of the sixteenth century.

The 'great gun', a cannon that could fire over a long range, revolutionized naval warfare, with warships able to engage enemies from a distance.. The *Mary Rose* was constructed at Portsmouth but fitted out on the Thames in 1512 with bronze cannons made in a London foundry. A state-of-the-art warship, it became the flagship of Henry's navy, perhaps the first to carry the great gun, and served in his navy for over thirty years. In 1513 Henry commissioned what was at that time the largest English ship afloat, the *Henri Grace-á-Dieu* (Henry, Thanks be to God) but popularly known as the *Great Harry*. It was built at Woolwich, downriver of Greenwich, which had the advantage of a ready supply of wood from the forests of Kent to build new ships.

During the Middle Ages most of the merchant ships sailing from London were built in Holland or Flanders but the growth of Henry's shipyards brought many of the necessary skills to the River Thames. Therefore a local shipbuilding and repair industry grew at yards downstream of London at the riverside hamlets of Wapping, Shadwell, Blackwall and Rotherhithe. Few, however, were permanent yards employing permanent staff; more often vessels were built on available land by transient shipwrights.

Despite progress, shipbuilding on the Thames and elsewhere throughout England would continue to be rather small-scale until the advent of long-distance trade, with most vessels less than 100 tons. During the Dutch wars of the mid- to late-seventeenth century around 2,000 merchant ships on either side were captured. The Dutch were the leaders in merchant ship design, building 'fluits' (known as 'flyboats' in English) that moved under less sail. They required a smaller crew, and were more space-efficient and thus carried a greater cargo. English merchants preferred to use captured Dutch ships rather than locally-built vessels and shipbuilding yards in England received fewer orders during the latter part of the century. In response the English yards began to copy the Dutch designs and as the captured ships came to the end of their working lives business once again picked up in the English yards. There was also new competition from shipyards in the American colonies, which under the Navigation Acts qualified as English until Independence, where there was the advantage of abundant supplies of timber. In the 1770s around a third of all British ships had been built in America but American Independence once again gave British shipyards a boost in business. Even though many of the ships on the river during the eighteenth century had been built elsewhere, ship-repairing continued to be a thriving business.

The Elizabethan reform of the Port

In 1552, during the reign of Edward VI, the Commission on the King's Courts of Revenue issued a report and, as a result, customs duties were increased and many more commodities added on which duty was payable. This made the collection of duties more complex and smuggling more profitable. Therefore a reform of ports was initiated by the Lord Chancellor, William Paulet, Marquis of Winchester. An Act of Parliament was passed in 1559 establishing general regulations for loading and unloading and a commission was appointed to survey the ports. The outcome was that, with the exception of fish, goods could henceforth only be unloaded during daylight and only at certain quays at London, Southampton, Bristol, Newcastle and certain other ports where customs officials were present. In London, arrivals of overseas goods were to be limited to particular wharves along the riverbank in the City and these became known as 'Legal Quays'. Incoming vessels were forbidden to touch land after passing Gravesend. Those wharves at the ancient Queenhithe – in use since Saxon times – as well as Gravesend, Barking, Blackwall and many other places, ceased to be used for goods on which duty was payable.

The Legal Quays, which lined the southern side of Thames Street, were to maintain their monopoly on the landing of foreign imports into the Port of London for the following 250 years. Their names changed over time, often according to their ownership. A survey of 1584 listed them as:

Three Cranes Wharf	The largest of the Legal Quays and located at Vintry, it was used for landing wine and 'waynscotts'.
The Steelyard	For the exclusive use by the German Hanse. By the time of the survey a crane was in use.
Fresh Wharf	For eels and fish.
Gaunt's Quay	A very small wharf where barrels of fish were landed.
Cock's Quay	For foreign merchants, including lodgings.
Botolph's Wharf	Used by the Russia Company as well as coastal traffic.
Sommer's Quay	Located on the west side of Billingsgate and owned by the City, it was used exclusively by Flemish merchants.
Billingsgate and Smart's Quays	Both forming the Billingsgate harbour and owned by the City. Fish, vegetables, fruit and grain were landed. Smart's Quay was on the east side of Billingsgate.
Old Thurston's Quay	For coastal trade and Flemish goods.
Dyse Quay	An open and unprotected quay used for coastal trade.
Raff's Quay	For imports and exports of general merchandise.
Young's Quay	Where Portuguese cloth was landed.
Gibson's Quay	For lead, tin, and other coastal trades.
Sabbe's Quay	Cargoes of pitch, tar, 'soap ashes' and other goods were landed. The property was generally in a poor state at the time of the survey.
Thurstan's Quay	For imports and exports of general merchandise. It no longer existed by the time of the Great Fire, presumably amalgamated with its neighbours.
Bear Quay	Used by merchants from Portugal who lived there, as well as coastal trades.
Crown Quay	For coastal trade in wood and corn.
Greenberry's Quay	Used for imports and exports from France and coastal trade.
Custom House Quay (or *New Wool Quay*)	Purchased by the Crown in 1558 and leased out, it was used for general imports and exports such as fine wares and haberdashery. It later returned to private ownership.
Old Wool Quay	This was one of the oldest quays on the riverside, dating back to the thirteenth century or earlier and named after the wool ships that loaded there in previous times. It had been purchased (from the Coopers' Company) by the Crown two years before they acquired Custom House Quay. At the time of the survey it was used for landing wood and by coastal trades.
Galley Quay	Formerly a place for shipbuilding but by then for unloading general merchandise.

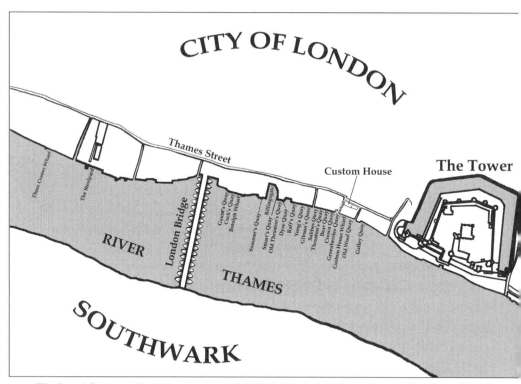

The Legal Quays, as listed in a survey of 1584. Of those originally registered, Bussher's Wharf and Thomas Johnson's Quay, each located between the bridge and the Steelyard, were no longer mentioned after 1559.

In some cases the Legal Quays were separated from each other by small wharves that were unregistered and therefore presumably only handled goods on which duty was not payable. Bridgehouse at Southwark was the only authorized landing place on the south bank. It was there that grain was unloaded for storage in granaries and for baking.

After creating the Legal Quays, Winchester turned his attention to improving customs administration throughout the country, detailed in his Book of Orders, issued in 1564. These set out the hierarchy of responsible officials within the Port. The Exchequer would henceforth issue port books – special parchment books – to the senior collectors in which details of ships, their cargoes and revenues were to be entered. The system included two separate controls in order to reduce the possibility of fraud. All goods were to arrive at the wharves by lighter (a barge for moving cargoes to and from ships), except in cases of those that were so large they had to be unloaded by crane. By the 1560s mechanical cranes were being used at Three Cranes Wharf, each operated by a man inside a cabin in the crane's structure.

An Act of Parliament of 1663 provided the width of river frontage of all the City quays, varying from the widest – Custom House Quay at 202 feet – to the narrowest – Hammond's Quay (between Botolph's and Cock's Quays) at just 23 feet. Three years later the Tudor-era wharves and warehouses from the Tower to Temple church were swept away during the Great Fire but by then some people had anyway thought the rotting timber wharves, the disorganized mass of warehouses and narrow lanes, were due for renewal. Visionaries including Sir Christopher Wren proposed a new broad quay running the entire length of the City, details of which were included in the second Rebuilding Act in 1670. Plans were drawn up by Robert Hooke but disputes with wharfingers regarding compensation delayed the project, which was only properly implemented along the Thames end of the River Fleet, Blackfriars, Dowgate and Puddle Dock. In the event, most individual wharfingers, notably those owning the Legal Quays below the bridge, rebuilt as they saw fit.

New trade routes and Chartered Companies

The need to find new markets became critical in the second half of the sixteenth century when the lucrative Antwerp trade collapsed, although exploration for new lands and routes had already begun in the previous century. The Spanish and Portuguese initially dominated the transatlantic trade routes. The earliest voyages westwards from England were undertaken from Bristol where John Jay the younger made an unsuccessful attempt to find the 'Island of Brazil' in 1480. Englishmen managed to reach Newfoundland and, later, continental North America under the Italian Giovanni Caboto (John Cabot) in 1497, partly supported by merchants from London. Giovanni's son, Sebastiano, made several voyages to North America in English ships, including unsuccessful attempts to discover a north-west passage to the Far East.

In May 1553 Sir Hugh Willoughby and Richard Chancellor set off from the Thames in three ships with the aim of finding an alternative north-east passage to the Orient without interference from the Portuguese who controlled the route to the Far East around Africa. Whereas Portuguese exploration and trade was state-led, that of the English was to be almost entirely private-enterprise. To fund the voyage, London merchants purchased shares in the joint-stock 'Mystery and Company of Merchant Adventurers for the Discovery of Regions,

Dominions and Islands and Places Unknown'. Two of the ships became trapped in Arctic ice and Willoughby and his crew perished but Chancellor reached the harbour of Nikolo-Korelsky from where he was invited to Moscow by Tsar Ivan IV (Ivan the Terrible). They made an agreement that took English cloth to Russia in return for Russian furs, timber, tar and other commodities. In 1555 Chancellor returned to London and a charter was granted to the Russia (or Muscovy) Company by Queen Mary and her husband King Philip of Spain. In 1558 representatives were able to travel by way of Moscow to reach the great Persian market of Boghar, where goods from China and India could be traded. Queen Elizabeth confirmed a new charter in 1566 and in the following years the Company was granted a monopoly by the Tsar on goods passing beyond Moscow to Persia. The Russia Company was the first English long-distance joint-stock company and its influence on the future of London as a trade centre was enormous. In 1557 Chancellor's successor at the Muscovy Company, Anthony Jenkinson, opened a new route through Russia to Central Asia, diverting trade from the old Silk Route. In 1613 the Company was granted a patent by James I giving them a monopoly on whaling off the coast of Greenland, although they had strong competition from the Dutch. The Muscovy Company continued trading with Russia, importing iron, tar and copper as well as fur, and survived until the Russian Revolution in 1917. It continues today as a charity. The Company sponsored the explorer Henry Hudson to seek a north-west passage to the Orient. Although unsuccessful in that quest he did make discoveries in the North-East of America, including what was named Hudson Bay.

Other English chartered companies were formed in the sixteenth century either as groups of merchants similar to the Merchant Adventurers or as joint-stock companies, each granted a monopoly on trade within a certain area of the world. The Eastland Company was formed in 1579 to trade around the Baltic, overlapping with areas monopolized by the Merchant Adventurers, and competing directly with the Hanse. There were several attempts by London merchants to create a Spanish Company to regulate English trade with the Iberian Peninsula. They ultimately failed due to either war or opposition from provincial merchants who were very active in trade with the near-Continent.

A group of English merchants were keen to establish direct business with the Ottoman Empire in order to avoid the high price of oriental goods passing through Venice and Antwerp. The Grand Dukes of Tuscany opened the port of Livorno in north-western Italy to foreign merchants and an English base was established there in 1573. Five years later a treaty of reciprocal safe conduct was agreed between the Sultan in Turkey and Queen Elizabeth at a time of mutual opposition to Spain. Elizabeth issued letters patent and the first English ship arrived at Constantinople in June 1584. Cloth was sent and spices, silks, dyes, grapes, currants and other merchandise brought back. In 1592 a charter was issued to the Levant Company, amalgamating the former Turkey and Venice Companies, with a monopoly on trade for its members from Venice to the 'newly discovered' East Indies. A flourishing trade developed thereafter, particularly in currants, as well as cotton and other exotic merchandise. London became a major base of trade with the Mediterranean, exporting cloth, tin, lead and fish and importing wine, cotton, dried fruit and other luxury goods. The Levant Company continued until the early decades of the nineteenth century. Many of the same merchants who comprised the Levant Company were also members of the Barbary Company, which was formed in 1585 and primarily imported sugar from along the Atlantic coast of Morocco.

The Guinea Company initially dealt in redwood from around Sierra Leone and became a joint-stock company in 1618. It turned its attention to the search for gold with limited success and its interests in Africa were taken over by the East India Company in 1657. In the 1640s sugar plantations were established on Barbados creating a demand for slave workers. The Company of Royal Adventurers into Africa was formed in 1660 by the Duke of York (later King James II) and Prince Rupert, establishing a fort in Gambia. Its main business was in gold, which it minted into coins, but it soon found slavery to be a lucrative additional business. Its intrusion into Dutch trading territory led to the Second Anglo-Dutch War and the company ceased to trade from 1665. It was succeeded by the Royal African Company, dominated by merchants, primarily supplying slaves to Virginia and the West Indies. Its monopoly on slave-trading ended in 1698 when that was opened up to other British companies.

Unsuccessful attempts were made to establish English colonies in North America in the 1580s. The first was founded by Sir Humphrey Gilbert at St John's in Newfoundland in 1583 but it collapsed due to disease and Gilbert drowned on the return voyage. Two years later Gilbert's half-brother, Walter Raleigh, attempted to create a colony further south at Roanoke, off the coast of what is now North Carolina. The war between England and Spain prevented supplies from reaching the colony between 1588 and 1589 and English ships arriving in 1590 found it deserted. Despite the setbacks during her reign, the area along the eastern seaboard, from what is now South Carolina and north to Maine, was nevertheless named 'Virginia' after the Queen.

In 1606 King James issued royal charters that established the Virginia Company of London and the Plymouth Company, both joint stock companies whose shares were traded in London. Their aim was to establish permanent colonies in North America and they were each granted rights to certain areas in which they were able to create settlements. The following year three London Company ships set sail from Blackwall to establish Jamestown on the James River in Chesapeake Bay, the first successful permanent British colony in North America. When the Plymouth Company's Popham colony failed, its territory was handed to the Virginia Company. A later charter gave the Company additional ocean territory including the island of Virgineola (Bermuda). It became ever more obvious that the London Company could not meet its obligations and King James changed the status of Virginia to that of a direct colony of the Crown in 1627, as it remained until the American War of Independence in 1776. New colonies were also established in New England, Massachusetts and Maryland. Virginia and the Bermuda Islands exported tobacco; new colonies at Barbados, St Christopher, Nevis and Antigua found greater success growing sugar. The initial impact of the colonies in North America was small but during the first half of the seventeenth century, particularly once the slave business was established, their importance to Britain's trade became significant. In 1660, shortly after regaining the throne, Charles II signed an Act stipulating that all goods imported from the colonial plantations should be carried in English ships.

Yet another unsuccessful attempt to find a north-west passage to the Far East was made on English ships in 1668 by the French traders Pierre-Esprit Radisson and Médard Chouart des Groseilliers. They nevertheless brought back to London beaver furs from north-east America and gained backing from Prince Rupert. Charles II granted a charter that founded the Hudson's Bay Company with a monopoly in trading in all the lands that have rivers and streams draining into the Hudson's Bay, which later proved to be a vast area from the Arctic Circle south to Dakota and west to the Rockies. Some of their trading forts, such as Winnipeg and Edmonton, grew into major cities. In a similar way to the East India Company, Hudson's Bay governed the lands in which it traded until handing them to the British Crown in 1869. The Hudson's Bay Company is the last of the early London-based Chartered Companies still in operation and the present monarch still retains a shareholding. Its headquarters moved from the City of London to Toronto in 1970. Shopping bags in their stores throughout Canada continue to boast 'Incorporated 2 May 1670'.

The reign of Queen Elizabeth was dominated by wars with Spain. English vessels were licensed as privateers, to plunder the ships and ports of the enemy. The onset of peace, in 1604, left shipowners with large, well-armed vessels, well-suited for long-distance trade, as well as the reopening of previously closed markets.

Sir Thomas Gresham and the start of London as a financial centre

Maritime commerce and voyages of discovery required finance but by the sixteenth century Europe's major money market was at the Antwerp bourse. It was largely through the efforts of Thomas Gresham that a new financial exchange was established in London, laying the foundation for the City to become the world's foremost commercial centre.

The growth of trade in London, including the funding of voyages of exploration in the sixteenth century, led to an increasing number of merchants and syndicates raising finance within the City. International shipping and trading was a lucrative but risky business and merchants needed to share that risk rather than possibly losing everything by borrowing. Initially they would do business with each other in the streets. Lombard Street, named after Italian financiers from Lombardy who had settled there, was the main centre for this. Other locations used were in and outside St Paul's or within the halls of the Livery Companies.

Two of London's leading men of the mid-century were the Gresham brothers, John and Richard. They were hard-working members of the Mercers' Company who both amassed a fortune and rose to become Mayor of London. John was one of the founders of the Muscovy Company. Richard, who lent money to Henry VIII, was knighted in 1531 and John six years later. Richard proposed a new establishment in Lombard Street where merchants could meet to do business with each other but he died before the plan could be realized.

It would be left to Richard's second son to accomplish the idea. Thomas was born in Milk Lane in around 1518. At 17 he joined his uncle John's drapery business, working in both London and the Low Countries. Living between the two, Thomas was able to speak both English and Flemish as well as French and classical languages. He also studied law at Gray's Inn. While still an apprentice, he came to the attention of Henry VIII's chief minister, Thomas Cromwell, and began undertaking errands on the Continent for the King. Following his apprenticeship, Thomas gained the right to membership of the Mercers' Company in 1543. Three years later he took control of the family business in the Netherlands, exporting woollen cloth from England and importing fine cloth and armaments. When English cloth became less competitive at the Continental markets in the 1540s he diversified into metals.

Gresham was appointed as the royal agent during the reign of the young Edward VI, responsible for borrowing at the Antwerp bourse where he was able to play the market in order to successfully reduce Crown loans. His moment of glory was cut short when the young Edward died and was succeeded by his sister Mary. Gresham and his fellow Merchant Adventurers were suddenly out of favour due to their association with the Duke of Northumberland, who had attempted to put Lady Jane Grey on the throne, and he returned to his commercial activities. When Gresham was reinstated as royal agent following Mary's death he was able to borrow more favourably for Queen Elizabeth and again greatly reduce the Crown's loans. Now with the full support of the monarch and her chief minister, William Cecil, he became involved in several government services and initiatives. Gresham was knighted in 1559 for his services to the Crown and continued as the royal agent for the first nine years of Elizabeth's reign.

Tragedy struck in 1564 when Thomas's son died in a riding accident. Without a male heir, and already in poor health, Thomas decided to use some of his large fortune to create a lasting legacy for the general good, reviving his father's idea of a public building where businessmen could carry out transactions to rival the bourse of Antwerp. A site was chosen at the junction of Cornhill and Threadneedle Street, and over £3,700 raised by subscription to purchase and demolish thirty-eight houses. The new exchange was completed at the end of 1567. Initially the idea was slow to take off and it took some years before it was fully used. In January 1571 the Queen visited to officially open the building. The market was given a royal charter and thereafter renamed the Royal Exchange.

Antwerp's golden period as the cultural and financial centre of Europe ended when that city was sacked by the Spanish in 1576. A large part of the population fled following a siege in 1585. Many of the bankers emigrated to London and thus enhanced London as a major European finance centre to supersede its Continental rival. After his death in November 1579 Gresham was buried at St Helen's Bishopsgate, with a still-extant tomb that may have been shipped from Antwerp. The Gresham family symbol of the grasshopper continues to be used by Gresham College, which he founded as London's first university-style institution, and on the weather vane of the Royal Exchange.

In the early part of the eighteenth century Joseph Addison was able to write in his *Spectator* magazine: 'There is no place in the town which I so much love to frequent as the Royal Exchange. It gives me a secret satisfaction, and, in some measure, gratifies my vanity, as I am an Englishman, to see so rich an assembly of country-men and foreigners consulting together upon the private business of mankind, and making this metropolis a kind of emporium for the whole earth.' Nearly a hundred years after its foundation, the original Royal Exchange was a victim of the Great Fire. It was subsequently rebuilt on two occasions and its successor of the 1840s, facing the Bank of England and Mansion House, continues today as an upmarket shopping centre.

The Far East and the East India Company

A significant factor in the immense growth of the Port during seventeenth to nineteenth centuries, as well the increasing business and prosperity of London, was that it was the home of the East India Company. For over 200 years the capital had a monopoly on trade with the Far East.

For centuries Asia was the world's greatest manufacturing area, with spices and exotic luxury goods sent overland from there to Europe via Istanbul and on to Venice. Thus a camel was incorporated into the heraldic device of London's medieval Grocers' Company. Vasco de Gama was the first European to open a direct sea route with the Far East in 1499 and the Portuguese monopolized maritime routes with India and China for the next century. The Dutch reached Bantam in Java from where they returned with spice, leading to the formation of the Verenigde Oostindische Compagnie (VOC) in 1602. It established a dominant position during the following century, particularly under the brutal Jan Coen, founder of Jakarta and the Company's Governor General from 1619. With a fleet of over 100 ships, the VOC accounted for half the world's shipping. The Dutch were eventually expelled from India by the British, ceased operations following the Anglo-Dutch War in the 1780s and the Compagnie was declared bankrupt in 1799.

English merchants had made exploratory voyages to the Far East under a royal charter granted by Elizabeth I in 1581, most likely to make raids on other European traders rather than trade in their own right. A group of English ships set out from Plymouth in 1591 under Captain George Raymond but it was a disaster, with all three ships lost. Only a handful of men, under the command of James Lancaster, one of the ships' captains, arrived back in England, having been rescued by French vessels. Nevertheless, the booty the survivors had amassed, and the information they conveyed, encouraged English merchants in their desire to carry out better-prepared voyages.

At least two expeditions set out from England carrying letters from Queen Elizabeth to the Chinese Emperor requesting trade agreements. Sir Robert Dudley dispatched three ships under Captain Benjamin Wood in 1596 but they never returned. Another expedition the following year was headed by merchants Richard Allen (or Adam) and Thomas Broomfield, although evidence of success is lacking. An early attempt to trade with China in 1637 was blocked by the Portuguese.

When the Dutch first returned from Java laden with pepper in 1599 its price almost tripled in England, which made London merchants determined to create their own monopoly of the trade. A meeting was chaired by the Mayor at Founders' Hall and an association was formed. On New Year's Eve 1600 a royal charter was granted to the 'Company and Merchants trading to the East Indies', or 'East India Company', giving them a monopoly on English trade between the Cape of Good Hope and Magellan's Strait.

A small fleet of well-armed ships carrying around 500 crew, many of them Thames watermen, sailed from Woolwich, backed by 218 subscribers. The Company was given the right to export silver – something that had previously been illegal – in order to purchase spices. The first voyage was not made until a peace agreement with Spain allowed English ships to safely navigate south. The vessels set sail from Woolwich in February 1601 under the command of James Lancaster, who had survived the doomed expedition of 1591. A variety of goods, including metals, fabrics, lace and gifts for foreign officials, as well as bullion, were sent on the outbound voyage. Despite poor sailing conditions that made for slow progress and many of the crew succumbing to scurvy, they arrived at Achin on the Indonesian island of Sumatra in the spring of 1602. A trade agreement with the Sultan was struck and a small settlement established as a base. Pepper, cloves, indigo, mace and silk were brought back, providing substantial returns for the investors. Continuing voyages ensured that spices were thereafter widely available in Britain, changing the nation's cuisine.

In 1608 the Company established a transit point at Surat, the main port of Gujarat on the north-west coast of India and another two years later at the town of Machilipatnam in the Bay of Bengal on the east coast. The Company's ships often clashed with those from the Netherlands and Portugal and in 1612 they won an important victory at the Battle of Swally. In 1613 an agreement was made with the shogan to establish a trading post on Japan's southern Hirado island (although it closed a decade later when Japan shut itself off from the world). Two years later a diplomatic mission sent on behalf of King James made a commercial treaty with the powerful Mughal emperor, who ruled much of the subcontinent, giving the East India Company exclusive trading rights with the Surat region. By 1640 the English and Dutch had broken the Portuguese monopoly on trade with the Far East.

Each of the early voyages were funded as individual ventures but in 1657 a permanent joint-stock corporation was formed, allowing the shares to be publicly traded. They could initially be purchased from the East India headquarters and later at the Royal Exchange. After a further two years, following a charter to the Company from Oliver Cromwell, an important supply base was established on the island of St Helena in the South Atlantic, en route between England and the Far East. An additional base was later available from the time when Cape Town became a British colony during the Napoleonic Wars.

Once they had been expelled from the Spice Islands by the Dutch in 1682, the East India Company instead focussed their attention on India and its textiles. A trading station was created at Bombay on the west coast of the Indian subcontinent. It had originally been established by the Portuguese but transferred to Charles II in 1661 as part of the dowry of Catherine of Braganza and rented to the East India Company for £10 per year. (Oddly, the letters patent that sealed the agreement placed Bombay 'in the Manor of East Greenwich in the County of Kent'). In the 1690s another base was established at the commercial centre of Calcutta on the prosperous Bengali coast of India and the area was soon providing over half the Company's imports from Asia. The original Indian base as Surat declined in importance as Calcutta, Madras and Bombay became pre-eminent. Local regulations ensured that business was conducted through intermediaries known as 'banians' and not directly with the producers.

By 1700 the East India Company was making 20 to 30 sailings per year to the Far East and was England's largest corporation. The Indian subcontinent accounted for substantially more than twenty per cent of the world's gross domestic production, compared with less than two per cent by Britain. The Bengal region in the north-east was the richest part of the Mughal empire.

Its weavers had for centuries efficiently produced a vast range of the finest textiles in silk and cotton. These colourful products, such as muslin, calico, chintz, dungaree and gingham, became the East India's primary imports into England. Business boomed and in the early eighteenth century East India-imported calico overtook native British wool as the most popular textile in English homes. This was to the great detriment of the local weaving industry, leading in 1697 to riots by London's textile workers and assaults on the property of the Company and its directors. Two decades later there were attacks on London's streets against women wearing calico. The government's response was to restrict its importation and ban the use of powered looms in Bengal.

Between 1699 and 1774 the East India Company's business increased to as much as fifteen per cent of total annual imports into Britain, its taxes and other payments often keeping the British government solvent. From its headquarters in London, instructions were sent around the world regarding what goods should be purchased and the price to be paid. Local Company governors in India were given autonomy as to how those purchases could be achieved.

One of the Company's strengths was its sophisticated fleet, its handsome and heavily-armed East Indiamen equal or superior to ships of the Royal Navy, with gilded sterns and flying the Company's striped flag. Initially it purchased existing craft but from 1610 commissioned its own ships from a yard at Deptford, next to the Royal Dockyard. As business grew, vessels of up to 1,000 tons were required, larger than could be constructed at Deptford, so the Company took the decision to create new yard. A marshy area slightly downriver on the opposite bank was chosen, by the fishing hamlet of Blackwall where Bow Creek flows into the Thames. Work began to create the yard in May 1614. It was operational within a few months, although not completely developed until 1619, by which time it was employing up to 400 workers. By then the Company operated a fleet of 10,000 tons, with 2,500 seamen. As with the royal dockyards on the opposite bank, the East India site at Blackwall was self-sufficient in all the needs of their ships, including the manufacture of its own ironwork and ropes. Employees were housed on site with their own victualling house where they could eat and drink. For security, a large wall and water-filled ditch surrounded the premises.

For customs inspections, imported goods were required to be discharged at the Legal Quays until the opening of the East India Docks in the early nineteenth century. The ships would moor at Blackwall and their cargoes would be unloaded onto 100-ton hoys to be taken upriver for inspection. From there the goods were moved to the Company warehouses in the City.

The Blackwall yard was a large fixed cost for the East India Company and when business became more difficult in the 1630s it proved to be a financial burden. After 1637 the Company ceased building its own ships and instead leased them from individual owners. The yard was sold in 1653 to a shipwright named Henry Johnson for considerably less than the Company had invested. The company did however continue to own a yard at Deptford until the latter part of the eighteenth century.

The East India merchants initially met in the City at the home of the Company's first Governor, Sir Thomas Smythe, in Philpot Lane, before setting up nearby at Crosby Hall at Bishopsgate until 1648. 'The East India House is in Leadenhall-Street, an old, but spacious building; very convenient, though not beautiful' is how Daniel Defoe described their headquarters in the early eighteenth century, by then one of the landmarks of the City. In 1729 it was rebuilt to include warehouses and cellars and enlarged yet again at the end of the eighteenth century with a 200-metre neo-classical frontage decorated with statues. Its vast size included the Court Room hall, Finance and Home Committee Room, the Sale Room for auctions, and a museum and library. From East India House clerks known as 'Writers' produced orders and other communications in longhand using quills and written in 'Indian ink', the replies to which would take a year to arrive back from the Far East. To ensure their safe arrival they were written in triplicate and sent on three separate ships. From 1806 Writers were trained at the East India College in Hertfordshire and it became an alternative to university education at Oxford or Cambridge. The method of their recruitment and practices formed those of the Civil Service from the mid-nineteenth century.

The imports brought back to England were stored in the Company's warehouses in various locations in the City. To cope with expanding business in textiles, tea, spices, ivory and other goods, a new Bengal warehouse was opened at Bishopsgate in 1771. It was incorporated into the massive Cutler Street complex, which opened in 1782. Over 640 staff were employed there in 1800.

In 1756 the young and imprudent new Nawab of Bengal seized the East India base at Calcutta. The Company's governor retreated, leaving a small number of British to defend their position, leading to the 'Black Hole of Calcutta' incident. The Company had from the start operated an armed security service

East India House in Leadenhall Street, illustrated by Thomas Hosmer Shepherd in 1829.

to defend its ships and warehouses, which evolved into a private army. The following year this small but effective force defeated the Nawab's much greater army at Plassey (Palashi), north of Calcutta. The victory was achieved in large part through bribery of the Nawab's commanders, as well as deceit, undertaken by the Company's Robert Clive.

The East India competed against a number of other European traders in Bengal, including the VOC and the French Compagnie Française des Indes Orientales. The conditions on which the 'kulah poshan', or hat-wearers, could trade were imposed by the Indian rulers who ensured that business did not disrupt the fine balance of local commerce. Goods could only be purchased with silver bullion. The East India had ambitions to trade on its own terms however, without the hindrance of competition, and England was anyway at war with France. Having defeated the Nawab, the French and Dutch were largely expelled and Bengal was systematically looted of its treasures, many of which were shipped back to England. A series of malleable puppet rulers was installed, each replaced according to the Company's needs. To increase profits an internal and external monopoly was enforced, driving out competitors, buying direct from local manufacturers, and paying weavers the minimum possible for their labours. The Company also took control of local taxes, draining the province of its wealth.

At the end of the eighteenth century up to ninety per cent of Bengal's trade was in the hands of the East India Company. Within a decade it had reversed the direction of wealth, from India to England. Profits flowed back to shareholders, as well as the British government by way of annual payments. From its base in London, trading goods halfway around the globe, from the Orient to the eastern seaboard of North America, the East India Company was rapidly transformed into the world's largest business entity, but it did not have the internal structures to manage its distant staff or rule a large and highly-populated nation. Corruption was endemic. Clive and his fellow executives enriched themselves through private trading. When Bengal suffered drought and famine in 1770 in excess of a million inhabitants perished while vast wealth continued to be transferred back to London. The following year Warren Hastings was appointed as Governor of Bengal and during his tenure a much greater part of India was brought under Company control. His eventual recall and trial in Westminster Hall 'in the name of the people of India, whose laws, rights and liberties, he has subverted, whose properties he has destroyed, whose country he has laid waste and desolate' was the most talked about event in London of 1788.

In the second half of the eighteenth century there was a dramatic increase in the size of the East India Company's army in India and by 1806 it employed over 150,000 soldiers, with mainly British officers and native conscripts. A separate navy had been developed around the coast of India to combat piracy. During the French Revolutionary and Napoleonic wars three regiments of 1,500 Company workers were maintained for the defence of Company properties in the City of London. In 1809 a military seminary was opened near Croydon where cadets studied infantry, artillery engineering, surveying and languages.

A Company trading post was established at Singapore in the early nineteenth century under the local governor, Stamford Raffles, as part of an Anglo-Dutch treaty. Raffles was especially interested in botany and zoology and became a founder of the London Zoological Society. Under Governor-General Richard Wellesley, and the army commanded by his brother Arthur (the later Duke of Wellington), more territory in India was brought under the Company's control. In the seventy years until the mid-nineteenth century the area of the Indian subcontinent ruled by the Company rose from just 7 per cent to 62 per cent, which also included Ceylon (Sri Lanka).

By then the Company had for some years faced strong competition within its home market. Mechanisation in Lancashire's cotton mills meant that by the end of the eighteenth century English-woven muslin was cheaper to produce than that imported from India. Whereas at the beginning of the Company's rule India had been the world's leading supplier of textiles, it later became the largest importer of cotton goods from England due to lack of industrial progress. Opium, grown by the East India Company, was then its main export. India was the only source of diamonds until their discovery in Brazil in 1725 and those imported by the East India Company led to London becoming a leading trader in the precious stones. In 1849 the East India Company won control of the Punjab and its defeated Sikh rulers were forced to surrender the famous Koh-i-Noor diamond to become part of Queen Victoria's Crown Jewels.

Tea, grown exclusively in China, overtook textiles as the East India's most profitable commodity by the mid-eighteenth century, doubling in volume every eighteen years. The beverage was first brought to England by the Portuguese wife of Charles II. When mixed with slave-harvested sugar from the West Indies it changed the drinking habits of people in Britain as an alternative to gin and beer, transforming from an expensive luxury to an essential beverage. It was also popular in the colonies of North America. Especially large ships of 1,200 tons carried it to London, where quarterly auctions lasted up to six days, with over a million pounds in weight sold per day.

As they had in India, European merchants in China faced problems with the conditions under which they could trade. The Manchu emperor kept tight control and stipulated they must only make their purchases through local merchants at Canton on the Pearl River and pay in silver bullion. To evade the latter edict, the East India instead grew opium in India that could be used to pay for Chinese tea, silk and other exotic goods. In order to claim it was not involved in the importation of the illicit drug it was smuggled into China by private traders, with the collusion of corrupt local officials, and proceeds paid to the Company at Canton. Chinese styles caught the imagination of the British public, with porcelain and furniture made to order at workshops in Jingdezhan and Canton.

Despite the Company's charter that gave it a monopoly of trade with all regions east of the Cape of Good Hope, much of the tea arriving at the American colonies was smuggled by merchants to avoid British taxes paid in London. In response, the government passed the Tea Act whereby taxes were instead paid locally in North America. Colonists resented the payment of taxes without representation. In December 1773 tea from three East India Company ships was dumped into Boston harbour, signalling the start of the American War of Independence.

In the early seventeenth century a return voyage to the Far East would take about two years but by the end of the eighteenth century that had been reduced to an average of 114 days. In the times of sail, East India ships left Blackwall each January in order to be in time for the winds required to carry them across the Indian Ocean. Convoys gathered in mid-stream at Gravesend where live animals and victuals were taken on board for the journey and passengers and outbound Company staff and soldiers embarked. It was not unknown for ships to perish at the very first or last stage of their journey, grounded on the sands around the Kent coast. The worst such incident occurred in January 1809 when three East Indiamen headed for Madras were lost on the Goodwin Sands.

Iron steamships were introduced in the Company's last decades and thereafter they could sail at any time of the year. 'Blackwall Frigates' were introduced, carrying passengers and mail as well as cargo. Sailing ships continued to be active long after the East India's trading days were over however, particularly with the introduction of the fast clipper-style ships that brought tea to London in record time. The journey was shortened further with the opening of the Suez Canal in 1869. General ships' crews tended to be recruited from amongst London's poor but many died on the outward journey so locals were often employed for the return. These were known as 'lascars', a word first used by the Portuguese to describe any Asian crew. Arriving in London in the autumn they had to survive the cold, often without lodgings, until embarking on an outbound ship early the following year. By the end of the eighteenth century they were a common sight on London's streets.

In order to provide a degree of accountability and combat corruption within the Company the government passed the India Act in 1784. The charters that provided the East India Company with its monopolies on business with India and China were renewed by the British government every twenty years. By the time the India charter came up for renewal in 1813 there were many calling for the liberalisation of trade and the monopoly of 200 years finally ended. Thereafter the Company continued to govern in India as an agent of Parliament. The China monopoly ended in 1833.

With the ending of the monopolies, the Company shared its business in the Far East with aggressive independent merchants such as the Scotsmen William Jardine and James Matheson who joined the triangular opium and tea traffic. After 1834 the East India no longer imported tea from China but

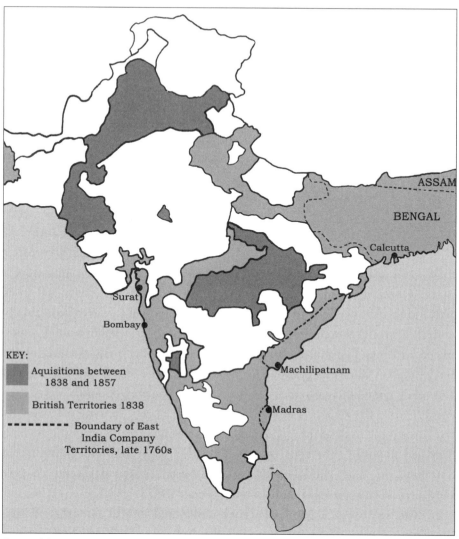

Areas of the Indian sub-continent controlled by the East India Company during the nineteenth century.

continued to grow the opium in India that fed the trade. In the meantime they finally infiltrated the Chinese tea-producing areas to learn the secrets of its cultivation. Following the East India's conquest of the Assam region of India, local varieties of the tea plant were discovered and Company plantations created there, the first harvest arriving in London in 1839.

In 1857 the Company's Bengal Army mutinied, leading to a general uprising in India. The savage war lasted for two years, after which Parliament decided it was time for a change in the governance of the subcontinent. The East India was stripped of its administrative powers and replaced by the British Raj, managed from the magnificent new India Office in Whitehall. Queen Victoria became Empress of India and the Company's forces became the British Indian Army. The head office in Leadenhall Street was demolished in 1861. Shareholders continued to be paid a guaranteed dividend until being bought out in 1873 at the expense of Indian taxpayers.

During its nearly 260-year existence the Honourable East India Company, often called 'John Company', went through four phases. First it brought spices directly from the Far East. In its second phase it revolutionized the fabric industry, bringing cheap, quality cottons and silks to Britain. Next it changed the drinking habits of the nation, with tea from China. Finally, it ceased to be a commercial operation but continued as the administrator of large parts of the Indian subcontinent. At its best it was highly efficient and the world's largest trading organization, directly employing 4,000 workers in London alone. Yet the large-scale corruption and its voracious appetite for excessive profits without accountability led to the plundering of the Indian economy and the near-enslavement of its people, opium addiction of huge numbers of Chinese, and a part in the loss of Britain's American colonies. To this day, Bengal, once one of the wealthiest regions of the world, remains one of its poorest.

The Age of Empire and the Industrial Revolution

The combination of the growing British Empire around the world and the Industrial Revolution at home had a profound effect on the Port of London. New methods of producing iron and the introduction of the steam engine brought mechanization on a massive scale, while the creation of canals allowed materials and goods to be transported in large quantities around the country. Raw material could be imported from the colonies. New types of product, or ones that could be machine-finished more economically in mass quantities, could be exported in return. Britain was on its way to becoming the 'workshop of the world' and by the mid-nineteenth century was producing forty per cent of the world's manufactured items.

The wars against the French during the reigns of William III and Queen Anne gave a great impetus to the growth of colonies and trading posts, particularly in North America and the Caribbean, Africa and the Far East, and a greater influence in the Mediterranean with the new possessions of Gibraltar and Minorca. The establishment of the Bank of England in 1694 laid a financial foundation for Britain as a great nation.

France and the Low Countries had long been the major western European mercantile nations but from the end of the seventeenth century Britain overtook the Netherlands to become an equal of France in what became known as the 'commercial revolution', a phrase coined by Viscount Bolingbroke in the 1730s. In the 1690s France took the decision to focus its military efforts on its land campaign, concentrating resources on the army rather than large warships, effectively giving up control of the seas. By 1715 Britain's navy of 182 ships in excess of 300 tons was larger than the French and Dutch navies combined. A larger navy helped to protect merchant shipping as well as assisting the growth of the empire by means of 'gunboat diplomacy'.

The Navigation Acts introduced by the Commonwealth Parliament and under Charles II did much to shift trade away from foreign to English ships and crews, as well as Scottish after the union of 1707. In 1600 half the ships entering London were English but by the 1680s that had risen to seventy-five per cent.

Although London was by far the biggest British port there were others benefitting from the increased trade. The new Atlantic routes benefitted towns on the western side of Britain. Liverpool grew from nothing to become the largest port in the north west by the end of the seventeenth century due to exports of cloth and salt. Bristol benefitted from imports of sugar, and fish from Newfoundland. Exeter became a major exporting port for cloth. Glasgow and Whitehaven in Cumbria also grew rapidly in size. On the east coast, shipments of coal from Newcastle rose dramatically in order to feed the growing demand from London and elsewhere and Hull became prominent. There was a five-fold increase in the amount of shipping passing through the Port of London between the beginning and end of the seventeenth century. Yet at the same time certain trades were moving away from London, such as tobacco in which the capital had an 80 per cent share in the middle of the seventeenth century, falling to 50 per cent in the 1680s in the face of rivalry from other ports.

Initially London was the leading port in the triangular slave trade in the early part of the eighteenth century. Ships would leave Britain bound for Africa where goods were traded for human cargo that was then taken to the Caribbean. They returned from there to Britain loaded with sugar and tobacco. Later in the century Bristol, and then Liverpool, became the prominent ports for this trade.

All the major European nations were at war with each other for a sixty year period from the second half of the eighteenth century. At the end of the Seven Years' War between 1756 and 1763 Britain had greatly enlarged the territory that it controlled in America, the Caribbean and India, either directly or through the East India Company. France lost almost all its vast territories in America and India to either Britain or Spain. Australia, New Zealand and Western Canada began to be colonized by Britain following James Cook's voyages around the Pacific in the latter eighteenth century. At the conclusion of the French Revolutionary War and Napoleonic Wars between 1793 and 1815 Britain was left as unquestionably the greatest European power, with an empire that spanned the globe, patrolled by the world's strongest navy and financed by a manufacturing economy.

Coffee houses and the origins of Lloyd's Insurance and the Baltic Exchange

The growth of international shipping created an increasing market for finance and marine insurance. London's merchants, financiers and marine insurance underwriters were primarily based at the Royal Exchange. At the turn of the eighteenth century specialist financial traders also began to congregate at certain coffee houses.

At the very end of the seventeenth century insurance underwriters met at Edward Lloyd's coffee house in Lombard Street to gather information and do business with one another. Information began to be published and read out from a pulpit within the coffee house on sailings and maritime disasters, which continued as 'Lloyd's List' after Lloyd's death in about 1713. In 1760 an association of underwriters was formed to set up a scheme to classify ships according to their condition in order to better quantify their risk. The result was the annual Lloyd's Register of Shipping which was first published in 1764, listing merchant vessels according to their name, home port, master, tonnage and equipment. A classification was devised to denote the condition of the ship according to the association's surveyors. As the organization began to expand internationally, surveyors were recruited around the world.

Official ship registration began in Britain from the seventeenth century and was the responsibility of customs officers. It was not until 1786 however that registration became fully obligatory for decked vessels above fifteen tons. In the latter part of the century around 200 large ships of over 360 tons were registered at London but also many smaller vessels.

Businessmen at coffee houses such as Garraway's and Jonathan's bought and sold commodities. At the latter, shares in joint-stock companies were traded after stockbrokers were expelled from the Royal Exchange in 1697, eventually leading to the establishment of the London Stock Exchange in 1802. Maritime merchants, ship brokers and ship captains met at John's on Birchin Lane, established in 1683, where ship auctions were held. Traders in goods from the American colonies met at the Virginia Coffee House, behind the Royal Exchange. The business of these merchants was to match cargoes with available ships arriving and departing from the Port. They were gradually joined there by brokers in merchandise to and from the Baltic and in 1744 the establishment changed its name to the Virginia and Baltick Coffee House. There was much risky speculative dealing in the 1820s and the brokers regulated their business. In 1823 a committee of brokers and merchants was formed; membership was restricted to 300 and a new headquarters established, known as the Subscription Room. This later evolved into the Baltic Exchange.

Custom House

At each major English port the officials responsible for collecting duties on behalf of the monarch were based at a building known as Custom House. At the Port of London it has always been located on the riverside immediately upstream of the Tower. The first recorded building was constructed at Wool Quay by the Sheriff of London in 1385 during the reign of Richard II. The poet Geoffrey Chaucer, Comptroller of the Customs of Wools, Skins and Tanned Hides from 1374 until 1386, was based there for his work as manager of tax collectors.

Those officials appointed as collectors and controllers during the mid-fifteenth century were from amongst London's leading merchants and stayed in their posts for short periods, often then rising to higher civic offices. The senior London customs officials during the latter years of Edward IV and reign of Henry VII, however, were royal servants who held their positions for many years.

The medieval Custom House was rebuilt in red brick in 1559 with three storeys, of which the lower level was an open arcade. Inspectors from Custom House known as 'tide-waiters' boarded each ship as it arrived to obtain a

Custom House in the early nineteenth century prior to its rebuilding by Robert Smirke. This engraving first appeared in Bernard Depping's *L'Angleterre, ou Description Historique et Topographique de Royaume Uni*, published in Paris in 1824.

certificate of the vessel's cargo, to be recorded at Custom House and the duty calculated. With confiscated goods stored inside, often of a flammable nature, fire was always a danger. When the Elizabethan property was destroyed in the Great Fire it was the first building that Charles II proposed to be rebuilt from public funds and the King surprised everyone by appointing Christopher Wren, a professor of astronomy from Oxford, to oversee the work, his first design project in London.

Wren's building was in turn devastated by fire in 1715. Its replacement, designed by Thomas Ripley, was constructed in a U-shape around a courtyard. Daniel Defoe wrote of it: 'As the city is the centre of business, there is Custom-house, an article, which, as it brings in an immense revenue to the public, so it cannot be removed from its place, all the vast import and export of goods being, of necessity, made there ... The stateliness of the building, showed the greatness of the business that is transacted there: the Long Room is like an Exchange every morning and the crowd of people who appear there, and the business they do, is not to be explained by words, nothing of that kind in Europe is like it.'

With growing trade in the port, and being somewhat dilapidated, a larger building was already being planned when it met the fate of its predecessors in 1814. Surrounding properties east of Billingsgate were purchased for the larger site with a waterfront almost 150 metres long. Much of the current building, completed in 1817, was designed by David Laing, Surveyor to the Customs and a pupil of John Soane, featuring a much-praised triple-domed hall in a French style. Unfortunately Laing had not foreseen that the piling underpinning the building had been poorly and fraudulently carried out by a contractor and in 1824 part of the river façade and the floor of the main hall collapsed. By then such work was the responsibility of the Office of Works and their surveyor Robert Smirke was commissioned to put things right. He created a new façade featuring Ionic columns that remain today.

In the early nineteenth century the 'tide-waiters' boarded inbound ships at Gravesend and stayed on board until their cargoes were discharged in the Port. In the docks and wharves 'landing-officers' took note of goods as they came ashore and once duties were paid a receipt was given. This information was then taken to the Long Room at Custom House. The system was modified in later decades whereby the master of each ship arriving or leaving the Port was obliged to attend the Long Room to report on its cargo and necessary payment made. In 1840 London's Custom House collected almost half of the total duties from the United Kingdom's ports. Throughout that century customs duties were progressively simplified. In 1853 there were over 1,100 rates of duty, yet most income came from just a small number of types of goods. Towards the century's end the number of rates had been greatly reduced and focussed on those imports that created most income, namely tobacco, spirits, tea and wine. Ships' masters today no longer arrive at Custom House to pay their duties but the building remains a rather grand office of HM Revenue & Customs.

The downriver hamlets before the nineteenth century

Immediately to the east of the Tower of London lay the Precinct of St Katharine, to which we will return in the next chapter. Further east still, the hamlets directly on the north bank were quite isolated from the city and surrounding districts until at least the sixteenth century. They were most easily reached by boat and evolved into communities employed in maritime industries, looking outwards to the river.

In Anglo-Saxon times a church dedicated to St Dunstan was established in the manor of Stibenhede. The village of Stepney, as it later became known, gradually grew in all directions around it, including down to the riverside hamlet of Ratcliff where Stepney's port developed, with cottages inhabited by fisherman and ferrymen.

Most of the nearby area had been marshy until the Middle Ages. It was then held by the bishops of London and in the reign of Edward II their bondmen converted much of Stepney Marsh – the Isle of Dogs – to meadow, with the alluvial deposits making it a rich pastureland. There were serious floods at various times, the most significant in March 1660. Three days after it occurred Samuel Pepys was passing by boat and recorded: '... in our way we saw the great breach which the late high water had made, to the loss of many 1000*l* [£1000] to the people about Limehouse.'

The process of draining Wapping Marsh, between Ratcliff and St Katharine's, was undertaken in the early sixteenth century when Cornelius Vanderdelft, a Dutchman with specialist knowledge in land drainage, was commissioned to oversee the task. A wall of built-up ground as high as eight or nine feet above the level of the land was created along the riverside and drainage ditches dug across the low ground. Cottages and workshops developed along the water's edge, creating the hamlet of Wapping-in-the-Wose ('in the marsh'), with each householder responsible for maintaining the wall. The buildings were constructed in precarious and rickety fashion overhanging the wall, interrupted by numerous stairs down to the river, forming the street of Wapping Wall, as well as Foxes Lanes (now Glamis Road). Similarly, causeways higher than the surrounding fields were created with buildings along them. Thus Wapping evolved as a river-facing community, otherwise isolated by its surrounding marsh.

The riverside communities were connected by a country lane, which in the time of Elizabethan historian John Stow developed into the road known as Ratcliff Highway, north of which lay open countryside. By then there were hamlets around the northern part of the Isle of Dogs. 'Of late years shipwrights and, for the most part, other marine men, have built many large and strong houses for themselves, and smaller for sailors, from thence also to Poplar, and so to Blackwall,' Stow recalled.

Maritime industries, including shipbuilding, the manufacture of chandlery, and the fitting out of ships, developed at Ratcliff, then to its east at Wapping and Limehouse to its west. The entire population was in some way involved in shipping and river activities. Some inhabitants became relatively wealthy and larger houses were built along Wapping High Street. Sailors arriving during the summer and autumn on long-distance voyages over-wintered in the riverside hamlets as they waited for their next passage. Their money boosted the local economy.

By the seventeenth century the waterfront had become a busy area, reflected in the building of new churches for the growing, strongly religious communities of Wapping (1617) and Shadwell (1656). The East India Company built an elegant chapel at Poplar in 1650, rebuilt in 1776, consisting of materials imported from the Far East and with wooden columns made from the masts of East Indiamen. There was such a demand for timber for rebuilding the City following the Great Fire of 1666 that a community of Danish and Norwegian importers established themselves at Well Close Square to the north of St Katharine's. They built their own church in 1696, designed by their compatriot and colleague of Sir Christopher Wren, Caius Gabriel Cibber. It remained a Scandinavian church for more than a century and was converted into a British seaman's mission in the nineteenth century. Swedes established their own church close by, to the north of Wapping, in 1729. As the easterly hamlets grew in size, these small seventeenth century churches were joined in the early eighteenth century by Nicholas Hawksmoor's much larger and magnificent St Anne's at Limehouse.

The year after witnessing the breach, Pepys visited Limehouse where 'they have a design to get the King to hire a docke for the herring busses [small boats for herring fishing] to lie up in'. Three years later he was back again: 'With Mr Margetts to Limehouse to see his ground and ropeyard there; which is very fine, and I believe we shall imploy it for the Navy.'

At a slightly earlier time than Pepys' visit, the property businessman Thomas Neale, famous for developing the district of Seven Dials at Covent Garden, created the riverside hamlet of Shadwell, next to Wapping, with a church and market place. By the end of the eighteenth century there was a large waterworks at Shadwell that supplied all the hamlets, as well as ropewalks, a large distillery, three coal wharves and two docks.

Numerous carpenters and blacksmiths set up shop in the villages. Craftsmen and tradesmen provided vessels on the river with many of their supplies, everything from ropes and anchors to ships' biscuits. There lived stevedores and lumpers who loaded and unloaded cargoes, as did the women who took in sailors' washing and the men who went on board to catch the rats. Seamen would come ashore and squander their pay on alcohol and women. Wapping in particular was noted for its many alehouses, of which *The Prospect of Whitby* and *The Town of Ramsgate* still remain. For some centuries the gibbet for hanging convicted pirates was located at Wapping, initially at the western end of the village and later moving a little to the east. Near to Blackwall, where Bow Creek enters the Thames, was a centre of shipbuilding, notably Green & Wigram's, around which it remained rural until the 1830s.

The East India Company had warehouses at Ratcliff, between Broad Street and the river, the Shipwrights' Company had their hall in Butchers Row, and the coopers had their headquarters and a charity school, founded in 1536, in the village. The riverside part of the village, a total of fifty-five acres, was destroyed in July 1794 when a barge-builder's pitch kettle at Cloves' barge-builders overturned. A fire spread through wooden shacks to barges on the river and then to the East India warehouse containing saltpetre (potassium nitrate). According to a contemporary account, wind drove the flames through the narrow streets destroying 630 buildings and leaving 2,700 people homeless. It is said to have been London's most devastating fire between the Great Fire and the Blitz.

On the opposite bank of the river, the hamlet of Rotherhithe had existed since at least the twelfth century. Its medieval riverside church of St Mary was rebuilt in 1714. Like the communities on the north side, its people depended on seafaring and maritime industries. It was home to many ships' captains, most memorably Christopher Jones, master of the *Mayflower* that sailed the Pilgrims to America, who was buried at St Mary's in 1622. The local charity school, opposite the church, was founded for the sons of mariners in 1613 by the Elders of Trinity House and in 1731 seventeen of its trustees were captains. Many of those who made up the vestry – the parish council – were ship's masters.

During the seventeenth and eighteenth centuries the area was usually referred to by the alternative name of Redriff. At the turn of the nineteenth century the long waterfront was lined with shipbuilders and breakers' yards, wharves, and dry docks, as well as the entrance to the Howland wet dock. Numerous stairs led down to the water. There were about twelve shipyards, with some perhaps dating back several centuries, building ships for the Royal Navy and East India Company amongst others. The famous painting by J.M.W. Turner shows *The Fighting Temeraire* being towed to John Beatson's yard at Rotherhithe to be broken up. All these businesses were connected by Rotherhithe Street, which curved around the edge of the peninsula. In around 1800 the population was over 10,000 but 100 years later it was to swell to almost four times as many.

Eighteenth century Rotherhithe with the church of St Mary the Virgin.

Congestion in the Port

During the period from 1500 to 1700 London's population rose more than ten-fold, from 50,000 to over 500,000, overtaking Paris to become the largest city in Europe. An increased population required greater supplies of corn, salt and other provisions, as well as coal for heating and cooking and stone for building. This created a significant increase in coastal shipping into the port. The rapid population increase was fuelled by manufacturing and trade, by new colonies and trading posts, and by a nascent Industrial Revolution. At the start of the eighteenth century London was on the verge of becoming Europe's leading financial centre, the capital of a growing empire and a major port at the centre of the world. According to historian Gustav Milne, England 'now found itself in a central position on the enlarged world map, looking east towards the old world, and west, towards the new.'

The number of Britain's colonies continued to increase and new trade routes were created. Imports and exports became ever more concentrated on a smaller number of British ports, of which the most important was London. The city had the monopoly on trading with the Far East and by the beginning of the eighteenth century it had become the busiest trading port in the world. In

1700 it was handling a staggering 80 per cent of Britain's imports, 69 per cent of exports and 86 per cent of re-exports. Trade almost doubled between 1700 and 1770 and nearly doubled again in the following twenty-five years. Imports flowing into London rose from £4,876,000 in value in 1700 to £14,863,000 in 1795. As the Industrial Revolution took hold, exports during the same period rose from £5,388,000 to £16,579,000.

The arrival of sailing ships was quite unpredictable in the days before instant communication. They often sailed, and arrived, in groups, according to harvests in distant lands and seasonal winds, and moved in convoy during times of war. Bad weather out at sea, or even wind in the wrong direction along the Thames Estuary, could hold up ships for long periods, with the quays relatively quiet. Suddenly hundreds would arrive within a few days. The result was a backlog and vessels waiting at anchor for days or even weeks to be unloaded. Ships had to moor in mid-stream, waiting for their cargoes to be off-loaded onto a hoy or lighter. The larger the ship the further downstream it had to moor to prevent beaching at low tide. Coasters could moor in the Upper Pool up to London Bridge, middle-size ships in the Middle Pool up to Union Hole, larger ships in the Lower Pool up to Wapping New Stairs, ships above 450 tons in the Limehouse and Greenwich reaches, and large East Indiamen no further upstream than Blackwall. Colliers lay at Ratcliff and Wapping.

In the early eighteenth century Daniel Defoe wrote: 'That part of the river of Thames which is properly the harbour, and where the ships usually deliver or unload their cargoes, is called the Pool, and begins at the turning of the river out of Lime-house Reach, and extends to the Custom-house-Keys. In this compass I have had the curiosity to count the ships as well as I could, *en passant*, and have found above two thousand sail of all sorts, not reckoning barges, lighters or pleasure-boats, and yachts; but vessels that really go to sea.' The precise number may not be accurate but certainly there would have been many vessels waiting to offload at the Legal Quays.

For 200 years, from 1603, London had a mere 1,419 feet of Legal Quays, mostly unprotected from the weather, with both imports and exports passing across them. Bristol, with less trade, had 4,000 feet. The number of vessels entering the port annually rose from approximately 5,500 at the beginning of the eighteenth century to around 13,500 ships each year. At the same time the average size also doubled from 50 to 100 tons. Hundreds of ships were moored in the Pool of London at any one time, four or five abreast in midstream. Others waited or discharged their cargoes onto lighters further downstream. Cargoes were offloaded onto smaller boats that then negotiated their way around the other moored vessels to reach the designated Legal Quay. Following clearance, the goods had to be moved up the ten narrow and crowded streets that led away from the quays. Between 1700 and 1750 not only did the number of colliers arriving rise from around 300 to 450 but they were larger and carried greater volume. There were 3,400 lighters on the river, many used for simply storing coal. Further obstruction was caused by imported timber left to float on the river. Such was the congestion that commodities could become scarce in London when there was plenty waiting on the river to be unloaded. The wharfingers, who operated a cartel, profited while the shipowners and merchants lost money caused by delays.

The Legal Quays were a monopoly that was jealously guarded by the City of London Corporation, a body made up of many of the quay owners and also the licensor of lightermen and watermen. Since some time in the Middle Ages the City had also governed the porters who had a monopoly on unloading and delivering merchandise and set the rates for their services. They were freemen of the City and their history varied over time. By the early eighteenth century they had become formed into four brotherhoods: Ticket Porters who landed goods from America; Fellowship Porters who landed dry goods such as corn and salt; Tackle Porters who were furnished with scales and weights; and Companies' Porters who handled vessels from specific areas. (The privileges and organization of porters gradually faded away during the nineteenth century).

In the last decades of the eighteenth century the situation had become intolerable for merchants and shipowners. They complained to the City Corporation and Parliament about the delays in unloading and the extortions of quay owners, requesting extensions to the wharves and quays. Vested interests were too powerful however, and little came of it. As a concession, starting from 1663, twenty-one wharves with a length of about 3,700 feet at Southwark and St Katharine's were licensed for unloading imports on a temporary basis (or under sufferance of the right being rescinded) and these were therefore known as 'Sufferance Wharves'. Generally, they handled lower-values and bulkier cargoes such as timber, stone and grain, much of it coastal trade on which no duty was payable anyway.

New wet docks

A partial answer to the congestion on the river was the creation of wet docks where ships could be moored, out of the strong winds that could blow across the rural areas downriver. It would have been illegal, however, to unload imports there. London's first recorded wet dock was created by the East India Company at Blackwall, for fitting out ships following their launch. Samuel Pepys wrote in January 1661: '... went to blackwall and viewed the dock and the new wet dock which is newly made there, and a brave new merchantman which is to be launched shortly, and they say to be called the *Royall oake*.' The Company had sold the dock in the mid-seventeenth century. In 1789 a Mr Perry created the eight-acre Brunswick (or Perry's) Dock and the former Blackwall Dock was absorbed into it. Perry's Dock was used for masting and fitting out vessels, with warehouses for storing whalebone and blubber. A painting from 1803 shows many moored ships and the dock surrounded by open countryside, with a line of trees acting as a windbreak. Towering over the dock was the 120 feet tall Mast House for lifting masts on and off ships. Using the Mast House's crane a mast could be fitted in three hours and forty minutes. Many of the ships that fought against France in the Napoleonic wars were built at Perry's.

To further ease the congestion, a large enclosed basin was opened in 1700 downstream of Southwark on the south bank of the river. Known as the Howland Great Wet Dock, it was the first large commercial dock in Britain. Its purpose was simply to provide sheltered anchorage for ships waiting to load or unload, as well as for refitting and repairing, and it therefore had no warehouses. It was built by the Rotherhithe shipwrights John and Richard Wells on land leased from the Russell family, the Dukes of Bedford. The Russells had acquired the area when in 1695 Elizabeth, daughter of the wealthy Streatham landowner John Howland and granddaughter of the Chairman of the East India Company, married the 15-year old Wrothesley Russell, Marquis of Tavistock. A dry dock had previously existed on the site and in 1696 the Duke and Elizabeth petitioned Parliament to build the new wet dock, which would be 'of Use to the Publick'. Work began in the following year creating the basin of over 1,000 feet in length, 500 feet in width and 17 feet in depth. It covered 12½ acres, with a basin of 10 acres. The sides were lined with wood by Stepney carpenter William Ogbourne.

When it opened the dock had space for up to 120 ocean-going ships of even the largest size. It had a constant depth and vessels could enter at various states of tides through an entrance lock of 150 feet in length by 44 feet in width. The water was surrounded by lines of trees to create a windbreak and the company promoted the fact that vessels could be moored there safely. Facilities were available for fixing masts and careening (cleaning and repairing hulls). During the Great Storm of November 1703 there was much damage to ships anchored on the open river but those moored in the Wet Dock remained safe. There was greater safety because cooking facilities for crews were provided on shore and fires were prohibited on moored vessels. The Russell family had a mansion built at the head of the dock from where they could look over the ships. The house was rarely used however, fell into disrepair and was demolished in the early nineteenth century.

The Howland Great Dock's location away from the city provided a good space for the messy business of whaling. Whalers had been operating from London since at least Tudor times when the Muscovy Company were hunting the creatures off the coast of Norway. Their remains provided meat, oil for lighting, and bones for corsets and upholstery. Ships of around 350 tons left port each April to arrive at Norway and Greenland in May when the whales swam near the surface. Oil had to be extracted on board the ships at sea until the early 1720s when the Howland Dock installed large boilers and tanks capable of processing oil and blubber on land, a more convenient and efficient method for the shipowners. This became a major part of the dock's business and in 1763, when it was acquired from the Russells by the Wells family it was renamed Greenland Dock. As the whaling industry declined, the dock was given over to the importation of timber and corn. It became part of the Surrey Commercial Docks and remained largely unaltered until more than doubled in size at the end of the nineteenth century. It still remains today as the oldest surviving London dock, although used only for recreational purposes and surrounded by a residential area.

The Marine Police Establishment

The result of the congestion was that valuable cargoes were left on moored ships for days or weeks on end, guarded by skeleton crews. They were then shifted to the quay by low-paid watermen of often dubious character, and lay on the quaysides in chaotic circumstances waiting to be checked. In such conditions it is not surprising that theft was rife. Thousands of port labourers and even customs officers were profiting from dishonesty, controlled by receivers, apparently respectable businessmen, known as 'copemen'.

John Harriott, originating from Essex, returned from America in 1795 and settled at Goodman's Fields just to the east of the City. He was an active man, having by then served in the Royal Navy from the age of 13; as a seaman in the merchant navy; had lived with indigenous North Americans; was wounded while fighting for the East India Company; and, as a farmer, had reclaimed land from the sea in Essex. Harriott had a close relationship with his uncle, John Staples, a London stipendiary magistrate with a great knowledge of crime on the river. Discussions between the two led Harriott to draw up plans for a police force to protect shipping on the river. Yet when approached with the idea, the Lord Mayor of London gave the opinion that this was not the business of the City. The plan advanced no further with the Home Secretary, the Duke of Portland, when it was presented to him in October 1797.

Shortly afterwards, Harriott was introduced to the magistrate, social reformer and statistician Patrick Colquhoun. The previous year Colquhoun had published the first of two editions of his *Treatise on the Police of the Metropolis* in which he argued for a centrally-organized police force for London, separated from the judiciary, with publicly salaried officers as was the case in France. It was widely read, not least by George III. Colquhoun originated from Dumbarton in Scotland and was a successful merchant in Virginia before being elected as Lord Provost (mayor) of Glasgow. In 1789 he and his family moved to London and three years later he was appointed as a magistrate. Colquhoun was a prolific writer of pamphlets on social issues and he also established a soup kitchen at Spitalfields. He worked together with the social philosopher Jeremy Bentham to develop his views.

Colquhoun's theories and observations in his *Treatise* led to an approach for advice on theft-prevention by London merchants trading with the Caribbean. He estimated that there were at any time 8,000 vessels between four miles below and two miles above London Bridge; and that the amount of property afloat to be worth £75 million, all of which was vulnerable to theft. He listed the various categories of thief working in the port with the slang terms in use. A corrupt revenue officer was a 'game'; 'river pirates' bribed watchmen before making off with a ship or lighter's cargo; 'night plunderers' were gangs who stole from unprotected lighters at night; 'light horsemen' were organized gangs who worked with the help of corrupt customs officers; and 'scuffle-hunters' offered their assistance as porters but simply pilfered goods and made away. Colquhoun's estimate of goods plundered from the port during 1797 was valued at slightly over half a million pounds. He argued for the establishment of a river police force and the creation of docks, where goods could be unloaded behind high walls and securely managed, away from the congested, chaotic and insecure Legal Quays.

At the end of January 1798 the Committee of the West India Merchants and Planters considered Colquhoun's proposal for a river police that could protect their cargoes on the Thames. They agreed that the plan should proceed providing it had approval from the government. In March the Duke of Portland wrote to confirm that the Exchequer would contribute financial assistance for the scheme, most likely because the government itself was losing import duties when cargo was stolen. Colquhoun was duly requested by the West Indies Committee to put the plan into operation.

In July 1798 the West India Merchants and Planters Marine Police Institution came into being, essentially a private security force, operating from a riverside building at Wapping New Stairs. Wapping was where many ships were moored and it was to that area that large amounts of the stolen cargoes were taken. The Institution initially consisted of twelve staff, patrolling continuously by boat day and night from London Bridge down to Blackwall. Although part-funded by the government, most of the running cost was paid by the West India merchants. Its primary task was to protect the ships carrying cargoes from the West Indies but their presence on the river was reported as immediately reducing theft from all craft, estimated at over £100,000 in the first six months. Furthermore, a register of 900 labourers employed in discharging West India ships was created, who were to wear uniforms in which stolen goods could not be concealed.

In the next chapter we will look at the creation of the West India Docks. The jurisdiction of the Marine Police did not extend to inside the enclosed docks and the dock company employed constables to ensure that their regulations were enforced. The first Captain of the Watch at the West India Docks was Captain Robert Bartlett who was appointed in 1802. Theft was minimal and this model of supervision was to be copied in other docks. With the creation of their docks, the West India merchants no longer required protection from their security force. Yet its success led the government to pass the Police Act in 1800, transforming it into a public body covering all shipping on the tidal Thames and its tributaries. It is said to be the world's first organized police force. The magistrates attached to the station had to deal with crimes along the length of the tidal Thames. They were obliged to take oaths to empower them in each of Essex, Middlesex, Surrey, Kent and the City of Westminster (but not the

City of London), the counties through which the river flowed. Harriott was appointed as the first stipendiary magistrate in residence, a post he held until his death in 1817.

The introduction of the Marine Police Establishment was naturally unpopular with those who had much to lose in illegal income. When a coal heaver was arrested for stealing a sack of coal, a riot involving several hundred erupted while the case was being dealt with by Harriott in the courtroom in October 1798. Colquhoun and Harriott read the Riot Act on Wapping High Street and ordered them to disperse. Shots were fired by the police but one of the constables, Gabriel Franks, was hit and died two days later, the first British policeman to die while carrying out his duties. The ringleader of the rioters was hanged and six men transported to the colonies for life.

Colquhoun wrote of the success of the force in his *The Commerce and Policing of the River Thames*, which was influential in creating new police bodies in several cities around the world. Over thirty years after the establishment of the Marine Police the London-wide Metropolitan Police was created, with which the river force merged in 1839 as the Thames Division. They continue to be based at their original location in Wapping.

Chapter Four

The New Docks of the Early Nineteenth Century

Much of the great increase in imports into London during the eighteenth century consisted of sugar, rum and other goods from the West Indies. Due to prevailing winds there was a short season from July to October for ships to sail from there to Britain. Such was the congestion when they reached London that sugar could be piled as much as eight hogsheads* high and unprotected on the quayside for lengthy periods, waiting to be inspected by customs officers. That was particularly so during the wars with France when most ships sailed in convoy for their protection and therefore arrived in groups.

Frustrated by the continual refusal of the government, the City of London and other vested interests to address the problems, the West India merchants threatened to take their operations elsewhere. That was a not inconsiderable threat when their business could account for a third of annual trade by value arriving at the Port. Between 1717 and 1785 seven docks had been created at Liverpool, which was not impeded by the ancient monopolies enjoyed by City of London Corporation, wharf owners and the Company of Watermen.

The London insurer and Fellow of the Royal Society, William Vaughan, in 1793 published his treatise *On Wet Docks, Quays and Warehouses for the Port of London, with Hints Respecting Trade*, describing the problems. His solution was to create tide-free docks between the Tower of London and Blackwall, noting successful examples at Liverpool and Le Havre. In the spring of 1794 he called a meeting of London merchants and members of public bodies, which a year later resolved that wet docks at Wapping were the solution. A petition was started and in 1796, under increasing pressure, Parliament formed the Select Committee for the Improvement of the Port of London, including Prime Minister William Pitt the Younger, to consider the matter. Ideas were

---

* hogshead = a barrel containing between 800 and 1,500 Imperial pounds (360 – 680 kilograms)

invited for reform of the Port and eight separate schemes were reviewed. The committee sat for twenty-five days during which time it heard evidence from the wharfingers who owned the Legal Quays, Customs, Trinity House, the East India Company, the Admiralty, shipowners, merchants and lightermen.

Plans were submitted that included better mooring facilities along the centre of the river and many new quays each dealing in goods from particular locations. This solution by wharf-owner Edward Ogle required the government to purchase a large amount of riverside land and was therefore a non-starter. Architect and engineer Willey Reveley's plan was to straighten the Thames by means of a channel across the Isle of Dogs, with the bends at Limehouse, Greenwich and Blackwall converted into wet docks. The City of London promoted the extension of the existing Legal Quays, a dock across the Isle of Dogs, and another at Rotherhithe. The people of Rotherhithe proposed five docks there. Another idea, submitted by a Mr Spence, Maritime Surveyor to the Admiralty, was for twelve docks either on the Isle of Dogs or either side of the river, each dealing with ships according to frequency of arrival. The London architect Samuel Wyatt proposed a canal through the Isle of Dogs from Blackwall to Limehouse, creating a shortcut whereby ships would no longer have to pass all the way around Greenwich Reach. His idea was to include three new parallel docks there for different types of vessel, with floating wharves. A similar proposal came from one Ralph Walker, accepted as viable by Trinity House.

The West India Docks

The Prime Minister handed the reform issue to a Select Committee chaired by Lord Hawkesbury. They recommended a canal across the Isle of Dogs linked to a system of docks, similar to the proposals of Wyatt, Walker and Vaughan. The West Indies merchant and shipowner Robert Milligan, whose family owned a sugar plantation in Jamaica, brought together a group of investors at the Royal Exchange to form the West India Dock Company in order to create facilities on the Isle of Dogs. (Such was Milligan's contribution in the final outcome that after the completion of the docks a bronze statue of him was erected at the entrance, which now stands before the Museum of Docklands).

Parliament passed the West India Dock Act in July 1799 to create the new venture as a private enterprise. It was the start of a new era for the Port of London, setting the template for the Acts for the other docks that immediately followed. Over the next hundred years vast new artificial lakes would be created either side of the river behind high walls and out of site of the public in which an increasing volume of goods could be safely unloaded, loaded, stored and repacked. Customs duties on imports could henceforth be paid at these new docks as an alternative to the Legal Quays along the north bank of the river within the City.

The Act of Parliament gave the West India Dock Company the right to raise £500,000 in capital (later raised to almost £1,400,000), purchase almost 300 acres of land to create their docks, and to discharge imported goods and store them in warehouses, thus ending the 250-year-old monopoly of the City's Legal Quays. In return for its investment, ships bringing goods from the West Indies would henceforth be obliged to land them at the West India Docks for a period of twenty-one years. The only exception was tobacco, which had to be unloaded on the river at the King's warehouse. The West India merchant, City of London alderman and opponent of the anti-slavery movement, George Hibbert, was the first chairman and he remained so for more than twenty years. The court of directors was to consist of thirteen stockholders, four aldermen of the City and four members of the City's Common Council. Importantly, the company had the right to draw water from the Thames to fill the docks. It was however forbidden to build or repair ships or operate a dry dock in order to protect other such businesses on the river, a restriction that would be removed seventy-five years later. The Company dockmasters had to satisfy Trinity House they were competent and would have control of the river for an area of 200 yards beyond the dock entrances.

The Act stipulated that the government had the option to buy the freehold of the Legal Quays, for which they paid £468,087. They thereafter derived income from rental on the properties. Owners of warehouses, the City of London Corporation, porters, lightermen, coopers and others were also to be compensated for their loss of business. It took twenty years to conclude agreements and settle all the claims, which finally amounted to £860,000. Lord Gwydyr and others were paid the huge sum of £142,136 (£650 million at current values) for loss of income from mooring chains on the river.

During the eighteenth century Robert Walpole had attempted, but failed, to introduce a system whereby customs duties were paid only when imports left the port. The intention was for London to become an entrepôt port in which goods could be stored in sealed conditions in bonded warehouses, and thus pass through on a journey from one country to another without having to pay duties. This finally came to fruition with Chancellor William Pitt's Warehousing Act of 1803. As a preventative measure to ensure inbound ships did not land cargoes elsewhere on the river, the hatches were secured at Gravesend and only unlocked once in the dock. The West India Docks and, subsequently, the London Docks, were the first to be licensed to enjoy such a privilege. Thereafter vast amounts of precious goods, particularly alcohol and tobacco could be stored and pass through the Port of London.

The City of London Corporation was initially given the right to acquire the land for the West India Docks. That proved too cumbersome and the task was soon transferred to the Company. They began the process of buying land from the many property owners, which included ship-breakers' yards, rope-makers, timber merchants and cow-herders. The civil engineer William Jessop, who was also responsible for the Grand Junction Canal, was commissioned to create the docks and warehouses. He in turn left much of the work to Ralph Walker, one of those who had originally proposed the docks. John Rennie acted as a consultant, introducing steam power for the construction work.

The foundation stone of the West India Docks (still visible in the north-west corner of the complex), laid on the anniversary of the passing of the Act, stated in wonderfully idiosyncratic capitalization:

Of the Range of BUILDINGS
Constructed together with the Adjacent DOCKS, At the Expense of
public spirited Individuals,
Under the Sanction of a provident Legislature,
And with the liberal Co-operation of the Corporate Body of the CITY
of LONDON,
For the distinct Purpose
Of complete SECURITY and ample ACCOMMODATION
(hitherto not afforded)
To the SHIPPING and PRODUCE of the WEST INDIES at this
wealthy PORT.
THE FIRST STONE WAS LAID
On Saturday the Twelfth Day of July, A.D. 1800,
BY THE CONCURRING HANDS OF
THE RIGHT HONOURABLE LORD LOUGHBOROUGH
LORD HIGH CHANCELLOR OF GREAT BRITAIN,
THE RIGHT HONOURABLE WILLIAM PITT

FIRST LORD COMMISSIONER OF HIS MAJESTY'S
TREASURY AND CHANCELLOR OF HIS MAJESTY'S
EXCHEQUER
GEORGE HIBBERT ESQ, THE CHAIRMAN AND ROBERT
MILLIGAN ESQ, THE DEPUTY CHAIRMAN
OF THE WEST INDIA DOCK COMPANY
The two former conspicuous in the Band Of those illustrious
Statesmen
Who in either House of Parliament, have been zealous to promote,
The two latter distinguished among those chosen to direct
AN UNDERTAKING
Which, under the favour of GOD, shall contribute
STABILITY, INCREASE, and ORNAMENT
TO
BRITISH COMMERCE.

The VIPs attending the ceremony all travelled in a procession of barges and enjoyed a great feast at the London Tavern in Bishopsgate. It thereafter became the standard venue for dinners related to ceremonies associated with the laying of foundation stones and openings of new docks of the period.

Several problems had to be overcome during the planning and construction of the West India Docks. Firstly there were the negotiations with property-owners who held out for exorbitant compensation. Tens of millions of bricks were ordered for the construction but by then the London Docks were being created at Wapping and there was competition to receive supply, delaying both projects. There was violent opposition from watermen and porters who foresaw the end of their lucrative plundering and a military guard was laid on to protect the construction. And in July 1802 a coffer dam at the Blackwall entrance broke and eight workers drowned.

Two massive basins were constructed, lying side by side in parallel, in an approximately east-west direction. The one to the north covered 30 acres and was for ships arriving with imports from the Caribbean, while the southern dock was of 24 acres and used by ships loading with exports. Two smaller basins, one on each side of the Isle of Dogs, connected the docks to the Thames via locks at Blackwall Reach (for ships) and Limehouse Reach for lighters. The ship lock was of 45 feet in width, with a maximum depth of 21 feet, allowing for vessels of a tonnage of 350 tons.

As sugar and rum arrived from the West Indies it was to be stored at the West India Docks until required. Thus nine huge warehouses, nearly three-quarters of a mile long, flanked the Export Dock, capable of storing the entire annual import of sugar and vast quantities of rum. The warehouses were designed by George Gwilt the Elder and his son, also named George. Each of the blocks, five storeys high, contained a series of doors opening to each floor, with a crane above to lift merchandise, a design that became a regular feature of wharves and warehouses thereafter. In the early times cranes were powered by men, some using a treadmill. There was little need for warehousing around the Export Dock as most goods were loaded as they arrived at the docks. Henry Addington, Prime Minister, officially opened the docks in August 1802. The first ship to enter was one named after him, followed by another carrying a cargo of sugar.

Two hundred full-time waged labourers were employed by the company when the West India docks opened. As they were so distant from London a new remote community began to grow as a working-class suburb. In its early years the West India Docks were receiving around 500 ships each year, with the discharge of goods reduced from at least a month to three or four days.

Discipline and procedures were very strict. The original Act included the requirement to surround the docks with a tall protective wall, surrounded by a ditch of twelve feet in width and six feet in depth, with no other building to be erected within 100 yards. The wall was immensely strong, built according to Jessop's design of bricks, made in such a way that they became harder as they aged. A further security measure was that the captain and crew of inbound ships were obliged to leave their vessel as soon as they had berthed, leaving only one officer on board. Only West India Dock staff and revenue officers were allowed to handle the goods inside the docks, and would also accompany the owner of the goods for inspection. Wagons or non-company porters were not allowed within the complex. Much else was also included in the Act regarding security. Once weighed and counted, cargoes were put into storage within tall dockside warehouses or loaded onto lighters or carts for onward travel to their destinations.

As part of the West India Dock Act the City of London Corporation gained the right to create a canal through the Isle of Dogs in order to create a shortcut from Limehouse Reach to Blackwall Reach and save ships the inconvenience of the journey round the peninsula. It was completed in 1805. The reality was that no time was saved after ships were moored up, sails taken down, passed through the locks at either end, hauled through the canal by teams of horses and sails raised again for the short passage to the Pool of London. Tolls barely covered running costs of the City Canal and it instead became a useful berth for ships, particularly colliers, to moor while waiting to enter the port. In 1829 the City sold it to the West India Company. Two years later they obtained approval to transform the canal into docks but they merely widened part of it and used it as a timber pond.

Throughout the mid-nineteenth century there was a general inertia at the West India Docks, with few improvements to the estate. In 1870 the energetic Colonel J.L. du Plat Taylor was appointed general manager and a number of new initiatives were undertaken. The former City Canal was enlarged to become the South West India Dock. Three years later warehouses were erected for the sale of wool and for fifteen years the Company was able to dominate that trade (until finally seized back by the London and St Katharine Docks in 1887). The West India timber sheds were rebuilt to facilitate the handling of heavy mahogany and teak. Hydraulic machinery throughout the docks was also brought up to the highest standards. During the 1870s, under the leadership of du Plat Taylor, the West India Docks were popular with vessels of the colonial

The West India Import Dock shown in an engraving for Walks through London and published in 1817

and India routes but were thereafter increasingly hampered by their small entrance lock that limited them to vessels of 6,000 tons.

The 'free water' clause

There had been many objections to the idea of creating enclosed docks and ending the monopoly of landing imports at the Legal Quays and sufferance wharves. Amongst objectors were the City of London (who controlled the licensing of lightermen and porters at the Legal Quays), and the numerous independent operators of lighters and other craft who transported goods from ship to shore and between wharves. The Watermens' Company pointed out that it represented 12,000 men, of whom 4,000 were currently away on board men-of-war. If docks were created, less than half of those currently employed on the river would have work. Lightermen explained the great investment they had in their vessels and equipment and that much of their business would be lost without the need to ferry cargoes to the Legal Quays.

In order to pacify these parties the government included Section 138, the 'free water' clause, into the West India Dock Act, as well as those Acts that approved all subsequent enclosed docks. This proviso allowed lighters to freely enter the docks without charge for the purpose of delivering or receiving cargo or ballast, as they could on the open river. Ships were therefore able to enjoy the safety and facilities of an enclosed dock, yet unload overside onto the lighter as an alternative to using the dock's workers or warehouses. Thus riverside wharves continued to profit from the ever-increasing trade passing through London. In 1840 for example, 735 ships entered the Commercial Docks at Rotherhithe but so did almost 8,000 barges and smaller craft.

In the early years, the docks enjoyed monopolies, so profits were high and the effect of the free water clause was minimal. Much of their income came from warehousing landed goods or those waiting to be loaded. After the monopolies ended and ships were free to unload wherever they chose, the free water clause allowed the many wharves and newer docks to openly compete. The dock owners then found themselves in a position whereby they had to maintain their large warehouses, yet the lucrative income was instead going to competitors who offered lower charges. The dock companies attempted unsuccessfully to have the free water clause abolished in 1855 and again in 1899.

The London Docks

The West India docks were created by and for merchants dealing with the Caribbean, primarily the importation of sugar and rum. At the same time, general merchants who were not trading with the West or East Indies laid plans to instigate their own dock system. Their proposal, with less interest from the City of London and with greater complexities and costs, took a year longer to pass through Parliament. It was to be at Wapping, the area bounded by the river to the south, Ratcliff Highway to the north, Shadwell in the east and the old Hermitage Dock to the west. The scheme was named the London Docks, emphasizing that they were closer to the city than the more remote West India Docks being constructed to the east at the Isle of Dogs.

The Act of Parliament for their creation eventually passed into law in June 1800. Around 200 subscribers were named, including some who had opposed the idea of docks and others who were also involved in the West India Docks. The Act gave the Company a 21-year monopoly on the importation to London of tobacco, brandy, wine and rice, except from the East and West Indies, and excluding fruit. The Company was to elect twenty-four directors and managers, to be joined by the Lord Mayor of London as Conservator of the river. The Act set berthing rates for particular classes of ship and their destinations, including Ireland, the Baltic, Spain, Portugal, Newfoundland, the Mediterranean, Africa, and America. The promoters, along with those of the West India Docks, were to compensate the owners of the Legal Quays for loss of business.

At the inaugural meeting of the new company, held in July 1800, Sir Richard Neave was elected as chairman. William Vaughan, who had made proposals for new docks, was appointed to a five-man action committee. The Southwark-born Daniel Asher Alexander, at the time surveyor to Trinity House and designer of lighthouses, was commissioned as surveyor. (Several years later he created the colonnades at Queen's House, Greenwich in honour of Admiral Nelson). The choice of Alexander was no doubt due to his experience in designing high-security buildings, having previously been responsible for Dartmoor and Maidstone prisons. John Rennie also had a significant involvement while at the same time consulting for the West India Docks. Other engineers involved were the company directors Joseph Huddart (a respected harbour surveyor) and Robert Mylne who had begun his engineering career by designing Blackfriars Bridge. (For decades until his death Mylne held the post of surveyor of St Paul's Cathedral, and during the time the docks were being completed he managed the arrangements for Nelson's funeral).

Being closer to the City meant that the London Docks were to displace a more urban area than the West India Docks. Two thousand houses, businesses, Shadwell Waterworks, and part of the churchyard of St John's Wapping, were to be replaced by the new dock complex. According to later reports 24 'inferior' streets, 33 courts, alleys, lanes and rows were cleared, providing an improvement to the Parish of St George's, although much of the village had been destroyed less than a decade earlier in the fire of 1794 described in the previous chapter.

The Company seriously underestimated the cost of acquiring the land; it had to compete with the West India Docks for bricks; the war with France caused a shortage of manpower; and there was high inflation. All these problems resulted in delays in completing the work and the cost of construction was much higher than originally planned. The foundation stone was laid in a ceremony held in June 1802 attended by the Prime Minister and Chancellor of the Exchequer. Builders were employed seven days a week in order to accelerate the work but that caused protest from the Society for Suppression of Vice, who enlisted the Bishop of London against 'so alarming an evil'. Steam engines were used for draining the works and grinding mortar.

The first ship to enter the docks did so in January 1805, although not all the warehouses were complete at that time. Over the following thirteen years the company applied to Parliament on several occasions to raise further funds and to acquire more land to increase the size of the dock complex.

Vessels entered through one of two locks that led into basins and from there into any of three docks: Eastern, Western or Tobacco. These could hold up to 390 ships at a time. A third lock onto the river at the western end gave access to lighters. Each dock was surrounded by a spacious quay. Wines and spirits were stored in the vast undercroft of the bonded warehouses, created at various times during the nineteenth century and eventually covering about twenty acres, all joined by tunnels. Relief from alcohol fumes was achieved by a ventilation system that was part of the original design. Although constructed primarily of bricks the buildings were decorated with massive blocks of rusticated stone into which were carved sea shells.

The huge tobacco warehouse measured 752 feet by 160 feet and could hold 24,000 hogsheads (or 5,700 cubic metres) of tobacco. Up to 25,000 bales of wool were sold at public sales each week on the 'Great Wool Floor'. There was cellarage for 57,000 pipes of wine.* In the early 1820s the London Docks were

---

* pipe (or butt) = a half tun or 1,008 Imperial pints.

handling up to 212 ships at a time. Initially 100 permanent staff were employed, later increased to 300, with additional workers taken on as necessary.

Unlike the regime at the West India Docks, there were fewer authoritarian regulations at the London Docks regarding security and it was less regimented than at the East India Docks. Ships' crews, wine merchants and their agents were allowed to come and go and it was possible for cargo owners to take samples. It was quite normal for privileged individuals with suitable connections to bring a party of guests into the vaults and be escorted around by a cooper to take a glass of each of different kinds of wines and sherries from the many barrels. Management and workers and even seamen would visit the vaults for a tipple known as a 'waxer'. Visitors never failed to comment on the large amount of thick fungus that hung from the ceilings of the vaults. (Henry Mayhew gave a detailed description of a visit to the London Docks in about 1850 in his *London Labour and the London Poor*).

The East India Docks

The East India Company was in a different situation to other London merchants. It had already been trading as a single body for 200 years, whereas the West India and London Docks were created by groups of individual traders. Their ships, of up to 750 tons, were the largest arriving in the port. East Indiamen often loaded at Greenhithe, between Dartford and Gravesend. Incoming vessels discharged in deep water at Blackwall onto lighters that carried the cargoes to the Legal Quays. After inspection by Customs, the goods were transferred to the Company's own secure warehouses at Cutler Street. The Company also had the advantage of a well-paid and highly-trained paramilitary force to protect its cargoes.

The East India Company had attempted to open a legal quay for their exclusive use in 1786 but the plan had to be dropped after opposition from vested interests. It took no part in the lengthy fight to create new enclosed basins, yet when the West India Dock and London Dock companies gained the right to create their docks with bonded warehouses, the East India Company decided to follow, to be situated at their traditional base further downriver at Blackwall. The prospectus revealed it had been losing stock to theft in the past three years. It may well have been that thieves, inhibited from stealing goods now destined to the other new and more secure docks, were targeting East India cargoes.

The Act that approved the creation of the East India Docks was passed in July 1803, giving them a monopoly of twenty-one years for the discharging and loading of goods to the East Indies and China, whoever owned the vessel. Ships trading with other destinations were prohibited. Compensation was to be paid to dry dock owners at Northfleet and elsewhere whose business would be diminished. Two hundred thousand pounds of shares in the newly-formed East India Dock Company were easily sold to investors, including some who were directors of the West India and London Docks, and further funds were raised during the development phase. The East India Company reserved for itself the right to appoint four to the Board of the dock company, which initially comprised thirteen directors. At the first meeting, held at Throgmorton Street in August 1803, Joseph Cotton was appointed chairman.

Being the third set of docks gave the East India the advantage of the expertise of their predecessors and the Company commissioned John Rennie and Ralph Walker to carry out the work. A wet dock – Brunswick, also known as Perry's Dock – already existed at Blackwall. It had originally been created by the East India Company but sold off in the seventeenth century. Since then it had become one of the largest businesses on the river, capable of simultaneously refitting a number of ships. For the expansion into a new dock complex it was reacquired for £35,600 from the then owners, the Wells family, together with sixty-five acres of Bromley marsh.

The original two Brunswick basins were merged to become the new Export Dock, with a larger eighteen-acre dock created in parallel to the north for imports. As work progressed it was decided that a third basin would be needed to hold ships waiting to enter the docks and prevent congestion. The entire dock space could handle 250 ships at any time, somewhat less than the London Docks. The complex was surrounded by 20-foot high walls for security, with a formal gateway of classical design. There was ample quayside but, unlike the West India and London Docks, very little warehousing. Many of the Company's imports were high value goods, such as silk and spices, which were immediately transported to Cutler Street. The giant Brunswick Dock Masting House was kept as part of the new complex until demolished in 1862.

The biggest challenge for Rennie and Walker in creating the enlarged dock and warehouses was the remoteness of the location, which was only accessible by river, with no road connection to London. It was therefore decided to produce the necessary bricks on the spot and two contracts were placed, each for 9 million bricks. Temporary accommodation had first to be built for the brick makers and contract labourers due to the location's isolation. Word also reached the contractors of builders at the London Docks being press-ganged into the navy for the war against France, so protection from forced enlistment was sought. A steam engine was acquired from Hull to be used for the construction work.

Preparations for the work were lengthy and it was necessary for the dock company to seek authorization to raise additional capital. The first stone was eventually laid by a director, Captain Joseph Huddart, in March 1805. Operations thereafter progressed swiftly. The grand ceremony for the opening of the new docks in August 1806 was attended by thousands of people, including shareholders and nobility. The first ship to enter was the East Indiaman *Admiral Gardner*, flying the flags of every nation (with France flying below the others) and with the Company's band on board playing *Rule Britannia*. It had been preceded by the Trinity House yacht.

The dock's entrance lock was 48 feet wide, which was adequate to accommodate the largest sailing ships of the time. It was however too small for the larger ships of fifty years later and in the 1870s a second lock was created of 65 feet and the dock rebuilt to accommodate vessels of up to 8,000 tons.

The East India Docks were managed by the 'Captain of the Dock' in command of six officers who supervised a hierarchy of waged workers for the loading and unloading of cargoes including 100 'lumpers'.

Being isolated from London, the Company built its own hotel at the docks for merchants who had overnight business there. The elegant Brunswick Hotel, located exactly on the meridian line, became well-known in the 1830s for its whitebait dinners. Politicians, fashionable young men and aristocrats, including William IV, would travel out of London to dine. Later in the century emigrants on the way to Australia and New Zealand would stay there while waiting to embark. The hotel survived until it was demolished in 1930.

Commercial Road and West India and East India Dock Roads

Until the early nineteenth century the villages along the north bank of the river to the east of London were linked by former country lanes, most notably Cable Street, Ratcliff Highway and Poplar High Street. They were unfit to carry heavy traffic and to transport goods from the more distant West India Docks into the City so a much larger and direct east-west highway was required. A new, straight and broad road was planned from Aldgate to the gate of the docks.

The Commercial Road Company was formed to create the thoroughfare, with income from tolls. The chairman of the company was George Hibbert, who also held the same position in the West India Dock Company. Even before the docks had been completed a map was published in October 1801 to promote the enterprise. It was created by the map-maker and former resident of the West Indies, John Luffman. As well as the docks that were then under construction, the map shows the proposed route passing largely through open fields between, and roughly in parallel to, Ratcliff Highway, and to the south of Mile End Road.

Problems in constructing the road through the suburbs to Whitechapel, including across a churchyard at Stepney, resulted in the Commercial Road not being completed until 1804, two years after the docks were opened. Following the decision to create the East India Docks, the decision was taken to extend the route to that new complex. Thus the Commercial Road went as far as St Anne's church at Limehouse and thereafter split into the West India Dock and East India Dock Roads. The raising of £10,000 of capital to finance the creation of East India Dock Road was included in a stock issue in 1806 by the East India Dock Company.

Valuable goods were transported along the Commercial Road, particularly from the East India Docks to their warehouses in the City. The Company sent their cargoes in convoys of horse-drawn wagons carrying padlocked containers, accompanied by armed guards. The horses were allowed one five-minute stop on the four-mile journey.

It took a further half a century however before Commercial Road joined Whitechapel High Street, and thus direct to Aldgate and the City. During the interim it reached only as far as Berner Street in Whitechapel and thereafter traffic was required to take a detour through smaller streets. In 1830 a stone tramway was constructed, made from Aberdeen granite, allowing horses to pull heavy wagons of sugar from the West India Docks.

The Surrey Docks

As the three new dock systems were being constructed on the north bank of the Thames to the east of London, the same was happening south of the river, at the Rotherhithe peninsula between Southwark and Greenwich. Whereas each of those on the north bank were created by a single company, the numerous docks, timber ponds and canal on the opposite side covering 300 acres were developed almost side by side by several competing enterprises that eventually merged over a period of time.

In the first years of the nineteenth century the engineer and entrepreneur Ralph Dodd was creating a waterway from the peninsula. He hoped the Grand Surrey Canal would connect the Thames to Epsom, with branches to other towns, and its primary aim was to bring market garden produce to the capital. By 1803 the canal stretched from Rotherhithe as far as Peckham but never extended further than Camberwell. As it was being dug, the shipowner Sir John Hall planned a new dock, created by widening the Thames end of the canal into a basin of three acres. For this, a ship lock of 140 feet in length was opened onto the river at Warlter's Wharf. The Grand Surrey Basin opened in November 1804 when Hall's ship the *Argo* entered.

As we have already seen in the previous chapter, the Howland Wet Dock had been opened at Rotherhithe in 1700. From the 1720s it was used by whaling ships and its name changed to the Greenland Dock. The whaling trade declined in Britain but there was a growing demand for timber for construction of the fast-expanding capital, with 800 ships unloading annually. It was for the importation of softwood from Scandinavia and Canada that in 1806 the wealthy timber merchant William Richie formed the Commercial Dock Company and this acquired Greenland Dock from the Wells family. Richie's aim, which was never achieved, was to gain the right to a monopoly of the importation of timber, hemp, flax, pitch and tar from the Baltic, in the same way that the other docks had been given such rights for various types of goods or regions. The Greenland Dock was renamed the Commercial Dock in 1810. Between 1811 and 1815 the Company created four smaller basins to the north of the Greenland Dock, later named Norway and Lady Docks and Acorn and Lavender Ponds. Timber was floated in the ponds, as both a method of storage and to remove sap. To emphasize their timber business, the warehouses around the dock were constructed of wood, including granaries made of Canadian pine. Some years later company director Nathaniel Gould wrote of the 'Esquimaux Indians' who arrived on timber ships from Canada and paddled their canoes around the dock during the winter months until they could return home in the spring.

Another company also sought the Baltic timber business. The East Country Dock Company opened their own small basin in 1807 to the south of Greenland Dock, holding just twenty-eight ships. The Commercial Dock Company attempted but failed to acquire this competitor, which kept its independence until 1850. When it was finally taken over, the East Country Dock was enlarged, becoming the Commercial Dock's South Dock, with a new, larger entrance lock onto the river. Yet another company, the Baltic Dock Company, was formed in 1809 by Rotherhithe landowner Joseph Moore but for the purpose of floating timber under bonded conditions instead of as a ship dock. It was a further threat to the Commercial Dock Company and in this case they were successful in acquiring the company and amalgamating the facilities into their own.

Port workers

Prior to the creation of the enclosed docks, the loading and unloading of ships had for centuries been a closed shop, monopolized by various groups known as 'Ticket Porters' (so called because they wore the badge of the City of London to show their membership of their brotherhood), Billingsgate Porters, Tacklehouse Porters (who dealt with weighing) and Companies' Porters. There were frequent demarcation disputes between these different groups. Porters vigorously opposed the creation of the docks, where they would not be employed. Ultimately their protestations were unsuccessful but they received compensation from the earliest of the dock companies. Some of them moved out of the City to work in the new docks.

Cargoes had been discharged into lighters and ferried to the riverbank from the time during the early Middle Ages when ships became too large to moor at London's quays. This was the work of skilled lightermen. When the river became congested in the eighteenth century it was necessary for ships to moor some distance from the Thames-side wharves. Lightermen became skilled at moving their craft up and down the river using tides and currents and with long oars for manoeuvrability. When the enclosed docks came into being, much of the cargo was carried into and out of the docks by lighter rather than on congested roads. Lightermen were distinct from watermen, the latter being those who conveyed passengers along or across the river by wherry, the predecessors of taxis. With their knowledge and skills, both were liable to be pressed into the Navy during times of war. In the sixteenth century Thames watermen formed the Watermen's Company guild to offer some protection. An Act of 1700 dictated that lightermen operating between Gravesend and Windsor should also be members of, and regulated by, the Company. Owners of quays between Hermitage Wharf and Wapping were thereafter only to employ qualified lightermen. The creation of bridges across the river, improved roads, and steam trains led to the demise of the watermen's trade but the continuous growth in cargo business increased the need for lighters. In 1827 a new Act incorporated the former guild as the Company of Watermen & Lightermen of the River Thames. Only those who were members, having served an apprenticeship of seven years, were licensed to ply their trade. Throughout the century numerous anomalies regarding cargo-carrying came into being however, leading to regular adjustments in the rules. A beverage popular throughout the port until the nineteenth century was 'purl'. It was a mixture of hot beer and gin, flavoured with ginger and sugar, sold from licensed purl-boats – or 'bum-boats' – up and down the river, equipped with a brazier. Passing continuously from quay to quay and barge to lighter, the purl-men knew all the news and gossip of the river.

The loading, unloading, warehousing and security in each of the new nineteenth century docks was managed by a dockmaster, sometimes known as the dock superintendent, and below him were hundreds of permanent staff and labourers. He would live in a fine company house overlooking the docks or entrance, as can still be seen beside the riverside lock at the St Katharine Docks. The company secretary managed the office, which was usually in the City. The complexities of importing and exporting a vast range of commodities to and from places around the world, in days before instant communication, with all the regulations and duties, and when records were kept in handwritten ledgers, required many clerks and bookkeepers. Within the port, imports and exports required different skills and handling, such as customs clearance for imports. Several of the companies therefore arranged their docks with different basins dealing with each process. Loading ships was a highly skilled process, which was quite different to unloading. In the former, cargoes had to be arranged in a way that they maximized available space and, in cases where a ship was off-loaded at several ports on its journey, were in the correct order for unloading. Most importantly though, the cargo had to be positioned in the hold in order to maintain the ship's balance while at sea so that it did not capsize. The loading was dealt with by skilled stevedores, a name anglicized from the Spanish equivalent of 'estibador'. Not only did it require a specialist knowledge but it took place in the tight confines of the ship's hold and with some measure of danger, under pressure of time, and requiring physical strength and agility. Stevedores were the elite amongst dockers, highly regarded, better-paid and living in the more salubrious areas of East London. Loading was not carried out by the dock companies and was under the control of the ship's captain. He would hire the stevedores, who were self-employed and advertised their service in the form of a brass plaque outside their home.

At the Surrey Docks (and later at the Millwall Docks) the companies handled neither loading nor unloading and there stevedores supervised both processes. British timber-carrying ships were unloaded by 'lumpers' and foreign ships by their crews. After it was unloaded, highly-skilled gangs of 'deal porters' carried the timber to warehouses where they stacked it before dispatch to its destination. The work, which involved carrying long lengths of wood across narrow planks between high stacks of timber, was quite dangerous and liable to cause serious injury. Shorter pieces of wood, such as that used for making barrels, were carried by 'stave porters' who had experience in the most efficient carrying and stacking of various shapes and sizes. Untreated lengths of wood were sorted according to length, quality and customer and floated in ponds or the open river to prevent them drying out and splitting, by skilled men known as 'rafters'. Rafters undertook a seven-year apprenticeship and were licensed by the Watermen's Company. They were fully employed during the busy July to October season when the timber ships arrived but had to seek work elsewhere in other months.

As with the deal porters, working as a meat porter was a difficult and specialist job carrying heavy carcasses. It required men who were very strong, agile and could work quickly. After refrigeration was introduced the meat had to be handled in a frozen state and it was important not to bruise it.

Many goods were shipped in wooden barrels, casks, hogsheads, puncheons or crates and when necessary these were repaired by coopers. Merchandise stored in wooden packaging included alcohol, tea and foodstuffs, as well as ivory, perfume and tobacco. Each time a cargo was inspected, a cooper was on hand to open and close the packing. They did not necessarily work exclusively for one dock but travelled around between them to carry out work as required. Experienced 'box knockers' opened cargoes for inspection and then resealed them again.

Ordinary dockers and warehousemen were experienced in lifting, moving, and storing cargoes, marking up exports and dealing with customs staff. Much of the work was physically demanding, skilled and dangerous. Deaths and injuries, such as those caused by treadmill cranes, were frequent and there was little if any compensation or support for the families of those who died or for those unable to work.

As we will come to later, from the 1820s the dock companies cut back on permanent staff and employed mostly casual labourers. They dealt with the unskilled and tough work of unloading the ships, wagons or railway trucks as well as the mundane tasks such as tidying the warehouses and clearing rubbish. These jobs tended mostly to be in the open in all weathers, the workers having often waited outside the dock gates for several hours beforehand. In some cases the only refreshment was beer that could be purchased from the company and was brought around on carts.

Coal shipped around the coast from Newcastle was excluded from the requirement to land goods at the Legal Quays and consequently it had always been discharged at numerous quays along the river. The task of unloading was dealt with by 'coal-whippers' who normally worked in teams of nine men. Four of them filled baskets in the vessel's hold, another four used pulleys and their own body-weight to raise the baskets onto the deck, while the team leader caught each basket as it rose. It was dirty and strenuous work that required perfect coordination between the team members. Coal-whippers were known as heavy drinkers but this was not simply to clear their throats of coal dust. In the 1840s there were around 2,000 living around the Wapping area. About 70 or 80 local pub landlords – 'coal-whipping publicans' – had gained a monopoly on the discharge of colliers and allotted work to only those coal-whippers who spent a large proportion of their wages in their pubs on overpriced and inferior beer. That led to the passing of William Gladstone's Coal-Whippers Act and the creation of a central employment office at Shadwell. The Act expired in 1856, however interested parties ensured it was not renewed, and the oppressive system resumed for decades.

The St Katharine Docks

Immediately to the east of the City and the Tower of London, on the north bank of the Thames, was located the ancient Precinct of St Katharine. In the early twelfth century a hospital – a resting place for the sick or travellers – had been founded there by Matilda, wife of King Stephen, linked at that time to the Priory of Holy Trinity at Aldgate. In the mid-thirteenth century, from the time of Queen Eleanor wife of Edward I, the Foundation of St Katharine's came under the patronage of each queen consort, queen dowager or reigning queen.

A French visitor to London in the 1570s, L. Grenade, commented:

As for the suburb called St Katharine, it is one of the largest and most populated [districts around London] of them all. It is inhabited by a large number of sailors and of craftsmen of varying trades such as hatters, makers of harquebuses [a sixteenth century rifle], shoemakers, brewers and many others like these. This suburb is also the destination point for a vast quantity of wood, which is brought there by boat to supply the city.

The earliest threat of redevelopment of the Precinct came in 1796 when the Corporation of the City of London applied for an Act of Parliament to convert the area into wet docks in order to improve the terrible congestion that had grown on the river. When they approached her legal advisors the Corporation received a diplomatic reply that Queen Charlotte, the Hospital's patron,

> having no wish to impede any measure which may be deemed necessary for the attainment of the Object proposed her Majesty will acquiesce in whatever plan the Parliament in its wisdom shall think proper for the purpose trusting however that all due Care will be taken that the Interest of the Community under the Queen's Patronage shall not be prejudiced.

Whatever Charlotte said publicly, it was most likely her discreet influence over Parliament that ensured the failure of the plan. As we have already seen, the City's merchants instead turned their attentions elsewhere, successfully creating in the following years the London Docks at neighbouring Wapping and further downriver.

The twenty-one-year monopoly granted to the proprietors of the West India Docks was due to expire in 1823 (and those of the London and East India Docks in subsequent years). They naturally applied for an extension of that privilege and a Parliamentary Committee was formed to consider the matter. Surprisingly, the renewal was challenged by the owners of the London Docks, supported by the Commercial Dock Company, who both believed they could profit from taking away some of the West India business if there was free trade. The committee held the view that the West India Dock Company had been making excess profits against the interest of consumers. They concluded that henceforth there were no grounds for anything other than open competition.

At least two Parliamentary Bills were prepared for new docks to take advantage of the end of the monopolies and the growing trade. Isambard Kingdom Brunel prepared plans for his father Marc Isambard to create the

South London Docks at Bermondsey, although they never came to fruition. Likewise, a plan for a new coal dock on the Isle of Dogs failed to proceed.

It was also at that time that the shipowner and dock developer John Hall turned his attentions to the Precinct of St Katharine's, by then sandwiched between the Tower of London and Wapping's London Docks. As we previously observed, Hall had been the instigator of the Grand Surrey Basin at Rotherhithe. Other directors of the newly-formed St Katharine Dock Company were businessmen including Thomas Tooke, a well-connected economist who became its first chairman, and two MPs: the banker William Glynn, and John Horseley Palmer who later became the Governor of the Bank of England.

According to the promoters of the new dock scheme at St Katharine's, in the thirty years between 1794 and 1824 the number of ships entering the port rose from slightly under 14,000 per year to over 23,600. Despite the creation of four major dock complexes, in 1808 over 8,000 ships had to moor in the river, which in 1824 had almost doubled to nearly 16,000 (although in reality many of those were likely to have been colliers bringing coal from Newcastle). The aim of the St Katharine Dock Company was to create a fifth major dock for the Port in which ships could be loaded and unloaded and for goods to be stored. Although they realized that a dock on the St Katharine's site would be relatively small compared with the existing basins, they knew that it would be the closest to the City of London, which would reduce transport costs considerably.

The timing couldn't have been worse for the Precinct. Queen Charlotte died in 1818 and the Hospital was temporarily without a patron. Her husband had long been debilitated with porphyria – or 'madness' – and the country was effectively reigned by the Prince Regent, who was estranged from his wife Caroline. George III died in 1820 and Caroline in 1821 so, for a rare time in its long history, St Katharine's lacked the royal protection of a queen consort. In April 1824 a Bill was laid before Parliament for the St Katharine Dock Company to acquire and raze the Precinct, as well as part of the parish of St Botolph, and replace them with a set of docks. It was opposed by many, including the neighbouring London Dock Company, who feared the direct competition, and by some antiquarians who wished to preserve the ancient Hospital and its church. In the face of such opposition the Bill was withdrawn before becoming law, leading to great rejoicing by the local community.

John Hall persisted in his efforts, however. Dubious accusations were made that the district was dilapidated and unsanitary, with brothels and opium dens, and home to 'ruffians'. The Bill was again presented before Parliament, together

Coal-whippers show their solidarity with striking dockers during the dock strike of 1889. (*Photo: By permission of the People's History Museum*)

The Main Gate of the East India Docks opening onto East India Dock Road. To the left of the gate in this photo stood Poplar Hospital (the 'Dockers' Hospital'), which was originally opened to treat injured dockers.

The Port of London headquarters on
Tower Hill.

The Royal Albert Dock.

Goods being sorted at a typical dock transit shed.

The fortress-like Cutler Street warehouse near Bishopsgate was originally built by the East India Company and at the time of this photo in 1930 continued as the PLA's main storage and sorting facility in the City of London. (*Photo: © PLA collection / Museum of London*)

The PLA's 150-ton floating crane *London Mammoth* is here unloading the Atlantic Transport Line's *SS Minnetonka* in the King George V Dock, probably sometime around 1930.

The PLA's grain elevator 'Rapid', built in 1906, is seen here discharging grain overboard from a vessel into lighters at Surrey Commercial Docks. (*Photo:* © *PLA collection/Museum of London*)

The Royal Docks looking west in 1946. In the foreground are the King George V Dock (left) and Royal Albert Dock (right), with the Royal Victoria Dock in the distance. The buildings in the foreground are the Harland & Wolff ship repair works. (© *Historic England Archive*)

The Port of London Authority operated an extensive railway system from which goods could be transported in and out of London and connect with the national network. Here the PLA's Engine No. 203 waits beside the Clan Line's cargo ship *Clan Maclennan* at Tilbury Docks. (© *PLA collection / Museum of London*)

Above: This photo looking east along the Thames shows much of the extent of the upper docks as they were in 1959, including (from bottom to top) the London Docks, Surrey Commercial Docks, Regents Canal Dock, West India Docks, Millwall Docks, East India Docks and the three Royal Docks. (© *Historic England Archive*)

Right: Unloading a vessel in the days prior to containers was a slow business, as can be seen here in this ship's hold in 1960. (© *PLA collection / Museum of London*)

Dockers wait for the call-on in 1962. (© *PLA collection/Museum of London*)

The modern Port of Tilbury. (*Photo courtesy of the Port of Tilbury*)

The PLA's Port control centres manage the movement of vessels along the length of the tidal river. The Thames Barrier Navigation Centre shown in this photo ensures the safe passage of 33,000 vessels through the barrier each year. (*Photo courtesy of the Port of London Authority*)

The Danish-registered *MV Mærsk Mc-Kinney Møller* container ship discharging at DP World London Gateway. With a capacity of 18,270 TEU it is currently one of the world's largest container ships. (*Photo: Sean Frost, courtesy of DP World London Gateway*)

with six petitions that favoured the creation of the docks. One was from London merchants, bankers and tradesmen; the second from London shipowners; the third from shipowners from around the country; the fourth from victuallers; the fifth from seed-men; the sixth, it was said, from between three and four hundred residents. On examination the latter merely contained 125 signatures, only one of whom actually lived within the area set for demolition, yet this point does not seem to have been contested at the time.

The following year the real householders lodged their own petition. The opposition came to nothing and the St Katharine Dock Bill was passed by Parliament in June 1825. Hall was appointed as Company Secretary. Thomas Tooke became the first chairman and remained so until 1853. Thirteen acres of land were acquired by the dock company, only separated from the London Docks to the west by the width of a street: Nightingale Lane (later renamed Thomas More Street). Demolition began almost immediately. The medieval and historic Hospital, which had survived the sixteenth century dissolution of the monasteries and the Great Fire of 1666, together with its much-admired fourteenth century church and graveyard, were destroyed.

The Act of Parliament stipulated compensation for landlords and brothers of the Foundation but not residential tenants. At the time of the opening of the new docks *The Times* reported that 1,250 houses and tenements had been destroyed, displacing 11,300 inhabitants, although the latter number was disputed by the company. It paid for the Foundation of St Katharine to transfer to salubrious new premises in the new Regent's Park, becoming more or less almshouses for well-off people.

To create the docks the company commissioned Thomas Telford as chief engineer and Thomas Rhodes as resident engineer. By then Telford had long been an eminent builder of canals, bridges and docks in his native Scotland, as well as England and Sweden, but St Katharine's was to be the only project for which he would be responsible in London. He was already quite elderly and the trusted Rhodes acted as his deputy, with assistance from the architect Sir Philip Hardwick.

Telford's plan was to create a central basin connected to the tidal river by a lock. That led to either an east or west dock, each of which had its own gates and could therefore be separately drained when necessary. Up to 120 ships could moor within. James Watt built two steam engines that pumped water from the river into the lock in order to maintain levels within the dock at less than high tide.

The contract for the work was awarded to George Burge who hired 2,500 labourers and they began construction in May 1827. An account published a decade later quotes a Swedish engineer, Captain A.G. Carlsund, as saying:

I frequently witnessed a thousand men and several hundred of horses employed in the operations, besides several powerful steam-engines. At the beginning of the works wheelbarrows were employed to carry away the earth, but as the excavations proceeded and became deeper, iron railways and steam-engines were substituted. The earth was conveyed into barges, carried down [sic] the river, and deposited in convenient places.

That earth was actually carried upriver on barges and deposited on marshy land behind Millbank prison, enabling Thomas Cubitt to create the new suburbs of Pimlico and Belgravia on Lord Grosvenor's estate.

The total space at St Katharine's was relatively small and awkward so Telford had to utilize every inch available. Slightly over ten acres of the total were given over to the three irregular-shaped basins, providing as much quayside space as possible, being 4,500 feet, to accommodate the largest possible number of vessels. On the riverside the ancient Irongate Wharf was joined by the 170-foot-long Steam Packet Wharf for ships too large to enter the docks. In 1849 the dock company leased the wharves to the General Steam Navigation Company.

Despite the austere and monumental style, the warehouses, designed by Hardwick, were some of the finest that would ever be constructed in London's dock system. They were built of yellow-grey London bricks and white stone sills, six storeys tall and with two levels of underground vaults. To maximize storage space the six warehouses, totalling over 1,200,000 square feet in extent, were built directly up to the water's edge inside the docks and to the roadside on the exterior of the docks. Cranes, fixed to the warehouses and swinging out over the ships' decks, hoisted cargoes straight into the storage space without the need for transit sheds and, likewise, lowered goods down to carts in the roads outside the docks. By this method ships could be loaded or unloaded much quicker than the other docks. About two decades after its opening, Henry Mayhew explained:

Cargoes are raised into the warehouses out of the hold of a ship without the goods being deposited on the quay. The cargoes can be raised out of the ship's hold into the warehouses of St Katharine's in one-fifth of the usual time. Before the existence of docks, a month or six weeks was taken up in discharging the cargo of an East Indiaman of from 800 to 1,200 tons burden; while eight days were necessary in the summer, and fourteen in the winter, to unload ships of 350 tons. At St Katharine's however, the average time now occupied in discharging a ship of 250 tons is twelve hours, and one of 500 tons two or three days, the goods being placed at the same time in the warehouse ... This would have been considered little short of a miracle on the legal quays less than fifty years ago.

The original cranes were manual, powered by treadmill pulley systems, but were later replaced by steam and then hydraulic lifts. On the ground level facing into the dock were quays, covered by part of the upper floors of the warehouses, which were supported on cast-iron Tuscan colonnades. To the streets the tall warehouses, windowless in their lower parts, formed the impregnable walls of the complex, providing the necessary security for the goods within. A Dock Master's House was constructed beside the entrance lock, with an impressive Dock House office in the Grecian Doric order in the north-west corner facing Tower Hill.

The West Dock of St Katharine's opened in October 1828 and the East Dock the following year. Unlike the opening of earlier docks, there seems to have been only a modest ceremony, with no state officials of note attending. Taking part on that occasion was the *Mary*, a ship that traded with Russia. On its deck were forty veteran sailors who had served under Nelson at the Battle of Trafalgar, collected from the Greenwich Hospital.

Around 500 staff were employed in the docks, warehouses and offices at St Katharine's, including 225 permanent men and 200 preferred labourers, in addition to some 1,700 casual workers hired as required. There were regulations regarding the honesty and sobriety of workers, who were strictly prohibited from carrying any kind of vessel capable of containing a liquid and could be searched by their foreman or at the dock gates.

St Katharine's specialized mostly in importing tea from India and wool from Australia, New Zealand and the Falkland Islands. The warehouses could accommodate 600,000 bales of wool. Both the wool trade and the importation of marble were shared between St Katharine's and the London Docks. Seven hundred thousand chests of tea passed through each year, repacked on site before being distributed to wholesalers. There was also a large range of luxury and exotic items from around the world, including spices, ivory, china, ostrich feathers, tortoiseshell, oriental carpets, mother of pearl, raw materials to manufacture perfume (with an on-site extraction facility), guano (used as a fertilizer) and tallow (used in soap manufacturing and cooking).

Even at the time of the docks' opening, the entry lock, 45 feet wide and 250 feet long, with a draught of 24 feet, was too small for the largest vessels. With the introduction of ever bigger iron-hulled and steam ships in the following decades fewer ocean-going vessels were small enough to enter. With easy access to the City, St Katharine's was initially very successful. Yet it marked the end of the dock boom, and thereafter had to cut its rates to be more competitive and pay out lower dividends to shareholders.

Canals, railways and basins

From the early nineteenth century new transport links were created, first canals and then railways, that linked the port with areas far beyond London. The River Lea (or 'Lee') flows south from Hertfordshire and for centuries barges brought grain and other produce downstream. Canalization of the Lea began as early as the fifteenth century and the first mitred lock gates in the country were introduced on the river in 1571. As boats arrived at the southern end of the Lea they had to navigate the winding and tidal Bow Creek before entering the Thames and then take the long passage around the Isle of Dogs before arriving at London. The engineer John Smeaton recommended the construction of the two-mile Limehouse Cut as a shortcut across the north of the Isle of Dogs to join the Thames at Limehouse. It was largely completed in 1770.

During the second half of the eighteenth century, when Britain's roads were still in a poor state, the major ports and industrial areas became connected by a network of canals, helping to fuel the Industrial Revolution. In 1801 the Grand Junction Canal joined England's industrial heartland around Birmingham to the Thames at Brentford, with a branch to Paddington. A proposal was then made to cut a new link from Paddington, in a semicircle through the fields north of the capital, around the City and down to the river at Limehouse. After much delay the eight-and-a-half-mile Regent's Canal was opened in 1820. It joined the Thames at a point roughly halfway between the London and West India Docks. There the canal company created the ten-acre Regent's Canal Dock. Ships could enter from the Thames via a lock of 350 feet by 60 feet and cargoes transferred onto barges for passage to other parts of the country. One of the main cargoes to pass through the dock was coal.

Railways were to become integral to the movement of goods and raw materials into and out of the Port. One of the country's earliest was the London & Blackwall, which linked the City to the East India Docks. Engineered by Robert Stephenson, carriages were originally worked by stationary steam engines and pulleys over a distance of about 3.5 miles. At the time it gained the name of the 'four-penny rope', being the cost of a ride and that the ropes that pulled the carriages often snapped. The railway company acquired the East India Dock's Brunswick Wharf, renamed Blackwall Pier, and the line initially ran to there from the Minories in the City. A year later it was extended to Fenchurch Street. Steamers carried passengers from Blackwall, upriver to Greenwich or downriver to Gravesend and Margate, and even to the Continent. For the following century the railway connected the East and West India Docks and Millwall Docks to the City and later to Tilbury. Today it forms part of the Docklands Light Railway.

The Regent's Canal was one of the last to be opened during the great age of English canal building, and its golden period was short-lived. In 1837 Stephenson's London & Birmingham Railway opened, following the route of the Grand Junction from the Midlands into Euston. Other railways followed, linking London to all parts of Britain. They were much faster and more efficient and soon began taking long-distance freight traffic away from the canals. Perhaps the biggest nail in the coffin of the Regent's Canal was the opening of the North London Railway in 1846 from the railway goods yards at Camden over to the West India Docks. This allowed goods to pass speedily from the Midlands to London's docks, avoiding altogether the much slower Grand Junction and Regent's canals. In the following chapter we will deal with the major docks created in the mid-nineteenth century. Each of them was connected to the national railway system from the outset.

The West India Dock Company created a reservoir immediately to the north of their entrance lock in order to maintain the head of water in their docks. The Company was one of the shareholders in the North London Railway. They leased the basin to the railway and it was renamed Collier Dock where coal could be discharged from colliers to railway trucks. In 1877 the dock was enlarged and the name eventually changed to Poplar Dock. By the end of the nineteenth century the dock property covered 28 acres, with 14 miles of railway sidings. Goods were stored in warehouses, including stores for Bass Pale Ale.

The call-on

As profits came under pressure the dock companies looked for ways to reduce their overheads. Their main variable cost was manpower and in the remainder of the nineteenth century it was the dockers who increasingly suffered. The coming and going of ships was dependent on the weather and was therefore unpredictable. Their arrival or departure could be delayed for days or even weeks while at other times a large group of ships might arrive at the same time. Certain types of cargo, such as tea, wool, sugar, grain or timber, were seasonal and caused vessels to arrive in groups. In the 1860s arrivals varied from between less than thirty in one week to over two hundred in another. It was expensive to have a waged staff on standby, whereas as London's population rapidly increased, particularly with unemployed immigrants from Ireland and the Continent, there was an abundance of available men.

The dock companies and wharf-owners began to substitute expensive full-time labourers with cheaper and more flexible casual workers who could be hired by the half-day when required as the number of ships fluctuated. In the mid-century a staff labourer earned sixteen shillings and sixpence per week, whereas a casual labourer was paid only four pence an hour if and when he worked, plus a bonus known as 'plus money' if a ship was unloaded quickly

Some of the casual workers were 'preferred hands' who were more or less permanent dock labourers. The majority were others who arrived to take their chance of some work. Huge crowds of men, sometimes in their thousands and many hungry and poorly clothed, congregated at the dock gates at seven thirty each morning seeking work as casual labourers. They called the waiting 'standing on the stones'. There they desperately scrambled to catch the attention of the 'calling foremen' who selected a number from amongst them for a half or full day's work, a process known as 'the call-on'.

Selection depended on various factors: the ships that were being loaded or unloaded; the strength and skills of the individuals; opinion of the foreman – 'the quay ganger' - towards individual candidates; and even bribery. When a ship was unloaded faster than scheduled the foreman received a bonus – 'the share' – to distribute as he saw fit and it was therefore in his interest to choose the most suitable workers.

Along the dock walls were elevated stands that quay-gangers ascended to survey the men below, to call out those selected and instruct them as to where they should work. There were those who were known to the foremen and whose name was sure to be called. It will have helped to know which pub the quay-ganger frequented and to buy him a few drinks. Those remaining after the first calling would push and shove each other for the best position to be noticed and the quay-gangers would choose the most robust from amongst them. About forty-five minutes later a second call-on took place, then another an hour later, and yet a fourth some time later. The unchosen ones became more desperate until the last amongst them simply had to go home knowing they and their family would probably be left hungry and the rent unpaid yet again. The unlucky ones might have gone through the same routine for days or weeks without being selected. It was an age when there was no unemployment benefit, leading to a life of poverty for many.

According to Henry Mayhew, the numbers given casual work at each of the docks varied between 500 and 3,000 at the London Docks; 500 to over 1,700 at St Katharine's and, at the West and East India Docks combined, 1,300 to 4,000. The work for casual labourers was simple and required no experience and thus suited 'men of all grades' who could not find employment elsewhere, according to Mayhew. Many had trained for work in other industries but resorted to trying their luck at the docks when business was slack. They included former soldiers, bankrupts and even the elderly who arrived dressed in clothes and shoes that were barely held together; a large reserve of labour that was referred to as 'residuum'. Some lived a hand-to-mouth existence and were attempting to supplement their poor relief or charity payments. Even when hired, their work was usually hard, manual labour. It involved jobs such as turning winches or wheeling laden trucks. In the early years cranes were manually-powered and involved a group of six to eight men walking inside a wooden treadmill.

In the early part of the century shipowners who chose workers to unload their vessel often did so by arrangement with landlords of pubs located close to the river. The arrangement extended to the landlord paying the wages after the work was completed. This required the labourers to spend long hours in those establishments to be first in line for available work when a ship arrived, as well as to continually buy alcohol in order to keep the attention of and be favoured by the landlord. The practice was discontinued by Act of Parliament in 1843.

Competition and mergers

The expansion of Britain's economy and overseas empire ensured that manufacturing in London and beyond continued to increase and that the growing wealth of many individuals created increased demands for consumer goods. Raw materials were required and exported manufactured goods could be sold around the world. The new docks of the early nineteenth century provided the facilities that ensured that much of that traffic passed through the Port of London. In the mid-1830s around 3,500,000 tons of cargo was handled annually. Slightly less than a million tons was foreign trade, which was almost exclusively handled by the new enclosed docks. The remainder was coastal traffic dealt with by wharves on the open river. A significant cargo was coal, brought down the coast from the North East of England.

Following the loss of their monopolies, greater dock space after the opening of the St Katharine Docks, and the increased effect of the free water clause, the dock companies were achieving lower profits and dividends to shareholders. Overcapacity and a free market allowed shipowners to negotiate lower docking rates. The dock companies were under pressure despite increasing business in the port.

In a measure to ensure their survival the East and West India Dock Companies agreed to merge in 1838, authorized in one of the first Acts of Parliament approved by the new Queen Victoria. It made sense for at least one reason. The East India Company lost their monopoly on trade with India in 1813 and with China in 1833 and no longer traded with its own fleet of ships as they had for the previous two centuries. They now needed to operate in an open market yet their docks at Blackwall had been designed for simply loading and unloading and three decades later were without the important warehousing income. The West India Docks on the other hand had been created with a large amount of warehousing space they were no longer able to fill due to reduced business. Publicly the new joint company put forward the more altruistic rationale that ships would find it convenient to dock at Blackwall instead of continuing upriver to other docks, thus making the Thames more open and safer for the fast new passenger steamships that had recently been introduced.

As they were no longer importing goods, the East India Company put its warehouses in the City up for auction in 1835. Cutler Street was acquired by the St Katharine Dock Company and others by the East & West India Dock Company.

The situation deteriorated further for the dock companies in 1853 when Parliament passed the Customs Consolidation Act that increased competition by sanctioning further legal quays and bonded warehouses along the river. Between the 1840s and 1870s governments also drastically reduced the types of goods on which customs duty was due, thus further undermining the previous advantage enjoyed by the docks. The number of riverside wharves greatly increased; they were able to compete with the docks, with over one hundred having landing and warehousing rights by the 1860s.

Chapter Five

Towards the Age of Steam

The introduction of steam-powered, iron-hulled ships revolutionized the shipping world during the nineteenth century and had a major impact on the Port of London. Sailing ships had to travel according to seasons, when the winds were blowing in the necessary direction to propel them across the Atlantic, or around Africa on their journey from the Far East. Steam allowed ships to navigate whatever the wind, reducing the voyage from New Zealand from four months to eight weeks. Iron hulls allowed vessels to be bigger and thus carry more cargo and be more cost-effective. They could run to regular timetables and communicate by telegraph, so – importantly for the dock companies – there was no need for goods to be stored for weeks awaiting the arrival of a ship. When the first of London's docks were completed in the early nineteenth century the average size of a merchant ship was under 500 tons and the largest around 1,200 tons. By the end of the century vessels of over 7,000 tons were arriving.

Nevertheless, the introduction of steam and iron did not happen overnight and it took time for such craft to prove their reliability and cost-effectiveness. It was only in the 1880s that British-registered steam tonnage exceeded that of sail. Coaling stations had to be established and supplied at points around the world before long-distance voyages were possible. The early steamships were pushed by paddle-wheel but a wooden-hulled propeller-driven vessel was demonstrated on the Paddington Canal in 1836. It was tested for the Royal Navy on the Thames and out to sea between Blackwall and Folkestone the following year. That in turn led in 1843 to Isambard Kingdom Brunel's design for the much larger ocean-going iron-hulled *SS Great Britain*. In 1850 there were 1,200 steamships operating in Britain but by the beginning of the next decade the number had almost doubled.

One of the leading companies for the construction of iron-hulled steamships was the Thames Ironworks & Shipbuilding Company, based at Leamouth on the Thames close to the East India Docks. In 1853 they built what was then the world's largest passenger ship. The yard's lasting legacy is the staff football team, Thames Ironworks FC, which since 1900 has been known as West Ham United. The Brunel-designed *The Leviathan* (later renamed *The Great Eastern*) was launched on the sixth attempt at the Scott Russell shipyard at Millwall in January 1858. At 700 feet long, with a gross tonnage of over 18,000 tons, it was to be the longest ship to be built anywhere for a further forty years. Its large size required it to be launched sideways onto the river. A workman was killed on the first attempt. The Thames was too narrow to launch the largest ships and too far from supplies of coal and iron ore so London went into decline as a shipbuilding centre. The Thames Ironworks yard eventually closed in the early twentieth century, by which time the country's largest shipyards were in the North East, Glasgow and Belfast.

Sailing ships tended to be owned by merchants but substantial capital was required to build and operate steamships. Large shipping lines developed during the nineteenth century. Larger, more stable and safer ships, travelling to more reliable timetables, encouraged the growth of international passenger travel, for business, pleasure or emigration from one part of the world to another. Some lines were founded initially to carry post. The Royal Mail Steam Packet Company was granted a royal charter in 1839. Samuel Cunard established the British & North American Royal Mail Steam Packet Company in the same year, later renamed the Cunard Steamship Company. They competed on the North Atlantic routes with the White Star and Inman lines. During the 1830s the Peninsula Steam Navigation Company was sailing between Britain and the Iberian Peninsula. By the 1840s it had won contracts to transport mail and its ships were travelling to more distant destinations in the east, changing its name to the Peninsula and Orient Steam Navigation Company, generally known as P&O. All these companies operated regular mail and passenger services to a fixed timetable, offering levels of passenger comfort ranging from luxurious first class down to steerage. By 1900 a third of Britain's merchant tonnage was owned by twenty-four companies.

The introduction of ever-larger steamships changed ports around Britain. Where it was possible, docks were enlarged and rivers and entrance-ways deepened. That was simply not possible or financially viable in many of the smaller coastal harbours. Inland ports and international trade became concentrated on a smaller number of major locations, each linked to an industrial centre and with good inland transport links. London, Southampton, Liverpool, Manchester and Glasgow were the beneficiaries, as well as Harwich and Dover for Continental crossings.

Despite the trend towards iron vessels for long-distance shipping, much of the local traffic along the Thames Estuary and around the coast during the nineteenth century was handled by Thames spritsail barges, with over 2,000 of them under sail at their peak. They were perfectly designed for the job, with flat bottomed hulls that could navigate in shallow water and lie on mud flats or sandbanks, sails that could be lowered to pass under bridges, able to travel up and down the river with the tides, and the ability to cruise empty without the need for ballast. The waterproofing, made of cod oil, red ochre and seawater, turned their flax sails a distinctive red colour. The barges could transport up to 200 tons and mainly carried farm products, bricks and other building materials. Their use gradually declined but some were still in use until the Second World War.

The Victoria Dock

When the London shipowners of the early nineteenth century had created their great new docks downriver between the Tower of London and Bow Creek they could not have foreseen a new generation of much bigger iron-hulled, steam-powered vessels. Nor did they imagine that goods would soon be swiftly carried far and wide by railway. By the mid-century new ships were being built that were too big to navigate as far along the Thames as the upper docks. Even if they could, they would be unable to enter through the relatively small locks into any of the existing docks that were also too shallow to receive them. Furthermore, some of the original docks were hemmed in and could not be easily expanded for railway sidings. If London was to continue to survive and grow it needed new docks or wharves for the steam age of the second half of the nineteenth century. A group of developers therefore obtained an Act of Parliament in 1850 to create a new enclosed dock to accommodate these bigger vessels, with a larger entrance lock and basin than its predecessors.

The new Victoria Dock was to be at Plaistow Marshes, east of Bow Creek, further downstream than the others. Being so remote from London had been a problem when the East and West India docks were created fifty years earlier. The new dock was linked to the rest of the country by rail from the outset, by means of the East Counties & Thames Junction Railway, so that was no longer an issue. Unlike earlier docks, its Act of Parliament included approval for the inclusion of a dry dock, although it was never implemented. The Bill was unopposed and passed in 1850.

The previous docks had been established by merchants and shipowners, whereas the men behind the Victoria Dock, such as Samuel Morton Peto, Edward Ladd Betts and Thomas Brassey, were civil engineers with experience of building railways. Peto was one of the heads of a business that was responsible for the construction of a number of new London buildings including the Houses of Parliament, Nelson's Column, the Metropolitan Board of Works' major new London sewers, and the Grand Crimean Central Railway. For certain projects he worked in conjunction with Brassey who was responsible for constructing many of the railways around the world during his lifetime. Betts was also one of the great railway developers of his time.

As the site was marshland, remote from London and with little purpose until that time, the developers were able to purchase the land cheaply. Much of the time it was below water level and flooded but that made excavation easier for the purposes of creating a basin. An early plan, never implemented, was to ship live cattle from Scotland, so the company acquired 200 acres of land beyond the dock for grazing.

The dock had half a mile of quay on each side of its vast single basin, the largest man-made body of water in London at that time. Railway tracks were laid alongside each side so that cargo could be loaded into goods wagons, to be taken into the dock storage sheds or out into the national railway system. The developers decided to line the basin with jetties onto which ships should berth, however. This made it easier to unload onto barges but not directly to and from railway wagons, a disadvantage that became more severe over time. On the north quay were the company offices, with tobacco warehouses, wine vaults and coal sidings. Storage for other types of goods such as salt, jute and guano stood on the opposite quay.

The dock's huge entrance lock, capable of handling ships of up to 8,000 tons, was 70 per cent greater than the nearby East and West India Docks. With a depth of 28 feet, it could accommodate ships up to 8,000 tons. The lock was at the western end of the dock, opening onto Bugsby's Reach, close to Bow Creek, and the Victoria was the first dock to use hydraulics for the lock gates and other equipment. There was a plan to acquire additional land so that a connection could be made to the east, downriver at Gallions Reach, but that never materialized.

The Victoria Dock was opened by Prince Albert in 1855. In order to attract the business of high-value cargoes away from the St Katharine Docks, the Victoria Dock Company acquired the Hansa's former Steelyard site in Upper

Thames Street in the City. The venture was not a success and they sold the land to the South Eastern Railway Company for their new Cannon Street railway station, which opened in 1866. By that time the Victoria Dock had become the busiest in the port, handling over 850,000 tons of cargo per year, far greater than any of the older docks.

Further consolidation of the dock companies

Sailing ships travelled according to the weather and their arrival was unpredictable. Warehouses were therefore vital to stockpile goods, having them ready to be loaded when vessels became available. The introduction of iron-hulled steamships sailing to fixed timetables, the ability to communicate their departure and arrival times by telegraph, and the possibility to speedily move goods in or out of the port by steam train, reduced the need for dockside storage. With a surplus of warehousing, there was a period of intense competition, when shipowners and merchants could negotiate lower charges from dock and wharf companies. The Warehousing Act of 1832 allowed bonded storage at riverside wharves and William Gladstone's Budget of 1860 reduced the number of dutiable goods to a mere forty-eight commodities. Thus, not only had the enclosed docks lost their monopoly on shipping, but also the ability to operate a bonded warehouse was thrown open to all, and fewer goods required them.

With so many fiercely competing docks offering low rates to shipping, with a decreasing requirement for long-term warehousing, and with an increasing amount of business going directly or indirectly to numerous factories and independent wharves along the Thames, the 1860s and 1870s were lean years for the major docks. Even at the time of its opening, the entry lock to St Katharine's was too small for the largest vessels. As ships became ever bigger with the introduction of iron hulls and steam engines, fewer freighters were able to access the dock. Under financial pressure, in 1864 the St Katharine Docks and neighbouring London Docks merged into the London & St Katharine Dock Company and the combined company acquired the Victoria Dock.

In the following year consolidation also took place at Rotherhithe. The Commercial Dock Company had already acquired its smaller neighbour, the East Country Dock, in 1850. In 1855 the Grand Surrey Canal was renamed the Grand Surrey Docks & Canal Company under a new Act of Parliament. They acquired additional land from Sir William Maynard Gomm and in 1860 completed their new Albion (or Main) Dock. At the same time they created four ponds in which timber could be floated to prevent it drying out, as the Commercial Docks had been doing since early in the century. By mid-century two companies owned all the Rotherhithe docks and ponds. Those on the western side of the peninsula belonged to the Grand Surrey Docks & Canal Company while those to the east were the property of the Commercial Dock Company. In 1865 the two companies merged to form the Surrey Commercial Dock Company and embarked on a programme of linking the various basins. In 1876 the Canada Dock was created to the south of Albion Dock, named after the country to which ships traded, with granaries able to hold 35,000 tons of grain. Twenty-three blocks of sheds were added, covering an area of forty-six acres. The company then had a system of nine docks and six timber ponds, with 176 acres of water and 193 acres of wharves.

Down by the docks

With the introduction of iron-hulled steamships the ancient maritime crafts associated with sail began to die out by the middle of the nineteenth century. Small, wooden riverside premises were replaced by larger brick-built wharves and riverside stairs fell into disrepair. As the docks and wharves opened they were joined by numerous manufacturing businesses. Consequently, hundreds of thousands of workers and their families moved to the areas around the docks. Some of the workers had previously been employed at the quays in the City, others arrived to build the docks and stayed to work in them. Step by step, what were market gardens, pastures, tea-gardens and marshes became residential and industrial districts. The ancient riverside Tower Hamlets of Wapping, Limehouse, Shadwell, Ratcliff, Poplar, and Blackwall became engulfed within new industrial suburbs that stretched out to East Ham and eventually beyond. The last of these areas to change from a rural character was the Isle of Dogs, largely in the 1850s, where heavy industry and chemical works replaced pastures, windmills and older riverside crafts. The same was happening on the south side of the river, with maritime and industrial premises all the way from Lambeth down to Greenwich.

Development was piecemeal and, unlike the earlier schemes on the west side of London, there was little overall planning in the creation of the new East End. Vast numbers of monotonous streets of terraced houses were constructed. Landlords often built larger dwellings in the optimistic hope of attracting clerks and tradesmen. In reality the middle classes preferred to live elsewhere, although a community of managers and clerks from the East and West India Docks remained in residence at Poplar until the 1870s. Mostly however, owners were forced to subdivide larger properties into two or three to accommodate workers' families.

The St Katharine's and Wapping districts had already existed and the arrival of the docks disrupted the area, causing residents and businesses to be displaced into the surrounding neighbourhoods. Those areas remained districts of small maritime industries, with rope-makers, ships' carpenters, biscuit-makers, sailors' outfitters, grog-shops and pawnshops. Along the Ratcliff Highway sailors could sell exotic creatures they had smuggled in. At the end of the century there was a mix of recent development and ancient buildings. The small, isolated area to the south of the London Docks had a distinctly maritime character according to Henry Mayhew writing in the mid-century but there was some redevelopment to residential use for workers in the second half of the century. The less salubrious streets were mainly occupied by thieves, prostitutes, and poor Irish families who had arrived following the potato famine. According to a policeman interviewed by Mayhew in the mid-century it was common for a sailor to arrive in the docks, spend all his money on women and alcohol around Ratcliff Highway (which bordered the north of the London Docks at Wapping) and sail off again penniless. That became less common towards the end of the century as sailors' missions were set up and as the Board of Trade created savings schemes with which sailors could deposit their money. Some ships' captains also began to insist that crews returned to their vessels overnight but the 1901 census still recorded that 8,000 sailors were being lodged in Bermondsey, Poplar and Stepney each night.

Charles Dickens described the area in around 1860:

Down by the Docks, they eat the largest oysters and scatter the roughest oyster-shells, known to the descendants of Saint George and the Dragon. Down by the Docks, they consume the slimiest of shell-fish, which seem to have been scraped off the copper bottoms of ships. Down by the Docks, the vegetables at green-grocers' doors acquire a saline and scaly look, as if they had been crossed with fish and seaweed. Down by the Docks, they 'board seamen' at the eating houses, the public houses, the coffee-shops, the tally-shops, all kinds of shops mentionable and unmentionable – board them, as it were, in the piratical sense, making them bleed terribly,

and giving no quarter. Down by the Docks, the seamen roam in mid-
street and mid-day, their pockets inside out, and their heads no better …
Down by the Docks, the pawnbroker lends money on Union-Jack pocket-
handkerchiefs, on watches with little ships pitching fore and aft on the
dial, on telescopes, nautical instruments in cases, and such-like.

At the end of the century, the writer and magistrate Montague Williams looked
back on the area immediately north of the London Docks of twenty-five years
previously:

Ratcliff Highway, running parallel with the river, extends from Little
Tower Hill to Shadwell, and is in close proximity with the London,
the Wapping, the Regent's Canal, and other docks, which at the period
I have alluded to were continuously crowded with shipping. In those
days the Highway was the scene of riots, debaucheries, robberies, and
all conceivable deeds of darkness. Such, indeed, was the character of the
place that it would have been madness for any respectable woman, or, for
the matter of that, for any well-dressed man, to proceed thither alone.
The police themselves seldom ventured there save in twos and threes, and
brutal assaults upon them were of frequent occurrence.

The inhabitants of Ratcliff Highway lived upon the sailors. There were
a great many lodging-houses there; still more clothiers and outfitters; and
any number of public-houses and beershops, nearly every one of which
had a dancing saloon at the back of the bar. Jack came ashore with his
pockets full of money, but they quickly emptied. He was ready enough
to spend his pay, but there were other persons still more ready to despoil
him of it. In those days there were no Government officials to board the
vessels and arrange for the safe despatch of Jack's money, and Jack himself
to his home. No sooner did a vessel reach her moorings than she was
swarming with boarding-house touts, crimps, outfitters, runners, and
other rapacious beasts of prey. Poor Jack was soon in the hands of the
Philistines.

From the public-houses in Ratcliff Highway there constantly issued the
sound of loud laughter, mingled with shouting and fearful imprecations.
Far into the night the women and the drunken sailors danced and sang to
the accompaniment of screeching fiddles. For the most part the women
wore white dresses and white shoes. If the sailors were not entirely fleeced

inside the saloons, the process was completed by bullies and fighting men when they staggered out into the street. The poor fellows were frequently drugged, and sometimes half murdered.

Sailors of every nationality were to be met in this thoroughfare, including a great many Portuguese, Spaniards, Italians, Greeks, Norwegians, and Scandinavians. The Highway was indeed a veritable modern Babel. Among the disreputable characters to be met there were men dressed as sailors who sold parrots and parakeets, many of which could blaspheme almost as naturally as their owners ...

After the great strikes the maritime prosperity of London began to wane, and one result was that the character of Ratcliff Highway somewhat improved. Other circumstances have assisted to purify that region. New docks drew the shipping lower down the Thames; the great liners are manned by a better class of men than were the sailing vessels of thirty years ago; and I am not sure that the changes brought about in the shipping world by the construction of the Suez Canal had not something to do with the transformation alluded to.

Much good has no doubt been effected by the appointment of certain Board of Trade officials. A sailor is now shipped in proper form. Articles are no longer signed in some disreputable little public-house.

The inhabitants of the East End were a melting pot of different people. Many had come seeking employment from Ireland, some from Scotland and the North of England. Some had arrived by ship from further afield, often fleeing poverty or war. Not too far away from the docks, around Spitalfields, a large community of Huguenots had settled, Protestants who had escaped persecution at the hands of Catholics in France. Later, large numbers of Germans and Jews settled around Leman Street and Whitechapel.

In the public perception, Limehouse was where you would find Chinese opium dens, due to some popular novels. In that there was some small truth but the reality was that there were far more public houses – over 100 on the East India Dock Road, West India Dock Road and surrounding area by the end of the century – for dock-workers and sailors. In the early twentieth century there was one pub per sixty households in the North Millwall area on the Isle of Dogs. The Chinese and Indians first arrived on East India Company ships during a period of manpower shortage in the Napoleonic Wars. The first arrivals were housed in a barrack accommodating upwards of 1,000 men located at Shadwell but later moved to Wapping. Indians settled around Cable Street.

Rotherhithe had less destitution than around Wapping in the second half of the century. Work prospects improved further with the opening of each new dock and of Tower Bridge in 1894. Many Irish also lived in the area, which was a mixture of housing and industry, including flour mills, as well as the Peek Freans biscuit factory at Bermondsey. Casual dock workers gathered each day at the corner of Rotherhithe New Road and Lower Road in the hope of work in the Surrey Commercial Docks.

Several districts took the names of those who urbanized them. In 1852 Samuel Winkworth Silver opened the India Rubber Works on the river south of the Victoria Dock and there he built terraced houses for his workers, known as Silvertown. The property developer William Cubitt, younger brother of Thomas who had earlier used the soil excavated from St Katharine's Dock to create the foundations for Pimlico, took leases on land belonging to the Countess of Glengall in the south-east of the Isle of Dogs. There he developed Cubitt Town, with timber wharves, sawmills, a cement factory, a pottery and residences for those working in the area. Cubitt financed the building of the local Christ Church. Canning Town to the north of the Royal Victoria Dock was largely developed by speculative builders in the 1870s at the time of the creation of the Royal Victoria Dock. It included no less than six schools, two music halls and numerous pubs. Only two roads led in and out of the Isle of Dogs. Cut off by docks and swing-bridges, these districts were largely self-sufficient, retaining a village-like remoteness from the general East End and the wider metropolis.

More obnoxious industries were established on the outskirts of the East End, around Bow Creek and Hackney Wick, including dye, glue and chemical works, all accessible by barges. Flour mills grew in number near Bow Bridge, an area that had a heritage of milling going back to medieval times. Over several decades the area lost its former rural tranquility, with its tea gardens and country houses, and the river waters became polluted.

The Victorian era, long before the introduction of the welfare state, was noted for its Christian missionary zeal and charitable efforts. Numerous missions were founded around the East End for the benefit of sailors and the local population. Organizations included the British & Foreign Sailors' Society, which operated the Passmore Edwards Sailors' Palace at Limehouse. The Methodists founded the Wesleyan Seamen's Mission in 1843 and the

Queen Victoria Seaman's Rest opened in Poplar in the 1890s. The Anglican ministry ran the Missions to Seamen Institute on East India Dock Road from 1893. One example of a project for the local population was the Malvern Mission. Funded by the private Malvern College school in Worcestershire, a centre for the residents of the area was opened at Vincent Street in a deprived area at Canning Town, north of the Royal Victoria Dock. It was at that time dubbed 'the worst street in London' by a newspaper. The original intention was to educate local boys and spread the Christian faith. With the arrival of Reginald Kennedy-Cox in 1905 it became the Docklands Settlement Mission and a number of other branches were opened around the East End and beyond in subsequent years.

Those who worked in the docks, residing in small streets sandwiched between the docks, became communities where father, son and grandson all worked as dockers, as did their neighbours, and they married local women. These people were in the middle of the most cosmopolitan of environments, with ships, cargoes, crews, large numbers of immigrants, and passengers arriving from every corner of the world. Yet they generally remained as static, tight-knit communities, isolated from the rest of London and the wider world.

The Thames Conservancy

Complaints had long been made that the City of London Corporation, responsible for the river, and receiving large amounts in tolls from coal and other goods, were doing little to maintain its condition, particularly in relation to dredging. The state of the tideway deteriorated with the introduction of steam-powered passenger pleasure boats, of which there were fifty-seven on the river by 1830. Their relatively high speed created a wash that threatened to sink barges, lighters and wherries. Furthermore, the wash and the action of paddle wheels swept away the foreshore mud, making it dangerous for wooden vessels to rest at low tide. A state of war ensued between the trip boats and lightermen. The issues became more critical as steamships began to be used for coastal cargo-carrying during the 1830s.

There had been a continuous increase in the number of colliers entering the Port. The greatest part of coal stocks arriving were transferred onto lighters where it was stored until required for sale. Thus the open river was congested with colliers and storage lighters. Because they had further to travel upriver, it affected vessels berthing at St Katharine's more than others. The Dock

Company complained of the ineffectiveness of the City's harbour masters in enforcing the by-law to maintain a 300-foot-wide navigable channel despite notification by Parliamentary committees on several occasions.

In 1836 a Parliamentary Select Committee was appointed to consider the issues. The solicitor to the Admiralty stated that the Thames, like all rivers, was the property of the Crown who granted the City the right of regulation and conservation. The neglect of the City however had resulted in the Admiralty becoming increasingly involved in the regulation of the river. The committee found that the City's Navigation Committee comprised members with little experience or interest in the river. Their opinion was that conservation of the Thames should be transferred to a new body created specifically for that purpose. Despite strong condemnation of the City's management of the Thames, no change was forthcoming. In the meantime, some of the problems were diminished by the introduction of the railways, which reduced the amount of coal arriving by boat.

The final impetus for the change in responsibility for the river was a dispute at the time of the building of the Thames Embankments. The City contested the Crown's ownership of the riverbed. An accord was finally reached with the decision to create a Conservancy Board, created by Act of Parliament in 1857, with title in the bed and shore of the river from Staines downriver to Yantlet Creek. The new Thames Conservancy was given responsibility for regulation, preservation and safety, including the laying down of buoys and beacons and dredging. Any works carried out on or adjoining the river were to be under licence from the Board. Income was to be received from such licences, with a third payable to the Crown, as well as from tolls on steamers calling at piers and on shipping.

The Thames Conservancy initially consisted of twelve members appointed by the City, Trinity House, the Admiralty and the Board of Trade. In 1864 the Board was increased to eighteen members, including representatives of vessels and dock owners. In 1866 the Thames Conservancy took over responsibility of the Upper Thames, with the size of the Board increased accordingly.

The Millwall Docks

Despite the fragile finances of the existing docks there were still those who believed that an opportunity existed for new docks. This was particularly the case following the repeal of the Corn Laws, which had blocked cheap imports of North American grain between 1815 and 1846. The West India Docks had opened across the north of the Isle of Dogs at the beginning of the century yet fifty years later the centre of the peninsula remained as meadow where cows grazed, much as it had done since it was drained in the Middle Ages. At its centre stood a former chapel that had been incorporated into a farmhouse. Around the surrounding embankment stood seven windmills and small independent wharves owned by shipwrights and maritime businesses.

In the late 1850s one of the Millwall wharf-owners, oil merchant Nathaniel Fenner, had the idea of creating a T-shaped enclosed dock behind the wharves, with the central basin leading northwards towards the West India Docks. His dock was to be connected to the river by locks to both the east and west of the peninsula. Fenner's business model was different to earlier docks in that its quays would be let out to individual businesses to run their own operations. The idea was that surrounding land would attract factories and shipbuilding yards, each paying rent to the company. He commissioned the engineer Robert Fairlie to draw up plans but, needing capital for the project, contacted the more eminent engineer William Wilson. Wilson submitted the plan to Parliament and attracted the interest of further developers and engineers. Fenner and Fairlie had in the meantime been sidelined so they raised objections to the Parliamentary Bill. In order to pacify them, Wilson and his partners paid the originators of the scheme substantial sums of money, with Fenner given a seat on the Board of the newly-formed Millwall Freehold Land & Dock Company.

Two hundred and four acres of land were acquired to the south of the West India Docks in order to create 52 acres of dock and 152 acres for associated purposes. Financing for the project proved more difficult than anticipated. (The long-established East & West India Dock Company was already struggling to raise more than half a million pounds in order to transform their City Canal across the Isle of Dogs into a new south dock. There was also a general financial crisis in London when the Overend, Gurney bank went bankrupt in May 1866). The Company was forced to enter into finance arrangement fees that increased the amount to be raised but still did not achieve the objective. Plans were scaled back to two basins and altered to make the project more affordable. Work to create the Millwall Docks began in 1866 and was completed in a year and a half, employing 3,000 construction workers and steam-powered pumping engines to drain the marshy land.

When completed in March 1868 the Millwall Docks had an unusual thirty-six-acre inverted L-shaped basin, with an entrance to the river on the west side of the peninsula. It was the first of the docks to be created with a dry dock, of 413 feet in length. The planned entrance to the east never materialized. While ships were beginning to get larger, the Millwall Docks were opened with an entrance lock of only eighty feet in width, which would never be enlarged due to the width and depth of the dock itself, restricting the size of vessels that could enter.

As with the Victoria Dock, Millwall had a rail connection, accommodating passengers from the beginning. By that time a branch of the Blackwall Railway passed through the West India Dock down to its terminus at North Greenwich station at the southern tip of the Isle of Dogs, serving the Millwall quays en route. Steam locomotives were banned from the West India Docks as a fire precaution however, so in the early years the trains were pulled by horses on the Isle of Dogs section of the railway. The line operated until it was abandoned in 1926.

In order to survive, the rates at the Millwall Docks were low from the start, so this added further competition to the port but without creating any significant profit for itself. Attempts to attract timber business away from the Surrey Docks were unsuccessful and in the event it specialized in grain from the Baltic. The Millwall Equipment Company, a subsidiary company, operated the finest granary facilities in the Port of London. A financial crisis occurred in 1898 when it was discovered that the dock's manager had been falsifying the accounts for several years.

In creating an industrial area on what had previously been meadows, the original developers were successful, progressing gradually as new businesses arrived and evolved. '[The whole Isle of Dogs] was given up to accommodating heavy industries that had replaced the old riverside crafts of Georgian days, such as boatbuilding in wood and the twisting of ropes by hand,' wrote East London historian Millicent Rose. 'In the new industrial town of Millwall, cables were manufactured by steam, out of Riga hemp and iron, of a weight suitable for use by the new iron ships. There were cement works, galvanized iron works and refineries of turpentine. The old windmills disappeared from the river-bank, and in the section opposite Deptford they were replaced by the yard of the well-known shipbuilding firm, Scott Russell & Co.' The shipyard actually predated the Millwall Docks. It was there that Isambard Kingdom Brunel's giant steamship the *Great Eastern* was launched.

Two notable businesses that were based at Millwall, both on the south quay, were Hooper's Telegraph Works, where from 1871 telegraph cable was

The illustration from *The Illustrated London News* of March 1868 that accompanied the news-piece of the opening of the Millwall Docks

produced and loaded directly onto cable-laying ships, and the McDougall's flour mill. Alexander McDougall began making self-raising flour in Manchester in 1865 following the discovery of a new type of baking powder. His five sons originally built a fertilizer factory at Millwall in 1871 but in the following decades they further developed their site for the milling of their famous flour. The original mill was destroyed in an enormous fire in 1898 and a replacement, the Wheatsheaf Mill, was completed in 1900. Further development took place in the 1930s and it continued to operate until closed by the Rank Hovis McDougall conglomerate in 1982.

Riverside wharves

The docks were mostly hidden behind high walls, so for the general public the riverside wharves were the visible sign of the busy port, particularly those in the Upper Pool seen from London Bridge.

The number of wharves along the river greatly increased from the 1830s following the ending of the docks' monopolies and the widening of customs bonding provisions. By the latter part of the nineteenth century there were about 300 wharves along the Thames to where around 75 per cent of goods arriving at the enclosed docks was syphoned off. With independent and often dynamic owners they became an important part of the Port. The dock companies each employed a certain number of permanent dock staff, or 'perms'. That wasn't usually the case at the wharves, where much of the work was carried out by casual labourers.

Some wharves had deep-water berths at which ships could directly unload, while others merely accepted goods arriving by lighter. There were those handling general cargo while others specialized in certain types of commodity. Raw materials could be directly discharged to riverside manufacturers of a particular kind of product and perhaps load whatever it was they produced. A major raw material was coal, shipped around the coast from Newcastle, and used to power many riverside gas, electricity and hydraulic power stations as well as factories. Following an explosion at the Victoria Dock in 1869, an Act of Parliament restricted the carriage of petroleum to no further upriver than a wharf at Shell Haven at Thurrock. From 1912 the Shell Oil Company operated a refinery there and petroleum and gas products continue to arrive, be stored and refined along that section of the Thames Estuary.

When the Butlers Wharf Company completed their wharves and warehouses at the Pool of London between Tower Bridge and St Saviour's Dock in 1873 they were the largest complex of warehouses on the river. They stretched from the riverside 130 metres inland. Shad Thames, a narrow street, ran behind the riverside wharves, separating them from the warehouses behind. Tall warehouses towered high each side of Shad Thames, crossed at various heights by lattice wrought-iron bridges across which dockers could move goods. The Butlers Wharf Company specialized mainly in general goods such as grain, rubber, spices, fruit, wines, spirits and tea.

A close neighbour to Butler's Wharf was Hay's Wharf in the Upper Pool, on the south bank of the river at Southwark. It had been established by Alexander Hay in the mid-seventeenth century, initially for brewing and wharfage and the latter proved to be more profitable. By the nineteenth century it was owned by the Humphrey family who stored tea and valuable cargoes. In 1861 a major fire began at nearby Cotton's Wharf, which spread along the riverside destroying three acres of property and contents estimated in value at £2 million. The Humphreys took the opportunity to rebuild Hay's Wharf with the innovation of refrigeration. In the twentieth century the Hay's Wharf business owned most of the riverside wharfage between Tower Bridge and London Bridge, handling a large part of the foodstuffs imported into the capital. Their total warehousing space by then occupied nearly 1,000 square metres, the largest such complex in the world. There they stored three quarters of London's provisions such as bacon, cheese, eggs, tea, coffee and fruit, and the wharves were known as 'London's Larder'. Until the Second World War, the quayside cranes at Hay's Wharf, the largest concentration in the entire Port and visible to anyone crossing London or Tower Bridge, were a reminder to anyone of the importance of London's international sea trade.

The Liverpool sugar refiner Henry Tate obtained the rights to produce sugar in cubes from its German inventor and purchased a derelict shipyard at Silvertown where in 1878 he built a refinery. The Scottish shipowner Abram Lyle opened a refinery a short distance along the river in 1883 at the former Plaistow and Odham's wharves to produce his famous Golden Syrup. (The two companies amalgamated in 1921 to form Tate & Lyle, after the deaths of their founders, who never actually met).

At the end of the nineteenth century there was an almost continuous line of wharves along both banks, downriver from London Bridge to the Isle of Dogs and Greenwich. They varied in size and type, from massive, brick blocks of warehousing to simple timber sheds. Some of the largest amongst them were Fresh Wharf in the City, which had existed since medieval times; Free Trade Wharf at Ratcliff; the Aberdeen Steam Navigation Company's Aberdeen Wharf at Limehouse; Morton's food factory (whose works football team became Millwall FC); Bellamy's Jetty at Rotherhithe, which could handle ships too large for the Upper Port; and Thames Tunnel Mills, also at Rotherhithe. Some had evocative and historic names, such as Black Eagle Wharf, King Henry's Wharves, Limekiln Wharf, St Saviour's Dock and St Olave's Wharf.

The Royal Albert Dock

In the mid-nineteenth century the economy was improving, demand for consumer goods increasing, and in 1869 the Suez Canal opened, increasing the amount of business with Asia and the Far East carried on large ocean-going ships. Liverpool, with superior facilities for larger steam ships, was prospering at London's expense. By the second half of the century the deep-water Victoria was the more successful of London & St Katharine's Thames docks, yet ships continued to increase in size, requiring even larger facilities. London & St Katharine therefore decided to expand the facilities at Plaistow.

When the Victoria Dock Company obtained their Act of Parliament in 1850 it included the option to acquire additional land to the east. The idea was to create a holding dock and shortcut from Gallions Reach, avoiding an additional four miles journey upriver along Woolwich Reach to their entrance lock. That plan was never implemented and the land was eventually purchased by the Victoria Dock's new owners, the London & St Katharine Dock Company.

In April 1879 the Company received royal assent to name this massive new dock after the Queen's late consort, to open as the Royal Albert Dock, with its older, smaller sister renamed the Royal Victoria Dock. The architect was Sir Alexander Rendel and the contractors were Lucas & Aird, whose partner John Aird had been one of the developers of the earlier Millwall Dock. The building methods were more modern than had been previously used, employing a steam dredger and cranes and using concrete instead of bricks. Nevertheless, 3,000 men were employed in the construction. The cost was relatively low, partly because concrete could be produced on site using excavated gravel.

The new dock was 1¼ miles in length, 490 feet wide, with 87 acres of water area and 16,500 feet of quays. The largest ships of the time could be accommodated, with a massive entrance lock measuring 550 by 80 feet, capable of accepting ships of up to 12,000 tons, double that of the West India Docks. Shortly after, a second, deeper entrance was created due to the threat of competition from a new dock at Tilbury. Ships could enter from the river at Gallions Reach in the east. Linked at its western end to the Victoria Dock, even ships from the latter could then avoid the journey along the tidal river at Woolwich Reach. The Royal Albert was the first to be lit by electricity, with lamps on 80-foot-tall poles allowing round-the-clock working. The cranes were hydraulically-powered. Railway tracks ran alongside each quay allowing cargoes to be directly loaded into wagons. The tracks ran into the company's sheds where the lines were sunk below the floor surface, allowing goods to be easily unloaded. The quays were lined with hydrants to provide docked vessels with fresh water. Ships could be repaired in either of the dock's two dry docks on the western edge of the south quay. The Royal Victoria and Royal Albert Docks together created a gigantic artificial waterway of 175 acres of water with 7 miles of quays.

The Great Eastern Railway passed through the dock property by means of a tunnel under the short canal that linked the Victoria and Albert docks.

Connaught Way passed over that same point and Manor Way over the dock entrance by swing bridge, where the basin opened to the east into Gallions Reach. By then international travel was increasing for the general public and a passenger terminus was established adjacent to the dock, together with the Gallions Hotel.

The new Royal Albert Dock was opened in June 1880 by the Duke and Duchess of Connaught, on behalf of his mother Queen Victoria. At the same time the chairman of the London & St Katharine Dock Company, George H. Chambers, was knighted. The dock specialized in grain and, after refrigeration was introduced, frozen meat, fruit and vegetables.

The Tilbury Docks

The success of, and the envy caused by, the large new Royal docks spurred the rival East & West India Dock Company into action. The Suez Canal was bringing increased business to the Port but not to the East & West India with their old, shallow, outdated docks and entrance locks too small to accept the new, larger vessels. Telegraphic communication by underwater cable resulted in better communication regarding a vessel's arrival and therefore less need for warehousing. There was also a threat from yet another company that had in 1880 successfully put a plan before Parliament for new deep-water docks at Dagenham in Essex. A breach in the river wall there as far back as 1707 had created a pool that could be converted into a dock. (That plan never proceeded and the site was eventually used by the Ford Motor Company for their new factory).

The East & West India chairman, the merchant Harry Dobree, and his engineer Augustus Manning, carefully chose the site for a new dock. Ships had for centuries moored at Gravesend in Kent, twenty-six miles downriver of London Bridge, while they waited for the incoming tide that would sweep them up to the city. The Company used agents to secretly take options on marshland around Tilbury on the opposite bank in Essex before making its intentions public by announcing them to shareholders. The advantage of creating docks there was that an entire day was saved in each direction for passengers or freight transferring to railway, compared with continuing upstream to London. Pilotage on the long journey upriver would also not be necessary. Cargoes were to be swiftly transferred to or from railway wagons and ships and thus large-scale warehousing was not part of the plan.

An Act of Parliament was passed in July 1882. The Company were highly optimistic about their new dock. They planned on such a large scale that they must have believed that either trade in and out of London would increase dramatically or that they could steal away the majority of the business from the Royal docks. The area of the site acquired was 450 acres.

Unfortunately, the work did not proceed according to plan. The Company and its contractors, Kirk & Randell, underestimated the scale and cost of the work, from a budget of £1,100,000 to a final cost of £2,800,000. The contractors requested large advances and, when they unexpectedly found blue clay, claimed additional costs. The exasperated dock company had them ejected from the site in 1884, leading to years of expensive litigation. For a while the East & West India continued with their own men until new contractors, Lucas & Aird, were appointed.

When Tilbury opened, ships entered a tidal basin of 19 acres, through an entrance lock of 700 by 80 feet, then passed into one of three parallel docks – the East, Central and West – totalling 56 acres of water space, allowing vessels to enter at any time, whatever the tide. Colliers unloaded fuel for ships at a jetty in the tidal basin; two dry docks were incorporated between the tidal basin and docks, and round the basins were 24 sheds, each measuring 300 by 120 feet.

As it was such a remote location the Company created tenement-block residences for the workers and managers. The only land connection to the world beyond the docks was by railway and initially there was no road link other than a track to supply food to the workers from local farms. Fifty miles of railway sidings connected the quays to London and the wider country, with trucks able to pass under the cranes. The London, Tilbury & Southend Railway ran passenger trains every thirty minutes to Fenchurch Street in the City, a journey of thirty-five minutes. Freight was carried to a newly-created depot at Whitechapel, later known as the Commercial Road Warehouse. The railway company undertook to charge no more to send goods to Tilbury than to other docks.

The Company considered that a hotel for passengers was an important part of their image and they opened the Tilbury Hotel. Under the stewardship of Leopold C. Bentley and, with a spectacular riverside location, it became an opulent institution.

The work was finally completed and the first ship, the *Glenfruin*, entered the docks at the end of its voyage from China in April 1886. Celebrations took place in the hotel, attended by the Company chairman, the Lord Mayor of

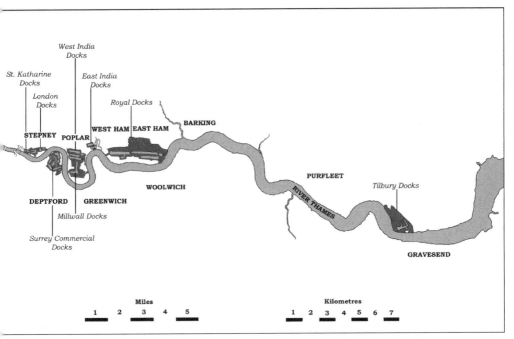

The River Thames from the Upper Pool downriver to Lower Hope Reach showing the locations of the major dock groups as they existed between the 1890s and 1950s.

London and the shipowner Sir Donald Currie of the Castle Shipping Line. Tilbury was to be the last dock system until the twenty-first century to be created by private enterprise as part of the Port of London.

The Company's optimism was short-lived. Thames lighters were not designed to go so far downriver and the lightmen and wharfingers boycotted the new docks. While Tilbury was being built the rival London & St Katharine Company had been negotiating with merchants and offered inducements for goods to be landed at their docks. The shipping trade waited to see what East & West India would offer in return. In the meantime the vast new docks stood almost empty for the first few months. Their answer was to offer the Clan Line, which operated steamers to India and South Africa, to dock at Tilbury instead of the Royal Albert in return for half rates for ten years. Others followed but to attract the business the docks were operating at a loss. With Tilbury offering such low rates, other docks and wharves had to do the same to maintain trade. Thus it was to the advantage of shipowners, while both the London & St Katharine and the East & West India Companies suffered financially.

The plight of the dock companies and wharf owners

The lack of initial success at Tilbury was too much for the East & West India Company. The fierce competition between all the dock companies and the wharfingers had cut profits to the extent that it became impossible for them to attract new capital. In 1887 the East & West India cut salaries and maintenance budgets in an effort to stay afloat but in March 1888 they fell into receivership. At around the same time, unable to survive financially, a number of riverside wharves were disposed of by their owners.

During the following months a merger of operations with the London & St Katharine (but not ownership, assets or profits) was agreed. Both companies retained their individual boards of directors, although reduced in size. A full merger was not possible due to the complex financial position of the India Company and pending litigation. It was a structure that had previously been used by railway companies. The new organization was known as the London & India Docks Joint Committee and took effect from January 1889. Chair of the committee was C.M. Norwood, who at the same time chaired the London & St Katharine Company. That year the Joint Committee made a mutually beneficial agreement with the leading wharfingers regarding landing rates, known as the 'Dock & Wharf Produce Agreement'.

Charles Morgan Norwood was a maritime merchant and shipowner from Hull who held the Parliamentary seat of that borough for twenty years. He had taken legal action for libel against Samuel Plimsoll following an accusation of dangerously overloading one of the ships he owned. As a result, Norwood was involved in the creation of the ships' loading mark standard, which became known as the 'Plimsoll line'. He died in 1891.

In early 1898, nine years after the formation of the Joint Committee, a full amalgamation of the two companies was finally agreed with creditors and shareholders with a complex structure. The London & India Docks Company formally came into being on 1 January 1901.

The Surrey Docks at the Rotherhithe Peninsula on the opposite bank had remained profitable and independent. They primarily handled timber, as well as grain destined for the local mills and biscuit-makers. Handling eighty per cent of London's timber trade, in 1904 enough wood passed through to gird the equator to a depth of three and a half feet. The complex of docks was competently managed by timber and grain men who continually upgraded and improved facilities and their specialized trade meant they suffered less from the effects of the free-water clause. The ships that transported those goods were smaller than other ocean-going cargo ships. As such the Surrey Docks could for a long time survive without the need to adapt to larger ships like those on the north bank. However, by the end of the nineteenth century vessels of up to 8,000 tons were being employed in the timber trade from North America, too large for the Surrey Docks. The Company embarked on another phase of upgrading by adapting their Greenland Dock, which had been in existence since it was opened as Howland Dock 200 years earlier, for larger ships. The eminent Sir John Wolfe Barry, who was at the same time working on the new Tower Bridge, was commissioned as the engineer. It was not an easy project, with fine Thanet sand unexpectedly filling the foundations and entrance lock. The dock more than doubled in size, with an entrance lock of 550 feet long and 80 feet wide. The newly-enlarged Greenland Dock opened in 1904 spanning twenty-two acres and connecting with the Canada Dock. At a cost of £940,000 and taking a decade, the project had cost far more than had been budgeted and caused financial problems for the Surrey Commercial Docks Company. To increase trade they belatedly began competing with the docks on the north bank. Two Canadian shipping lines carrying butter and cheese were tempted away from the Royal Victoria Dock, who retaliated by offering rates to timber ships at a quarter less than the Surrey Docks. It turned out to be the final nail in the coffin of the independent dock companies.

The formation of trade unions

Even when jobs were plentiful a port labourer was unlikely to work more than four days in any week and the wages were low. It was not uncommon for casual workers to earn a pound or two in a week and then nothing further for a fortnight. To put that into perspective, a typical rent in the East End at that time was around 5 shillings (25 decimal pence) per week and it was common for families to fall behind with their payments. If a docker became particularly desperate he might walk the twenty miles each way from the East End to Tilbury in the hope of finding a few hours work. It was an insecure and precarious existence for workers and their families and attracted those who were already down on their luck and had failed to find employment elsewhere. Once they became part of the casual-labour dock pool of workers it was difficult to escape to take their chance elsewhere. The need to be constantly waiting for work from early each morning, and with little or no money in their pockets, meant they had to live within walking distance of the docks. The call-on became a way of life for generations of families and entire neighbourhoods.

Colonel G.R. Birt, general manager of the Millwall Docks, explained to a Parliamentary Committee that men would arrive outside the dock gates who were so poor that 'they cannot run, their boots would not permit them'. They arrived hungry, having not had food since the previous day and could only work an hour because 'their hunger will not allow them to continue'. They would leave with their hour's pay in order to buy some food. To those who complained that dockers would not work after four o'clock in the afternoon, he explained that was because by that time their strength had gone due to hunger. Dock work was also dangerous, with a high accident rate. A hospital chairman, quoted in evidence to a Parliamentary Committee towards the end of the century, stated that an accident occurred in the docks every quarter of an hour, day and night. A Home Office report in 1929 put only mining as more hazardous than dock-working, with twelve per cent of workers making successful claims for compensation during their working lives.

Labour was cheap and abundant in the nineteenth century, with more casual workers than available employment at most times. The Mansion House Committee, assembled by the Lord Mayor in 1889, estimated there were 20,000 unemployed workers in London. With such a perilous existence it was difficult for them to demand better conditions. The amount of work in the Port fluctuated according to the economy and the season however, and at busy times there was a shortage of labour. Workers occasionally exploited the situation when too many vessels needed unloading at the same time, taking the opportunity to demand increased remuneration. There were strikes at the shipyards at Deptford during the busy years at the end of the eighteenth and early nineteenth centuries while the wars against France were taking place. As early as July 1810, when workers were still employed on a full-time basis, around 1,000 men at the London Docks had struck for an increase from eighteen shillings to one guinea per week. They were unsuccessful in their claim and returned to work after several days. In 1821 casually-employed coopers at the West India Docks struck for increased wages. The dock company attempted to take on coopers from as far afield as Bristol and Liverpool but there was solidarity with the London workers amongst compatriots in those ports. The Company then appealed to the Duke of York to provide experienced men from the armed forces on the grounds that ships remained unloaded, sugar was deteriorating on board and customs revenues were not being collected. The tactics were successful and according to Henry Longlands, Secretary to the West India Dock Company, the coopers 'returned to their work unconditionally'.

Until the latter part of the century workers lacked a body that represented, organized and supported them; indeed 'combinations', what we now call trade unions, were illegal in Britain until 1824. Fifty years later, in 1871, the same year that the Trade Union Act was passed in Britain, Colonel J.L. du Plat Taylor, general manager of the ailing East & West India Docks, attempted to economize by reducing the pay of labourers from 20 to 15 shillings per week. A meeting of workers was held, presided over by Reverend Hansard, a rector of Bethnal Green. The dockers felt themselves to be in a weak position, however: they were already so poor they could ill afford to lose further pay by striking. That autumn the Irish trade unionist Patrick Hennessey arranged further meetings under the auspices of what became the Labour Protection League. Hennessey was appointed secretary of the union but several months later absconded with the association's funds.

Despite its setbacks, membership of the Labour Protection League gained momentum, with support from stevedores, wharf workers and those working in the tea warehouses in the City and East End. By the summer of 1872 the association had 12,000 members. Later that decade the men working on British ships that berthed in the port were joining the newly-formed National Amalgamated Sailors' & Firemen's Union.

In June 1872 the men at the West India Dock went on strike, demanding an increase from four pence to six pence per hour and they were joined by workers from the Millwall, St Katharine's and London Docks. It was a particularly busy period and a rare occasion of full employment. The dock company were unable to find other workers to replace those on strike, agreed a compromise of an extra penny per hour and work resumed. Great celebrations were held at Shoreditch Town Hall, attended by 20,000 people from all along the north and south banks of the river, with music provided by bands. Reverend Hansard presided over a meeting inside the building and those outside led a joyful march to Hoxton Market.

Joy amongst the workers over their five pence an hour was to last only a short time. The latter years of the 1870s saw a downturn in trade that continued for a decade, with workers laid off in the port. Requirements for greater skills within the docks had led to a small number of well-paid and experienced staff and fewer casual labourers were being taken on, leading to great hardship. Those who were hired were put under increasing pressure. With the advent of steamships that could sail in all weathers, shipowners demanded rapid turnaround. Rather than being hired for a half day, as they were previously, labourers were called on and laid off on an hourly basis. The 'plus money' bonus that had been paid in earlier decades became an arbitrary payment. Men could wait outside the dock gates for hours or even days for as little as five pence worth of work. To save the dock management the effort of hiring men each day, the task was instead delegated to ruthless contractors who in many cases had to be bribed in order to gain work.

In 1888 there was a well-publicized strike by female packers at the Bryant & May match factory at Bow, not far from the docks. That encouraged workers in other industries to agitate for better conditions. In the following year the National Union of Gas Workers and General Labourers was formed under the leadership of Will Thorne and they were successful in reducing the working hours at Beckton Gas Works, just to the east of the Royal Docks. Thorne was one of several eloquent and charismatic leaders emerging at that time who were able to negotiate with managers. Another was Ben Tillett who had experience as a sailor as well as a casual labourer at the docks where he endured the degrading call-on. He was working at the Monuments Quay Warehouse and heard that tea workers at the Cutler Street warehouses in the City were planning to fight a pay reduction. Attending a meeting where they discussed action to fight a pay cut, he was given the position of secretary of the Tea Operatives' Union. Despite being afflicted with a stammer he was nevertheless an eloquent speaker and was not shy of being in the limelight.

The 'docker's tanner'

On 13 August 1889 Ben Tillett met with some workers at the South West India Dock. Instructed to speedily unload the *Lady Armstrong* with a full cargo, the workers walked out when not paid adequate 'plus money', which they believed to be owed for their effort. Tillett gathered together various other leading union activists to meet at the dock the following day and they formed a strike committee under his leadership to represent the men and to organize and spread the industrial action. By the 15th the entire labour force at the East and West India Docks had walked out. What had started as a small dispute regarding the unloading of one ship led to one of Britain's first great industrial disputes.

During the following weeks *The Times* was to report extensively and reasonably objectively, perhaps sympathetically, on the strike, unlike some other newspapers that called for the arrest of the strike leaders. On some days *The Times* reports covered two pages, or more, yet they began modestly with a brief news item on the Monday following the commencement of the action. It informed its readers that on the previous day [Sunday] 2,000 of an estimated 10,000 strikers marched in procession from the East End, along Commercial Road to the City,

> with the intention of claiming for a deputation an interview with the London & India Docks Committee at their offices in Leadenhall-street. A party of six were introduced to Mr C.M. Norwood (the chairman) and some of the directors who happened to be in the building. A long interview followed, in the course of which the men urged their demands. In reply, Mr Norwood stated that the directors would always be ready to listen to any grievances which the men might have ... but he could promise them nothing until they were in a different frame of mind. He urged them to return to their work.

The processions along Commercial Road and through the City became a daily event. The following day, *The Times* continued:

> [the] whole of the proceedings ... by the men were very enthusiastic, and began early in the morning by the formation of a procession, which was a mile-and-three-quarters long, and a number of men in it carried poles with crusts, penny loaves, bones, vegetable tops, and other refuse fixed to them, to show the fare they lived on.

As the days went on the processions grew in size, numbering up to 100,000 and taking an hour to pass a given point. The marchers included many sympathetic workers other than dockers. They arrived at Dock House in Leadenhall Street at one o'clock each day and ended with a mass meeting at Tower Hill, Hyde Park or elsewhere. The purpose of the marches was to garner support from the public, maintain morale amongst the strikers and create some discipline amongst what was generally an undisciplined group. Each day City workers came out of their offices to see the spectacle, with its flags and banners, Doggett's race winners in their scarlet uniforms with huge pewter badges, and marching bands playing the *Marseillaise* – the national anthem of France, in memory of the French Revolution. Despite the vast numbers, the men marched peacefully.

At the head of the processions strode the committed socialist and flamboyant dresser John Burns, in his distinctive straw boater hat. Earlier that year he had won a seat representing Battersea on the newly-established London County Council in which he was to become a driving force in its early years. Despite growing up in poverty in Lambeth, the sixteenth child in a family supported only by their mother, Burns was an eloquent public speaker with a gift of expression, credited as coining the description of the River Thames as 'liquid history'. Along with Tillett, Burns was a tireless organizer and skillful negotiator but his greatest contribution to the strike was his powerful oratory at the many mass meetings that were to maintain the solidarity and determination of the strikers.

Tillett and Burns were joined on the strikers' organizing committee, which based itself at the Wade's Arms in Jeremiah Street, Poplar, by Tom Mann, a former colleague of Burns at the Battersea branch of the Social Democratic Federation. Mann was a committed trade unionist and member of the Amalgamated Society of Engineers who had been campaigning within the socialist movement for the introduction of an eight-hour working day. Earlier that year he had been a key person in the campaign to unite the gasworkers. During the strike, Mann ensured the effectiveness of round-the-clock picket lines at the dock gates as well as the issuing of food tickets that could be spent locally.

On Monday, 19 August, the strike at the East and West India Docks extended to the men of the Millwall, Victoria, Albert and Tilbury Docks. Significantly they were also joined by 1,800 members of the Amalgamated Stevedores' Union, led by the Irishman Tom McCarthy. Stevedores were the highly-experienced, self-employed and generally well-paid men hired by shipowners (rather than the dock companies) to oversee the loading of ships. They issued a statement that explained:

We, the union stevedores of London, knowing the condition of the dock labourers, have determined to support their movement. We do this not to inconvenience the brokers, shipowners, or master stevedores, as our quarrel is not with them, but we feel it our duty to support our poorer brothers.

By 22 August the industrial action had spread throughout the entire port, including lightermen, warehouse workers and wharfmen and other low-paid workers, numbering perhaps as many as 70,000. Unlike their counterparts on the north side of the river, dockers at the Surrey Docks largely dealt with unloading timber and had their own particular demands regarding how they were paid. The lightermen, who were employed by master lightermen, initially came out in sympathy with the dockers but during the following weeks began to air their own grievances and make their separate demands. Both these latter groups formed their own strike committees, working in parallel and in conjunction with the main strike committee. The leaders of the Surrey Docks men, led by James Sullivan, became known as the 'Sayes Court committee'.

Other union leaders and socialists came to the aid of the dockers, including Will Thorne of the National Gasworkers, Joseph Havelock Wilson of the National Sailors & Firemen, and the publisher Henry Hyde Champion. During the following weeks, workers in other nearby businesses, such as the McDougall's flour mill at the Millwall Docks, ceased work but in some cases they claimed their primary reason was due to intimidation from strikers rather than any demands of their own. The strike committee issued a statement that they 'strongly deprecate the rash action taken by unorganized workmen not directly connected with the dock workmen' and felt that it hindered their own efforts.

'The directors', as the dock-managers committee were referred to, were under pressure from both the workers and the shipowners whose vessels lay unloaded in the port. Thomas Sutherland, chairman of the P&O Company, wrote to *The Times* stating that both dockers and shipowners were being 'sweated by the dock company'. He proposed that in future shipowners should take responsibility for unloading vessels rather than the dock companies and even create their own docks. Norwood's opinion was that the shipping lines were 'spoiling his game' regarding breaking the strike, which further incensed the workers.

The strike committee worked long hours each day. They made demands to the directors that there should be only two daily call-ons; a minimum of four hours work each time men were hired; the ending of hire by contractors; six pence per hour in wages for daytime work; an increase from one penny to two pence per hour extra for overtime; and an end to the arbitrary 'plus money' bonus.

At a rally at Tower Hill Burns had used the phrase 'the full round orb of the dockers' tanner' to describe the hourly rate they sought ('tanner' being slang for six pence) and it became the rallying cry of the campaign. The daily mass rally on 25 August was held in Hyde Park where Tillett, McCarthy and others addressed the audience. As usual, the most rousing speech was given by Burns:

> 'The letters and speeches of the directors which had been published were unworthy of men, and were the language of ghouls in human shape, and the sentiments of financial Jack the Rippers.' (Loud cheers from the audience) 'But the women were setting a good example to them, for in one street they had erected a banner with the words on it 'No rent paid in the East of London till the docker gets his tanner" (Loud cheers)

Early in the strike the employers attempted to bring in blackleg workers. They were perhaps hired by William Coulson – 'the Apostle of free labour', financially supported by Randolph Churchill – who ran an organization to supply strike-breaking labour. Tom Mann organized pickets to prevent any non-strikers entering the docks. Blackleg workers from Liverpool, Southampton, Newcastle and Dundee were brought in to sleep in the docks but local butchers and bakers were persuaded to not supply them with food. When the strikers

> found 40 at the East India Docks, a great effort was made to induce the men to come out and not to remain in to injure the cause. The men said they had been engaged for a fortnight certain at 5s [five shillings] per day; but they were told they were wanted for railway metal work, and they were not informed that there was any strike on. There were more men, they said, to be sent on from Liverpool and the district. Eventually they all came out, and six were at once taken to Euston and sent back to try to stop other men from coming to London.

Furthermore, the strike committee announced they had received telegrams from each of the other major docks of Liverpool, Glasgow, Grimsby and Hull pledging to strike in support if any London-bound freight arrived at their port. Nevertheless, a certain amount of work continued throughout the strike, carried out by blacklegs. P&O and other shipping lines were successful in diverting their steamers to Southampton where the docks were kept busy.

The strike was a unique event, which caught the imagination of the general public. Trade unions were a relatively new phenomenon and strikes on this scale still unknown. Most Londoners knew the Thames, particularly because of the contemporary popularity of taking a trip down the river on a steamer. Yet hitherto few had understood the workings of the London freight docks and of the sufferings of the workers. In general, the public were sympathetic. In part that was because Henry Hyde Champion, one of the founders of the Fabian Society, acted as press officer to ensure the workers' side of the story was published by the British and foreign press who came to the strike headquarters each day.

There was great hardship for the workers who already struggled to survive and were unpaid during the industrial action, some coming close to starvation. As early as 24 October *The Times* reported that:

some of them declared that they had no food and were suffering already from hunger. A few charitable persons came and distributed 3d [three pence] tickets for food, whilst at one or two committee rooms small loaves of bread, with cheese, were issued. Many poor men were looking very haggard and serious, and were asking each other how long the strike was likely to last.

Two days later the same paper reported:

On account of the want severely felt by thousands of men, women and children in the East-end through the strike, General Booth [of the Salvation Army] opened his cheap food and shelter depot, 21a East India Dock-road, yesterday, until 1 o'clock to supply soup at half the usual price, and will open it again today. All the food at this depot is to be obtained at half-price for one week, or until the termination of the present difficulties.

By early September another nearby Salvation Army shelter on West India Dock Road was serving up to 8,000 men and children each day. Other churches also arranged soup kitchens. The numerous pubs in the districts that surrounded the docks were normally kept busy but they stood empty during the strike, the men having no income to pay for drinks. Three weeks into the strike *The Times* reported:

At the Wade's Arms, the headquarters of the Strike Committee, some 2000 poor labourers collected about 8 o'clock, and standing there in the drenching rain they presented a most woe-begone appearance. The ravages of hunger were clearly traceable on nearly all their countenances, and they waited patiently out in the wet for tickets which would be the means of procuring them food, of which they stood in so much need. An idea of the extent of the existing distress may be gathered when it is mentioned that yesterday upwards of 16,000 relief tickets were distributed …

Decisions on who was eligible to receive tickets must have been difficult. At the end of the campaign John Burns alluded to those who have made a living by false pretences and *The Times* mentioned 'idle loafers and corner men' who had benefitted from the strike funds. The strike committee were able to provide the tickets due to donations from far and wide. The radical *Star* newspaper, edited by the MP and Irish nationalist Thomas Power ('Tay Pay') O'Connor, had initiated a relief fund by its readers that raised £6,000. The British public contributed £10,000 with a further £1,000 from street collections. Workers in Melbourne, Australia, many of whom had emigrated from England and still felt a strong bond with the London dockers, sent the massive sum of £30,000 and there were small amounts from France, Belgium, New York, Philadelphia and Berlin. A total of over £48,000 was received by the strike committee, which was distributed to strikers in the form of one shilling food coupons.

By the end of August various issues between the Strike and Joint Committees had been resolved except the key point regarding the extra penny per hour. On the 30th of that month the 81-year old Cardinal Henry Manning, Archbishop of Westminster, took it upon himself to attempt to break the deadlock. His intention was to visit the dock company directors along with the Home Secretary and Lord Mayor of London but he could not locate either of them. Instead he was accompanied by the Deputy Mayor and acting head of the Metropolitan Police, yet found little sympathy for compromise from the employers. To his plea they should not employ imported labour from Holland, as was rumoured, they responded that it was their business who they hired. Manning departed with the thought that he had 'never in my life preached to so impenitent a congregation'.

The Cardinal's efforts seem to have at least achieved one thing of significance: several days later the Lord Mayor of London, Alderman James Whitehead, formed a Mansion House Committee, or 'Committee of Conciliation' as it became known, to arbitrate between the two sides in the dispute. It initially included the Cardinal as well as the Bishop of London, Sir John Lubbock MP (president of the London Chamber of Commerce), Sydney Buxton MP for Poplar, and Lord Brassey. Following discussion amongst themselves they proposed the dock companies pay the increase but that it be delayed until the following March. That evening they met with Tillett and Burns who agreed on the principal of a delay but that the rise should take place in January. Surprisingly, despite all their previous rebuttals, after a stormy debate, Norwood and the directors agreed to accept the compromise. When Tillett and Burns presented it to the strike committee however, it was rejected, to their surprise. The first months of each year were a slack period when casual labourers were anyway likely to be out of work and it was therefore important for them that an increase was given before the end of the year in order to get back on their feet. The rejection of the January compromise angered the Lord Mayor, the Bishop of London and the dock company directors.

The Bishop took no further part in proceedings. Tillett anyway found a lack of sympathy from both him and the Mayor but the elderly Cardinal Manning proved to be an effective reconciler. He was better qualified than the other committee members to understand both sides of the argument. His father had been a West India Company merchant, his brother a former dock chairman, and he therefore had a good knowledge of the docks from the management side. An estimated 40,000 of the strikers were Irish Catholics and the Cardinal was therefore well-acquainted with the deprivation around the docks. In the days that followed, the Cardinal, Mayor and Sydney Buxton had numerous meetings with the various employer and strike committees involved in the dispute.

On 7 September the strike committee set a new target of a raise from 1 October. A week later Manning persuaded Norwood to agree to a date of Monday, 4 November, although it would appear from contemporary reports that the directors of the Surrey Commercial Docks were less inclined to do so. Shipowners, who met together at the offices of the P&O Company in the City, were also far from accommodating an increase in berthing rates to pay for a rise in the dockers' wages.

An extraordinary meeting then took place on 10 September. The Lord Mayor delegated the power of negotiation to the Cardinal. Despite his age and frailty, Manning travelled out to the East End for a joint meeting with the Wade's Arms and Sayes Court strike committees. The Wade's Arms pub was probably seen as inappropriate for the teetotal clergyman so they instead met in a nearby school classroom. It was a meeting that was to last long into the evening. The Cardinal asked Tillett to state the reasons for not accepting the 4 November compromise and in the following twenty minutes replied to each of those points. He implored that they recognize the damage being done to the nation and the suffering of the men's families. Tillett was still not won over but Tom McCarthy recommended that the men accept the terms, backed by Tom Mann and Henry Champion. The Cardinal then gave an impassioned address, said to be the last great speech of his life, that brought tears to the eyes of some of the hardened dock labourers present. A vote was taken and the strike committee agreed by majority, although not unanimously, that the men would return to work providing that the penny per hour rise would come into effect from November.

The Joint Committee had insisted that their acceptance to the entire agreement was conditional upon all workers simultaneously returning to work and by then almost everyone was anxious to end the dispute. There were however still some further issues to be overcome regarding the specific demands of the lightermen, as well as the workers at the Surrey Docks. Further meetings were held during the morning of Saturday the 14th and these two latter groups agreed to return to work on the proviso that their points would thereafter go to arbitration.

Separate agreements could then be signed by each of the different groups of workers and directors: the London & India and Millwall Docks; Surrey Commercial Docks; independent wharves; and the lightermen. The end of the Great Dock Strike was finally announced on the afternoon of Saturday, 14 September, and work could therefore be resumed on Monday. Thus the dockers got their tanner, an extra two pence per hour overtime paid during the hours of six o'clock in the evening until six in the morning, and not less than two shillings each time they were called on.

In their final meeting on Saturday John Burns expressed, on behalf of the strikers, 'hearty thanks' to the Lord Mayor and his colleagues for their efforts to 'construct a golden bridge whereby the dispute could be ended'. The Mayor responded by voicing his admiration for the conduct of the strikers throughout the previous weeks. As for his efforts, Cardinal Manning was modest, merely stating that what he had done was 'for the love of his dear country and the love of all men joined together in the brotherhood of their commonwealth'.

On Sunday, 15 September, Burns and Champion led a triumphant mile-long procession from Canning Town to Hyde Park, cheered on along Commercial Road by their womenfolk. The final speeches of the campaign were made in the park by Tillett, Burns, McCarthy and Mann in which, ominously for the port managers, they predicted that the strike was only the first step for the labour movement. Special thanks were given to those in Australia who had supported the strikers.

The return to work was not the end of the matter. A specific part of the written undertakings with the Joint Committee was 'to unreservedly undertake that all labourers who have been at work during the strike shall be unmolested and treated as fellow labourers by those who have been out on strike'. Yet a couple of days earlier Tillett had told the day's mass meeting that when the men resumed work 'a look from a docker's eye was sufficient to paralyze a blackleg and they would be able to speak to those men when they [the strikers] returned to work.' During the following days there were major disturbances at the West India and Royal Victoria docks. On several occasions blacklegs who had continued to work were attacked by strikers and had to be protected by the Metropolitan Police. Union members blamed the disturbances on 'loafers' who were disappointed the strike had ended. At the same time workers complained that dock officials were favouring strangers with work in preference to strikers, a charge denied by the Company.

The following year the London & India Docks Joint Committee provided workers with further improved employment conditions. Permanent staff were henceforth entitled to sick pay, annual holidays and pensions for those serving at least fifteen years. Casual workers were divided into two classes: 'A' labourers were employed by the week, given annual holidays and the right to join the permanent staff when vacancies occurred; 'B' labourers were provided with numbered tickets that gave precedence to available work according to seniority.

The Tea Operatives' Union was renamed the Dock, Wharf, Riverside and General Labourers' Union of Great Britain & Ireland – generally known as simply the Dockers' Union – with Tom Mann as its president and Ben Tillett its general secretary. Representing port workers around the country, the union's membership increased to 57,000 in 1890. The dockers thereafter felt in a position of strength and began to take advantage of it, with frequent stoppages.

The strike had tarnished the reputation of the London & India Docks Joint Committee in the eyes of the public. Under pressure from shipping companies Norwood agreed from November 1890 to relinquish responsibility to shipowners for unloading their vessels at the Royal and Tilbury Docks, which did not particularly work in favour of the casual labourers who then had to deal with multiple employers. In fact the Joint Committee had handed on the poisoned chalice of dealing with militant labourers. Frustrated by the workforce, the shipping companies organized a mobile force of strike-breakers from other ports, with three ships able to transport them to wherever a strike broke out. It succeeded in breaking a dockers' strike in the autumn of 1890. The ships were still in operation until 1911, after the dock companies had ceased to exist.

During the decade following the Great Dock Strike, workers on the south side of the river separated from the Dockers' Union, forming the South Side Labour Protection League and thus, for a time, weakening the position of the original body. The National Amalgamated Sailors' & Firemen's Union lasted only six years before going into voluntary liquidation to avoid bankruptcy, due to expensive legal action. It reformed in 1894 as the National Sailors' & Firemen's Union and organized the first national seamen's strike in 1911.

Chapter Six

The Port of London Authority

The change from wooden-hulled sailing ships to iron and then steel steam ships in the second half of the nineteenth century meant that fewer vessels could carry a far greater tonnage of cargo. Prior to the First World War British-registered ships accounted for over a third of the world's total ocean-going tonnage, the largest of any nation by a wide margin. In 1815 the British merchant fleet consisted of nearly 22,000 ships, but in the early twentieth century less than 21,000 British ships carried almost five times more tonnage. Not only could greater loads be carried but they arrived faster, more predictably and at cheaper rates.

The Port of London had long been the largest dock complex in the world, handling the greatest volume of cargo, with a storage capacity of one million tons and over nine million tons of foreign cargo passing through in 1899, a third of all goods arriving in the country. This pre-eminence continued into the following decades until around 1913 when it was surpassed by Hamburg and then New York. In the early twentieth century the port was the biggest employer in the capital, with 20,000 men working in a wide variety of jobs and half as many again seeking casual work at the gates each day. Furthermore, the docks had become surrounded by manufacturing industries of many kinds, producing everything from domestic gas and electricity to consumer goods.

Ever larger ships had cut voyage times around the world, helped by the opening of the Suez Canal in 1869. The requirement for larger docks and harbours to accommodate these vessels concentrated Britain's maritime trade on a limited number of locations. At the end of the nineteenth century the largest of the country's ports were London and Liverpool. They were followed by Newcastle and Cardiff, both of which had a strong coal trade, the latter changing from a small harbour into the world's largest coal port. By the start of the Great War in 1914 Southampton had become the fifth largest port. In addition to cargoes, large passenger liners were sailing according to fixed timetables across the Atlantic and to other parts of the world, particularly from Liverpool and Southampton.

During the eighteenth century, exports from the Port of London exceeded imports but that had dramatically reversed by the early part of the twentieth century. In 1913 the value of imports was £253,879,000 but that of exports only £157,913,000. The principal incoming goods by value were wool, tea, rubber, metals, timber for construction, sugar, meat and butter. The major exports by value were cotton and woollen clothing, machinery and metal products. Around two thirds of the volume carried by British ships was with Europe and about a fifth with the Americas.

At the start of the twentieth century the complex of docks and wharves and the forest of cranes of the Port of London were symbols of the nation's wealth. A map of the city's principal businesses created in 1904 for the Royal Commission on London Traffic showed a continuous belt along the Thames-side, from Barking in the east to Brentford in the west. Wharves and factories had developed along all the navigable tributaries of the Thames, including the Wandle, Deptford Creek and Ravensbourne, Bow Creek and the Lea, Barking Creek and the Roding, as well as London's canals. Yet despite the great size of the Port, the vast amount of cargo that passed in and out, the large workforce, and its national importance, it was failing for both its shareholders, who were receiving a poor return in dividends, and the workers, many of whom lived on the breadline. London was becoming less reliable and cost-effective for shipowners. Business was going elsewhere, particularly to Liverpool, which was more convenient especially for the North Atlantic routes, or to Continental ports, some of which were subsidized by their local governments. The larger ocean-going ships had become so big that silting of the river meant that few could reach the upper docks and the Pool of London, all of which were restricted to small coastal steamers and lighters. Dock companies were therefore reluctant to invest in larger entrance locks for ships that were unable to navigate upriver, while the Thames Conservancy saw little point in dredging if ships could not pass through the small locks.

The Port of London Authority

In the late eighteenth century the main issue at the Port had been the lack of facilities for berthing and unloading ships, leading to lengthy delays and congestion. The government set up a commission to consider the problem at that time, leading to the creation of docks owned by individual companies. A hundred years later there were too many docks of the wrong kind, a lack of coordination between the multitude of docks, and no effective authority to manage the river. In 1900 the government once again set up a royal commission to consider the problems. During their investigation the eminent commissioners made visits to London's docks and wharves, as well as other major British ports, and made enquiries of Continental ports such as Hamburg and Rotterdam. One hundred and fourteen witnesses were questioned over thirty-one days.

Some of the findings during the review process were that the facilities in the port were outdated because of lack of investment; the river was too shallow to allow ships to reach the upper docks and wharves due to neglect by the Thames Conservancy; there were divisions of responsibility that obstructed improvement of the Port; the turnaround times for loading and unloading ships were too slow; railway connections were poor; and docking charges were too high. The docks were not up to modern standards but the commission believed they were capable of further development. The recommendation, published in June 1902, was that a single public authority should be created to manage both the docks and the river from Teddington down to the sea. The concluding words of the lengthy report included:

The deficiencies of London as a port, to which our attention has been called, are not due to any physical circumstances, but to causes which may easily be removed by a better organization of administration and financial powers. The great increase in the size and draught of ocean-going ships has made extensive works necessary both in the river and in the docks, but the dispersion of powers among several authorities and companies has prevented any systematic execution of adequate improvements.

The London & India Docks Joint Committee had done little during its tenure to improve their estate other than enlarge the Blackwall and South West India entrances of the West India Docks. They had, however, greatly increased the importation of frozen meat, with the addition of several specialized warehouses at the Royal Victoria. Perhaps to show they were not yet a dead force, or possibly wanting to enhance their takeover value in the case of their demise, they cut maintenance budgets, reduced wages, increased shipping dues by fifty per cent and submitted a plan to Parliament to extend the Royals with a large new deep basin to the south of the Royal Albert Dock.

It was too late. The government considered the problem and began the process of nationalizing London's docks. The creation of the Port of London Authority was introduced in the King's Speech at the Opening of Parliament in November 1903. It was then delayed for several years as discussions took place about how the Port should be organized. There were those who believed the plans were a dangerous move towards socialism. Some advocated creating new, more efficient and cheaper wharves instead of upgrading the enclosed docks. The first attempt at a Bill was abandoned by the Conservative government. In the meantime, alternative Bills were promoted by the London & India Docks, the Thames Conservancy and London County Council, and another was for the amalgamation of the London & India and Millwall companies.

In the summer of 1906 David Lloyd George, President of the Board of Trade in the new Liberal government, visited some of the Continental ports to investigate how they were managed. He came to the conclusion that a single nationalized authority was indeed the best solution and that the docks should be retained. He proceeded to strike a deal with the dock companies and the Port of London Act was passed in December 1908 despite some opposition. The final acquisition of the London docks and their storage facilities was concluded under Lloyd George's successor at the Board of Trade, Winston Churchill.

The management of the tidal River Thames and its docks were assigned to the Port of London Authority, which began operating in March 1909, and was accountable to the Board of Trade. It was headed by a Board consisting of between 15 and 28 members representing all the various interested parties, including the government, shipowners, wharfingers, lightermen, London's public authorities, Trinity House, the National Ports, the Admiralty and the workers. Up to four of the members could be nominated by the London County Council, two each by the City of London and Board of Trade and one each by the Admiralty and Trinity House. One each of the LCC and Board of Trade members were to represent the labour force.

Following the example of the Mersey Docks & Harbour Board, the PLA was created as a non-profit, self-governing trust in which any excess revenues would be used to improve the river and port facilities or to reduce charges. It was empowered to raise up to £5 million in fixed-interest-bearing stock to acquire the docks. Income came from rates on goods entering and leaving the Port, the licensing of craft, and on various services such as loading, unloading and storage.

The Authority took on obligations for maintenance of the river channels, provision of moorings, regulation of river traffic, the licensing of wharves, the removal of wrecks, and the prevention of pollution. It took over the duties of the Thames Conservancy on the Lower Thames, the latter thereafter having responsibility only for the upper, non-tidal river. Registration of licensing of craft, watermen and lightermen was taken from the Watermen's Company. Responsible for sixty-nine miles of tidal river downstream from Teddington to the Thames Estuary, the PLA had the authority and scope to solve many of the long-term problems, including dredging the river and regulating dock labour.

The PLA inherited almost 3,000 acres of estate, including that of the London & India, Millwall, and Surrey Commercial companies, with 32 miles of quays, as well as 17 London County Council passenger piers. The numerous riverside wharves remained in private hands. Towage within the docks was the responsibility of the Authority although on the open river it remained in the hands of private tug companies. At the time of its creation it employed over 11,000 people, almost all of them men. Most were ordinary dockers for cargo-handling but there were also those with specialist skills and training such as dockmasters, stevedores, timber porters, barge-handlers, coopers, divers and inspectors. Others undertook clerical work in the offices or packed and bottled. Over 1,000 worked in the headquarters and dock offices, more than 7,000 as permanently employed dock-workers, plus an average of around 3,000 casual labourers hired each day. The number of workers had increased by 1911 to over 13,000, remaining fairly constant until after the Second World War.

Several other bodies continued in their responsibilities alongside the PLA. Trinity House retained jurisdiction over pilotage on the river as well as for buoys and lighting. The City of London continued to deal with health issues regarding ships, passengers and cargoes. The Free Water Clause that was written into the Act of Parliament, which allowed lighters to freely enter each dock to load and unload overside, remained in place. However, each lighter was thereafter required to pay a registration fee.

Security on the Thames had been the responsibility of the Marine Police Establishment since its creation in 1798, which was later incorporated into the Metropolitan Police. Within the enclosed docks the dock companies employed their own security until the late-nineteenth century. When the PLA was established it held discussions with the Metropolitan Police regarding them taking over responsibility within the docks. The matter could not be resolved, and Tilbury Docks were anyway outside the Met's area, so in 1910 the PLA created its own police force and ambulance service. A Criminal Investigation Department was formed in 1913. A PLA police HQ was opened at the main entrance to the West India Docks. The hours were long and the pay was low; the police force was not particularly well-motivated or effective so theft by dockers was common and in the early years many officers were dismissed for being intoxicated or smoking while on duty. It was relatively easy for workers to carefully open a packing crate, steal some of the contents, replace them with an object of equal size and then reseal the crate. Pilfering was considered part of the way of life within the Port, to which it seems a blind eye was turned by the authorities. As has been mentioned in an earlier chapter, having a 'waxer', a sample of alcohol from the vaults, had a long tradition.

The first chairman of the PLA was the energetic and forceful Sir Hudson Kearley MP, which he undertook in an unpaid role. As Parliamentary Secretary to the Board of Trade he had been responsible for steering the Port of London Act through the House of Commons. Starting work at 16 for the Tetley tea company, he made his fortune as the founder of the tea importer Kearley & Tonge and the International Stores grocery retailer, which had 200 branches. He was elevated to become Lord Devonport in 1910.

As part of a move to create a strong and unifying public image, a coat of arms was approved by King Edward VII, including the motto *Floreat Imperii Portvs* (May the Imperial Port Flourish). The Board of the PLA initially met at the former Leadenhall Street offices of the London & India Dock Company. They had inherited the East India Company warehouse at Crutched Friars and obtained powers to clear the surrounding area containing eighteenth century houses, the whole to be used for the creation of a new headquarters. The leading architect, Sir Aston Webb, organized a competition for a design and the one chosen was from Edwin Cooper. John Mowlem & Company began construction in 1913 but there were delays from the start, not improved by the outbreak of war. Lord Devonport laid the foundation stone in June 1915 and the building was finally opened by the Prime Minister, David Lloyd George, in October 1922. After several increases in the budget, the final cost was over £2 million. Occupying a complete City block, the imposing building still stands beside the Trinity House headquarters, looking down Tower Hill onto the Tower of London and clearly seen from the river. Cooper's clever design consisted of a rectangular square, cut back at forty-five degrees on one corner to give an elevation facing Trinity Square. The grand classical entrance featured Corinthian columns, three storeys high, topped with a massive tower featuring a giant figure of Father Thames. A huge rotunda, with a larger diameter than the dome of St Paul's and claimed to be Europe's largest unsupported concrete dome, stood within the central atrium, connecting to offices on the four sides and maximizing light internally. For decades the Trinity Square HQ housed large numbers of bowler-hat-wearing clerks, female typists, and telephone operators, who rarely, if ever, visited the docks. Previously communication between the many PLA staff, located over a large area, had been undertaken by the Authority's own uniformed messenger boys. A telephone exchange was installed in the headquarters from the beginning and it had an extensive network that linked it to the docks.

The PLA's first Chief Engineer was Frederick Palmer, who had held the same position at the Port of Calcutta. He was tasked with proposing plans for works to make good on previous neglect and to upgrade the PLA's docks. In his report submitted to the Board in December 1910 he divided the plan into three programmes based on their importance and urgency, with the total cost estimated at £14,426,700. It was Lord Devonport's opinion that priority should be given to the West India Docks – close to the City and with excellent warehousing but with limited use due to the small size of its entrance locks and shallow depth – and the Royal Docks. He considered Tilbury to be too far away, beyond the cartage area of London, to be of importance. Simultaneously undertaking all the work of the first programme would have created much delay to shipping, so what was approved varied from Palmer's plan from the start. In particular, much of the work proposed for the West India Docks had to be delayed in order to minimize disruption to the Port, despite the priority given to it by Lord Devonport. Contracts were soon being put out to tender for a number of projects, the first being the East India and London Docks, where, when completed, shipping could be diverted while the more important work at the West India took place. As the work was getting underway Britain declared war on Germany and that was to cause serious disruption to the plans.

The older of London's docks had been constructed at a time when ships had round hulls and thus quay walls were curved. By the twentieth century ships had straight hulls and deeper drafts, with the result that they could not moor directly against older quaysides. As part of the new works, a false, vertical wall was constructed in front on the curved quay wall at the North Quay of the West India's Import Dock. New concrete transit sheds replaced the existing dilapidated timber-built facilities. The first section of this work was completed in October 1914 but thereafter work slowed due to the war and the entire project was not completed until May 1917. Similar work was carried out at the West India Export Dock and the lock between the East India Import Dock and Basin was widened to eighty feet. By far the cheapest tender came from a German company, who carried out the initial work, but the contract had to be transferred to a British firm at the outbreak of war and the work completed in 1916. Additionally, the width of the North and East Quays of the Import Dock was increased by twenty feet and new transit sheds constructed, three on the North Quay and one on the West Quay.

The North Quay of the London Docks was reconstructed using reinforced concrete, replacing the early nineteenth century wooden sheds with two-storey sheds, built onto a concrete-framed false quay in front of the existing dock wall. A new electric crane was installed. The size of ships entering the London Docks was still limited to 2,000 tons by the small 45-foot-wide entrance lock at Wapping and the Tobacco Dock Passage. By widening the passage, bigger ships could enter via the larger Shadwell New Entrance. This work was completed and the passage in use in April 1915 and, as it was taking place, a new reinforced-concrete jetty was constructed to replace the old timber jetty in the Western Dock.

The Tilbury Docks had originally been opened for the use of larger vessels but, as they continued to increase in size, the modern ships of the early twentieth century were having difficulty manoeuvring in and out of the three parallel docks. It was therefore decided in 1912 to extend the Main Dock, providing three new berths, together with sheds on the South Quay. The initial work proved to be difficult due to pressure from ground water. The solution was to sink fifty-three large concrete monoliths into the ground to form the quay walls. The change in construction method delayed the work, which was completed in 1916.

It was proposed to replace the equipment at some of the impounding stations that pumped water and regulated levels within the docks in order to provide greater depth. A new impounding station was completed at the Victoria and Albert Docks prior to the war; it was followed by those at the London Docks, in use by January 1915, and the East India Docks.

A cold store was built for the PLA at Smithfield market in the City and completed shortly after the outbreak of war. In 1913 work commenced on a large cold store with a reinforced-concrete frame at the Royal Albert Dock for the sorting of frozen meat from New Zealand. Work slowed during the war, the contractor went into liquidation in 1916, and the PLA completed it in 1918 using direct labour. Forty-three electric cranes were installed at the Albert Dock, which could lift substantially greater loads than those they replaced, and new timber sheds were created at the Surrey Docks.

There was concern owing to the poor state of the Port's dry docks, which could cause business to go elsewhere, so several new ones were planned. Millwall Dry Dock was lengthened to 550 feet and new pumping equipment installed, completed in March 1913. The Western Albert Dry Dock was enlarged to 575 feet in length by 80 feet in width, with new pumping equipment that reduced emptying to three hours.

In the opinion of Edward Sargent of the Docklands History Group: 'The PLA works programme was breath-taking in its scale and conception and would have undoubtedly made the Port the premier port in the world.' Although much modernization and improvement was achieved in the first few years, Palmer's original plans were heavily curtailed by the onset of war in 1914.

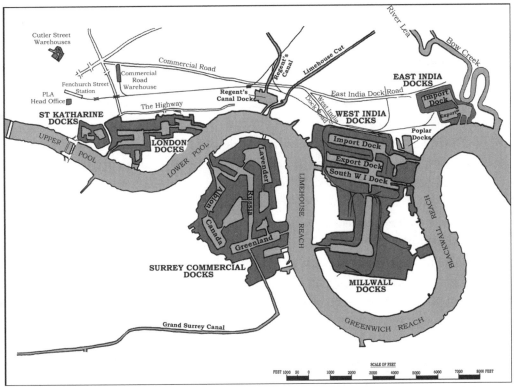

The Upper Docks shown at their greatest extent, which was reached in the latter part of the 19th century.

The National Transport Workers' Federation

No doubt it was hoped that the inclusion of James Anderson of the Amalgamated Stevedores' Union and Harry Gosling of the Lightermen's Union on the Board of the PLA would lead to greater harmony and inclusiveness across both sides of Port employment. Yet labour relations remained as fractious as in the days of the private dock companies. Much of the time of PLA committees became devoted to points regarding wages and related issues rather than improvements to the Port and the increase of business. The Dockers' Union, still headed by Ben Tillett, formed an affiliation with the National Union of Dock Workers, National Sailors' and Firemen's Union and fourteen other unions in 1910 to form the National Transport Workers' Federation, with Gosling as president and Anderson as general secretary.

The following July, taking advantage of a shortage of labourers, the Dockers' Union, supported by the other members of the NTWF, made a demand for an increase in the hourly rate from six pence to eight pence, other improved conditions, and formal recognition of all unions. For the first time, on one side of the negotiating table sat the united port workers led by Gosling and on the other all the employers represented by the PLA and its chairman, Lord Devonport. Gosling was a lifelong Thames man, whose father, grandfather and great-grandfather had all been lightermen. A naturally gentle man, he was highly respected by the port workers. With the employment situation as it was, the employers were in no mood for a fight and made concessions in what was called the Devonport Agreement. Under this plan the hourly day rate was increased to seven pence and overtime from eight to nine pence for various types of ordinary dock work, as well as a decrease in the length of the working day. The NTWF leadership's agreement however was rejected by their own members who demanded an extra penny an hour. Gosling and Tillett, though recommending acceptance, were voted down at a mass rally and were forced into calling a strike. It was a repeat of the 1889 strike, with daily processions through the City, ending at either Tower Hill or Trafalgar Square. There were calls for troops to be sent in to clear incoming food that was blockaded in the docks but they were resisted by Home Secretary Winston Churchill. Devonport famously declared that he would prefer to starve the men back to work, to which Tillett declared at a mass meeting on Tower Hill, 'Oh God, strike Lord Devonport dead.' After a month the union funds were exhausted and the government stepped in as conciliator. The workers returned to work on the terms of the Devonport Agreement but issues remained unresolved, in particular regarding the call-on. Union membership collapsed after the strike. The PLA henceforth held the call-on inside the dock gates, without a requirement to be a union member. They refused to reinstate striking workers on a permanent basis and instead continued to employ many blackleg workers used during the strike. They did however take on as permanent staff 3,000 casual workers.

The Great War

London was the largest city in the world as well as the leading manufacturing centre in Britain at the beginning of the twentieth century. When Britain went to war with Germany from August 1914, factories that made certain products switched instead to making munitions, or those producing garments to military uniforms. Economically, and leaving aside the great loss of lives of those who went to fight, London generally prospered from the Great War of 1914–18.

In the first years of the conflict, trade in the Port rapidly increased. Continental ports closed and shipments from allied countries were diverted to London. Troops and supplies were also being ferried to France from the Thames. The Port's warehouses were soon unusually full with produce. There were so many vessels coming and going in the first months that there was congestion, with queues of ships at anchor in the Thames Estuary waiting for berths. Fortunately, at around that time, improvements initiated by the PLA at the East India, London, West India and Tilbury Docks were coming to fruition to ease the situation. As labour became scarce, dredging of the river ceased early in the conflict.

The PLA was directly employing around 4,500 men prior to the war and that increased to 8,000 in 1915. With the port so important to the war effort, workers were selectively exempted from being drafted into the armed services. Many anyway signed up or left to work in local munitions factories where high wages were on offer. Over 1,200 were enlisted to assist in French ports. To best regulate traffic throughout the country, the Port & Transit Executive Committee was formed in November 1915, with Lord Inchcape as chairman. One of its initiatives was to form mobile Transport Workers' Battalions, consisting of soldiers, to provide labour whenever there was a shortage in a port. On occasion as many as 1,000 men from the battalions were employed in the Port of London.

In October 1914 the PLA's engineers were requested to create a temporary pontoon bridge across the Thames at Gravesend, supported by seventy lighters, to prevent enemy ships entering the river. It opened to shipping for three hours on each high tide. Torpedo nets and booms were also set up at dock entrance locks. The Admiralty sought additional equipment in the Port's dry docks for the repair of ships damaged by torpedoes but the PLA's facilities were at that time intended primarily for painting and cleaning. Following negotiation it was agreed that the Admiralty would pay half the cost of the equipment. Security of the Port became even more important during the war. It was a task entrusted to the PLA police force who worked together with government Alien Officers. Of particular interest were foreign nationals, especially sailors arriving on alien vessels.

Britain had a superior navy and, despite some setbacks and losses, generally kept the German surface fleet in check. Much of the nation's food and raw materials were imported, all of that arriving by sea, and it was therefore vital that the enemy was not able to blockade the ports. Understanding the importance of the Port of London to Britain, it became the target of Zeppelin air raids from the summer of 1915. The giant airships were notoriously ineffective in hitting targets and the damage was mostly psychological rather than physical. By 1917 the airships were being superseded by fixed-wing Gotha bombers. A shrapnel bomb dropped from one of them in the first big raid, in June of that year, hit a school in Poplar near the docks, killing eighteen of the children and causing shock and anger throughout the country.

One of the many factories that switched to producing explosives for the military was the Brunner Mond & Co. caustic soda works in the densely-populated suburb of Silvertown, close to the Royal Docks. The company was requested by the Ministry of Munitions to produce the volatile explosive TNT, which began in September 1915. In January 1917 a fire broke out in the plant during the evening and a massive explosion occurred just before seven o'clock, which devastated not only the factory but much of the surrounding neighbourhood. Seventy-three people were killed including seven PLA staff, and ninety-four seriously injured. It would have been worse if the works had not been closed for the night. The explosion was so great that it could be heard up to 100 miles. Nearly 1,000 homes, many housing people who would have worked in or around the docks and wharves, were totally destroyed and a further 70,000 damaged. Fires broke out along the Thames-side wharves. Sheds and other buildings were damaged or destroyed in the Victoria Dock, taking up to two years to re-erect or repair. The grain silos around Pontoon Dock were particularly badly damaged. One of the two gas-holders at the East Greenwich Gas Works on the opposite side of the Thames at the Greenwich Peninsula, at that time the largest in the world, was damaged and was thereafter reduced in size. A payment of £250,000 was made by the government to the PLA for repairs. This was a time when bad news was covered up or heavily censored and the Ministry of Munitions merely issued a simple statement. The following day the local council began to organize the clearance of the damaged area and provide temporary housing for those displaced. A relief office was set up at Canning Town where residents could apply for aid and seek compensation, which eventually amounted to £3 million. It was never established as to what had caused the explosion. The resulting enquiry, which was not made public until the 1950s, criticized both the Ministry of Munitions for producing explosives in a heavily populated area and the Brunner Mond management for not keeping a round-the-clock watch for fires. The immediate area remained undeveloped for many decades and is now the site of the Thames Barrier. A stone memorial marks the location of the explosion and there is a plaque in Postman's Park in the City in memory of a policeman who died during rescue operations.

Germany had developed submarine technology. In the first months of the war they restricted their attacks to Allied naval vessels but from October 1914 they were also intermittently targeting cargo and passenger ships. A London-bound ship carrying food was sunk as it left Falmouth. The government therefore decided it was safer for shipments to be sent to ports on the west coast of Britain and their cargoes forwarded on to London by rail. In March 1918 it became necessary to entirely close the Straits of Dover to shipping. As the West Coast ports were generally not suited to the types and volume of cargoes, however, the policy led to congestion and food shortages during 1917–18. Ongoing improvements to London's port facilities were put on hold from the beginning of 1916 as it became difficult to obtain suitable machinery. By 1918 the Port was handling only half the pre-war tonnage.

In May 1917 the British Workers League organized a great rally in Hyde Park in support of their comrades in the military at which one of the speakers was Ben Tillett of the Dockers' Union. Over 400 PLA employees lost their lives serving in the war, as did an unknown number of casual dock workers and those involved in other Port-related industries.

The threat of industrial action by British merchant seamen led to the government forming the National Maritime Board in November 1917 to regulate wages and working practices. The board brought together under government control the Shipping Federation from the employers' side and the National Union of Seamen and National Union of Ship's Stewards from that of the employees. It was intended as only a wartime initiative but in 1919 was re-established as a permanent organization for joint consultation, without government involvement.

The King George V Dock

Ships continued to increase in size and at the beginning of the twentieth century some were too large even for the Royal Albert Dock, which was restricted to those of 12,000 tons and 500 feet in length. Prior to their demise, the East & West India Company had planned to create a new Royal dock. Plans by Frederick Palmer were completed in 1911 for a dock to the south of the Royal Albert, where the PLA owned land acquired by compulsory purchase orders obtained in an Act of 1901, and contracts placed the following year. Work slowed down during the Great War as men went off to join the services and materials became scarce.

In 1918, when the Admiralty was in need of additional dry-docking facilities, a new priority was given to the planned dock. Displaced residents were provided with 204 newly-built homes on the west side of Prince Regent's Lane, opposite Beckton Road recreation ground. The existing road from the City to the Royal Docks was carried over the new basin by a bascule bridge. The King George V, the most modern dock in the world at that time, was finally opened by the King, accompanied by Queen Mary, in July 1921. They arrived on a steam yacht flying the white ensign that cut through a ribbon, watched by 8,000 invited guests, as well as crowds who lined the river to see them pass by. After berthing in the dock, the King and Queen disembarked to inspect the premises. As the King declared the new dock open, a gun salute was fired from the Royal Arsenal at Woolwich on the opposite bank of the river.

Six two-storey warehouses with storage space of 700,000 square feet stood along the northern quay of the George V Dock. The southern side of the dock was lined with 'dolphin' berths. These 520-foot-long jetties lay parallel to the main quays at a distance of thirty-two feet, allowing lighters to pass between jetty and quay. Forty-nine cranes on the dolphin berths allowed cargoes to be simultaneously discharged or loaded onto lighters on both sides of a vessel, which moored on the outside of the jetties, or onto the quayside. The dock was created with the most modern facilities of the time for loading and unloading, storage and transport, including large transit sheds with twenty-seven electric cranes of five-ton carrying capacity. Railway lines served both north and south quays as well as behind the warehouses. The cost of the project was £4,500,000.

At 64 acres the King George V was smaller than its neighbouring Royal Docks. Its length was 4,500 feet, the width varying between 500 and 700 feet, and with over 3 miles of quays, able to accommodate up to 15 of the largest ocean-going vessels of the time, of up to 35,000 tons. A passage linked it to the Royal Albert Dock. It also contained its own entrance lock onto the river at Gallions Reach of 800 feet by 100 feet, operational at all tide levels. In 1939 the Cunard liner *RMS Mauretania*, the largest ship to pass up the Thames, was able to enter through the lock. Harland & Wolff operated a ship-repair workshop

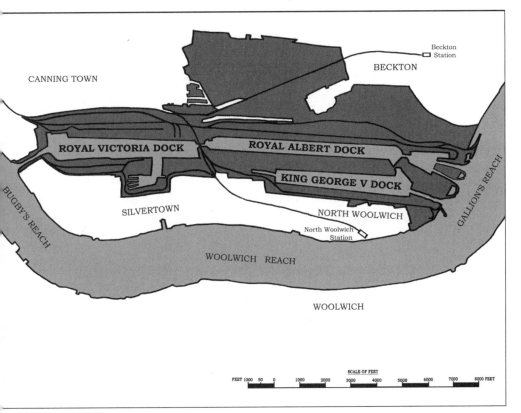

The Royal Docks after 1921.

from within the dock that could accommodate vessels up to 25,000 tons. The combined size of the three Royal Docks measured 230 acres, the world's largest surface of impounded water, with 11 miles of quays. The George V remains the only London dock to be created as part of a public service.

The PLA also considered the idea of siting a larger dock on open land to the north of the Royal Albert and Lord Devonport arranged the purchase of 202 acres of land and various shops and houses. A plan was drawn up in 1919 by Cyril Kirkpatrick, successor to Palmer, but by the time the project was revisited in the early 1920s the priority had changed to Tilbury so the north dock was never built.

Between the wars

The Great War ended with a diminished amount of trade passing through the Port. Traffic with Germany and Russia had disappeared, as had that with Belgium and the Netherlands, this having largely been of German origin. Business soon recovered however, rising from 15 million tons in 1918 to 33 million in 1920. At the end of that decade both London and Liverpool faced competition for the entrepôt business from Hamburg, as well as Antwerp and Rotterdam, all offering substantially lower berthing and handling rates. Shipowners were also facing difficulties as too many ships competed for too little business. In response, the PLA reduced their rates and undertook an advertising campaign in order to win back business, featuring aerial photographs of the Tilbury and Royal Docks and boasting of the PLA's expertise in handling cargoes. Lord Devonport, who had been so energetic in the early years of the PLA, retired from his position in 1925. His place was taken by Lord Ritchie of Dundee, vice-chairman under Devonport and head of a firm of East India merchants. Although not the first general manager, David Owen, appointed in 1922, was the earliest in that position to really make his mark on the development of the Port.

Between the First and Second World Wars London remained the largest manufacturing city in the United Kingdom, producing many types of general goods. Its population was growing, as was the number of visitors. As well as wharves, the Thames and its tributaries were lined with factories and power stations at which ships and lighters transferred fuel and goods. Vessels arrived in London from every country in the world and railways linked most of the docks with the metropolis and other parts of Great Britain. Continental ports such as Hamburg, Rotterdam and Antwerp were within easy reach by steamer. Finished goods were exported, although Liverpool had the advantage in that respect due to its proximity to the factories of Lancashire and Yorkshire.

The PLA's post-war plans for modernization and upgrading had been badly delayed by the war and the only project to be initiated during that period was the new headquarters building. The three phases of Frederick Palmer's programme of 1910 were in due course also highly modified by practicalities, the outbreak of war, and the ever-changing requirements of the Port. It was not until the second half of the 1920s and into the 1930s that further major projects were carried out by the PLA.

The intention in 1910 had been to undertake upgrading at the important West India Docks and from 1912 additional land was acquired by compulsory purchase powers. In the event, the plans were pushed back by more than a decade, finally starting in 1926. There was at least the advantage that by then the railway passenger service across the docks to North Greenwich had closed, so it was possible to considerably extend the original scheme. A new entrance lock to the South West India Dock was created; 80 feet in width, 955 feet in length and 35 feet deep, opening in August 1929. At the same time a new impounding station, built across what had been the old entrance to the former City Canal, raised the water level. Thus, larger ships with deeper draughts could enter. Wide passages were created between all the West India and Millwall Docks and new berths were provided with modern transit sheds.

Prior to the Great War a 1,000-foot-long, 50-foot-wide jetty was planned on the river at the Tilbury Docks. This would allow a fast turnaround for vessels that were only loading or unloading part of their cargo, without the lengthy time taken to lock in and out of the docks. A contract for the construction was agreed in 1912 but work was slow during the war and in 1918 the original contractors were released from their obligations. It was finally completed using PLA direct labour. Cranes were ordered in 1920 and the jetty opened in 1921. The original plan was to eventually double its length but the jetty proved unpopular, particularly with barge-owners due to the river current and tidal fall, and the extension never took place.

Unlike Lord Devonport, Lord Ritchie felt the need to invest downriver. By the 1920s ships were becoming larger and there was concern that those heading for the Royal Docks would cause congestion on the river. Also, the war had stimulated the use of motor vehicles and, by then, ex-military trucks were being sold off cheaply, becoming widely available for commercial use. Tilbury thus became a more attractive option for investment. A project for a larger entrance lock of 110 feet wide began in 1926, as well as a new dry dock, both completed in 1929.

In 1926 a South American meat berth was constructed at Tidal Basin in the Royal Victoria Dock. Three cold stores were capable of holding over 500,000 carcasses, along with all the equipment and staff required to process meat. From there the PLA's insulated railway wagons could transport the frozen meat to their stores at Smithfield market. The PLA had a combined cold-air storage of 11,000 tons. Bananas from Jamaica were a specialty at the Royal Albert, with a mechanized berth capable of unloading more than 80,000 stems each day. The first shipment arrived on board the *Jamaican Producer* in 1929. Three flour mills were constructed on the south side of the Royal Victoria Dock. The original jetties along the north side of the Royal Victoria were becoming an inconvenience and were removed, with new false quays constructed. Three quarters of a mile of linear quay and floating pneumatic grain elevators, discharging directly from ships into vast silos, were installed. New berths were added on the north side at what was known as the 'mudfield' and five new sheds built. The width of North Quay at the Royal Albert Dock was increased. The Connaught Passage that linked the Royal Victoria and Royal Albert Docks was deepened, a difficult and costly exercise due to the railway tunnel below. In 1934 the Ministry of Transport's two-mile Silvertown Way approach road to the Royal Docks was opened.

Some of the 7 million tons of grain that arrived in the Port annually was also being directed to the Surrey Commercial Docks where there were seven granaries. The three central ponds at Rotherhithe were converted into the deep-water Quebec Dock, which opened in 1926, with six timber-discharging berths. That brought the Surrey Docks up to 11 docks, 136 acres of water area, including 70 acres of ponds for floating timber, 9 miles of quays, 64 acres of open storage and 58 acres of storage sheds. Further improvements continued to be made at Rotherhithe and the Surrey Commercial Docks were the world's largest timber yard by the start of the Second World War. The St Katharine and London Docks, where new modern buildings were constructed, remained busy between the wars, although by then only with very small ships and lighters.

London continued to be the pre-eminent port for the importation and sales of both wool from Australia and tea from India, having the infrastructure and expertise lacking elsewhere. The amount of PLA warehousing at the docks and in the City was vast. In the mid-1920s they could hold one million bales of wool, 28,000 pipes of wine, 120,000 casks of brandy, 330,000 puncheons of rum, 125,000 tons of grain, 50,000 carcasses of meat, 35,000 tons of tobacco, 30,000 tons of tea and one million tons of other goods. There were acres of sheds at the Surrey Commercial Docks to store timber arriving from the Baltic and Canada. Millwall handled two-fifths of London's grain imports in the early part of the century. Wool was kept at the London Docks and wines, ports and sherries in their vaults. Sugar and rum continued to arrive at the West India Docks as they had done since their beginnings. Exotic and valuable goods such as spices, ivory, silks and oriental carpets, as well as tea, were stored at the former East India warehouses in the City at Cutler Street, Houndsditch, and at St Katharine's. Tobacco went to the north side of the Royal Victoria Dock and frozen meat to the Royal Albert Dock. Large quantities of fruit, butter, cheese, bacon and grain such as wheat, corn, oats, maize and barley arrived from overseas. A relatively new importation was cultivated plantation rubber. During and after the war motor transport had replaced horse-drawn vehicles and required a constant supply of fuel; Lord Ritchie therefore valued the petroleum trade. New terminals were opened at Thurrock and Canvey Island, with Esso at Purfleet becoming the PLA's largest customer. An important new development was when the Ford Motor Company built their factory and wharf at Dagenham in 1929.

The principle domestic and industrial fuel used in London was coal that arrived by sea from the North-East or South Wales. Much of it was brought into the Port on a fleet of colliers owned by independent companies. There were also a number of riverside coal-burning gas and electricity stations that operated their own fleet of colliers. In many cases their seagoing ships were designed to pass under London's bridges and these were known as 'flatirons'. An average of 13 million tons of seaborne coal arrived in London each year yet in 1936 petroleum imports overtook coal for the first time.

The river was busy with passenger steamers in the second half of the nineteenth century. In the first half of the twentieth century excursions from London to Gravesend, Southend and Margate remained popular during the summer months. The interwar years were the peak period of ocean-going liners. London had previously been a popular embarkation and disembarkation point but Liverpool and Southampton had taken a far greater share of that business, particularly to North America and France. Nevertheless, Tilbury was used by liners operating to and from India and the colonies and by ships that carried both passengers and cargo. The PLA were keen to develop services but shipowners were complaining about the time it took for travellers to disembark. Passengers had to be brought ashore on small boats, so even before the war Lord Devonport had considered a landing stage important. To open one required negotiation with the Midland Railway, owners of the Tilbury Riverside Station, which made slow progress. Agreement was finally reached in May 1919 but even then work did not begin until 1928. The landing stage, designed by the PLA's architect Sir Edwin Cooper, projecting 370 feet into the river and designed to rise and fall with the tide, was 1,142 feet long. A two-storey building was constructed to house a baggage hall, waiting area, customs and immigration facilities. The passenger terminal was opened in 1930 by Prime Minister Ramsay MacDonald. It became famous as a departure point for those emigrating to Australia and other Commonwealth countries and was used by ships bringing immigrants from the West Indies during the 1950s.

Dredging ceased altogether in October 1915 but resumed again after the war. Depths and channel widths had been fixed, varying from 30 feet depth and 1,000 feet of channel at Crayfordness to 14 feet depth and 450 feet of channel at London Bridge. New plant was acquired to undertake the work, including four dredgers. By 1921 over 1,500,000 cubic yards was being raised each year, rising to 4 million cubic yards in 1925. The giant, self-propelled steam-powered floating crane the *London Mammoth*, weighing 1,000 tons and rising 67 metres above the waterline, began operation in 1926. It could originally lift 150 tons, increased to 200 tons in the 1960s. It was in use at the Port until 1975 and its replacement of the same name is still in service.

A failure of the former dock companies, in which the PLA was to succeed, was that of better integrating the docks with the national rail network. In the 1930s the PLA had 140 miles of track, 40 locomotives and ran 120 train-loads per day. There were sidings at the Royal Docks, Tilbury, West India and Millwall. Rail played a key part before the Second World War but declined in favour of road transport thereafter.

During the nine-day national Great Strike of May 1926 each of the docks was blockaded by pickets. Supplies of flour for the south of England up to the Midlands were about to run out within the first week, while loaded ships in the docks were lying idle. The government therefore set up a base in Hyde Park and on the third day a convoy of 105 lorries manned by Grenadier Guards set out from there to surround and secure the Victoria Dock. Once the guards had accomplished their task, 150 volunteers embarked on a lighter at Westminster

Pier and were towed down to the dock. There they loaded lorries with sacks of flour that returned back to Hyde Park. This was repeated several times but it was not providing sufficient supply. The government therefore made an agreement with the Admiralty to operate lighters on the river flying the naval white ensign, carrying flour from the docks to where it could be safely discharged. In that way 17,000 tons of foodstuffs were removed from the docks in 48 hours.

The government was also concerned that the electricity supply from a Labour-controlled power station to the King George V Dock would be cut off. Three-quarters of a million carcasses of meat were stored at the dock and without refrigeration Londoners and many in the south of England would eventually go hungry. Two days before the supply was duly cut, two Navy submarines quietly crept into the dock and were able to connect to the dock's circuits from their on-board generators.

The USA was experiencing an economic boom during the first half of the 1920s and the amount of American trade passing through the Port of London increased accordingly. That came to a spectacular end in October 1929 when the Wall Street stock market crashed, temporarily diminishing the US economy during the early 1930s. Luxury exports destined for the US market were particularly adversely affected. Stock market investors, attempting to cut their losses, sold shares in European businesses causing financial problems for public companies associated with shipping and the Port. Pay was cut for British merchant seamen. With a surplus of available manpower the casual labour system continued, despite continued calls for its abolition. To alleviate hardship, a new method was introduced whereby workers of all types and skills were 'stood-off' on a rotation basis. Each dock was allocated its quota of workers daily according to the amount of work available.

During the nineteenth century heavy industries that involved iron and steel moved away from London to those areas where the raw materials were more easily accessible. Boat-building, repair and the manufacturing of marine equipment returned to the Thames when, between 1924 and 1972, the Belfast shipbuilders Harland & Wolff operated a major yard at North Woolwich, adjacent to the lock entrance to the King George V Dock. The works were noted for the building of the 'Woolwich' class of canal narrowboats for the Grand Union Canal Carrying Company.

London's many tugs were all steam driven until after the Second World War. Around 7,000 barges and lighters, owned by some 200 companies, were operating on the river, ranging from 50- to 500-ton craft. Many were designed for specific trades, such as oil or meat. When not being towed, they were manoeuvred by means of thirty-foot oars known as 'sweeps'. These craft were operated by skilled lightermen, work that was often passed down from generation to generation in the same family. Prior to the Second World War, flat-bottomed Thames spritsail barges were still operating, perhaps the last cargo-carrying sailing vessels on the river.

By 1931 the tonnage carried on British ships remained at about the same level as in 1919. Other nations were subsidizing their shipping lines. At the same time, unsubsidized British tramp ships – small vessels usually owned by private companies and which made up a sizable portion of the British fleet – were being laid up for want of cargoes, so the government introduced its own subsidies between 1935 and 1938. Nevertheless, the percentage of world tonnage carried on British ships decreased between the wars at the expense of those from the USA, Germany and Japan. In part that was because British merchant ships continued to rely on slower coal-burning engines, whereas new vessels of other nations were being fitted with faster and more competitive diesel-powered engines.

Mechanization and the Great Depression of the early 1930s reduced the number of people working in the Port from 52,000 in 1920 to 34,000 in the latter 1930s. The greatest degree of cooperation and harmony between workers and management was achieved in the 1930s. The surplus of labour at that time probably made it worthless to strike for better pay or conditions and joint committees made discussion and compromise easier. There were nevertheless numerous minor and local disputes.

A serious fire broke out in 1933 in the vaults of the old warehouses at the North Quay of the West India Import Dock where 6,500 casks of rum were being stored. To extinguish it took 65 pumps, 3 tugboats, and 378 firefighters 63 hours. Several warehouses were burned down and never rebuilt and over 3 million litres of rum destroyed.

By the 1930s the Port of London, after more than a century of expansion and with the world's largest man-made enclosed dock system, had reached the end of its growth, the maximum size it would ever achieve. An estimated 1,500 wharves, jetties and yards lined the river between Brentford and Gravesend. Every port in the world was served, either directly or by trans-shipment and the Port was more complex than it would ever be again in the future. The combined docks and wharves were the nation's principal storage centre for goods of many varieties. Around 100,000 men were dependent, either directly or indirectly, for employment. In 1938 thirty-eight per cent of the UK's trade passed through London, an all-time high that was never to be achieved again, with 63 million tons carried. During that period 50,000 ocean-going ships arrived each year, coasters were making 15,000 round trips, 250 tugs worked on the river, as did 10,000 lighters and 1,000 sailing barges. Three hundred thousand passengers arrived or departed annually. Larger ships primarily used the enclosed docks while coastal and Continental trade operated from riverside wharves. Twenty-eight graving docks operated for repairing ships. In the following forty years the world would go through dramatic changes however, as would the methods by which the world moved its goods.

Ernest Bevin

After the Great War, ports around the country attempted to create registers of dockers in order to regulate employment and the call-on, with the task organized by local committees. It proved to be unworkable. It was estimated that 34,000 men worked in the Port of London yet 62,000 came forward to register. One of those managing the registration on the London committee was Ernest Bevin who already had some success creating such a register at his home port of Bristol and Avonmouth. Despite the failure of the scheme, for the next two decades and more Bevin pursued his ideal of reforms of the port labour system and the end of casual working.

As the Port returned to normal and trade was brisk after the Great War, the National Transport Workers' Federation again took advantage of the strength of business, demanding a minimum wage for its members of sixteen shillings a day for a 44-hour week. The employers proposed a public enquiry to consider the matter. It was duly arranged by the government under the chairmanship of the Law Lord, Lord Shaw of Dunfermline. An expert in industrial legal cases, Sir Lynden Macassey KC, represented the employers and Ernest Bevin represented the workers.

Bevin's masterful opening speech lasted eleven hours, given over two and a half days. He claimed that a docker needed £6 each week to maintain a family of five. Macassey responded that was an exaggeration and called witnesses to testify to that effect. Sir Alfred Booth, chairman of the Cunard line, stated that a Liverpool docker could adequately manage on three pounds four shillings and tuppence. Professor of statistics at London University A.L. Bowley was asked to give his opinion and he responded that three pounds and seventeen shillings was enough. To resolve the point, Bevin and his secretary travelled to Canning Town and there purchased the amount of food that would be available each day on those levels of pay. They took their purchases to the union offices, cooked it, divided it onto five plates and presented the results to the enquiry. Bevin asked the court their opinion as to whether the small portions they saw before them were enough to feed a man who was asked to carry seventy-one tons of wheat every day. The court accepted the argument and the dockers received their minimum of sixteen shillings per day.

To celebrate, the workers marched from Temple station to the Royal Albert Hall where a rally was held in Bevin's honour. Yet again, it was a short-term gain. The post-war boom ended in the 1920s and wages fell back to ten shillings per day. Poverty around the docks was severe in the decade from 1921. In 1923 the employers proposed a reduction from eight shillings to five shillings and sixpence for the four-hour minimum period. The dockers responded by going out on strike for eight weeks until forced to return.

As a result of the public enquiry of 1919, the employers formed the National Council of Port Employers, headed by Devonport, which was able to represent their interests in labour disputes. Bevin was instrumental in amalgamating fourteen unions to become the Transport & General Workers Union in 1922, for which he became its first General Secretary, with the former lighterman Harry Gosling as its president. There was not full unity between workers in the port however, and the T&GWU continued to have a rival. Stevedores had been represented since the nineteenth century by the Amalgamated Stevedores' Union, which enjoyed a close relationship between its officers and members. They could not be persuaded to join the T&GWU and at that time changed their name to the National Amalgamated Stevedores, Lightermen, Watermen & Dockers' Union. Those who belonged to the T&GWU were henceforth known as 'whites' and NASLW&DU members as 'blues', each based on the colour of their membership card. Rivalry and disunity between the two unions continued until the closure of the docks in the latter twentieth century, with the T&GWU often losing members to the NASLW&DU.

Bevin played a leading role when the Port workers supported the General Strike of May 1926, which closed the Port. When the strike ended, Bevin was forced to sign an agreement admitting that the workers had broken previous agreements but nevertheless arranged for all the Port strikers to be reinstated on their previous terms.

When Winston Churchill was appointed Prime Minister in 1940 he formed a wartime emergency coalition National Government with representatives from all the major parties. Despite their differences of political opinion, he had been impressed by Bevin's work ethic and his opposition to both fascism and the pacifist element of the union movement and invited him to join the coalition cabinet as Minister of Labour. It was unusual in that Bevin was still General Secretary of the T&GW Union at the time and not actually a Member of Parliament. To overcome the anomaly Churchill arranged for Bevin to stand as Parliamentary candidate for the London constituency of Wandsworth Central. The other parties agreed that he could take the seat unopposed. Despite the war, Bevin took the opportunity to introduce a number of reforms in favour of British workers. Upon the defeat of Germany, Bevin joined Churchill for the VE Day celebrations in London. By then he had drawn up plans for the demobilization of the forces and their return into the civilian workforce.

After the war, normal party politics resumed and the Labour Party won the 1945 General Election. The new Prime Minister, Clement Attlee, appointed Bevin as Foreign Secretary and for the next few years he played a key role in international affairs including the formation of NATO, the United Nations and the State of Israel. There was a story amongst dockers that in 1947 a group of them discovered a hamper from an overseas government addressed to Bevin. Cold and hungry they consumed the contents, repacked it and sent it on with a card wishing him a Happy Christmas.

The Second World War

Following the declaration of war against Germany and its allies, on 3 September 1939 all UK ports were put under the control of Port Emergency Committees, responsible to the Ministry of Transport. The committee for the Port of London was headed by J.D. (later Sir Douglas) Ritchie, who had succeeded David Owen as general manager of the PLA in 1938. The Admiralty also created a Naval base for the Port of London, with its flag officer and staff based at the PLA headquarters, the control centre for the Port throughout the war.

Adolf Hitler was well aware that to cripple the Port of London was to weaken Britain's ability to survive and, as it was an entrepôt port, would furthermore affect the entire British Empire. Prior to the war, the Luftwaffe had been flying reconnaissance flights over London, taking aerial photographs, and had marked key points along the river as targets. For centuries the winding river and dangerous estuary shoals had long protected the Port. It was clear from contemporary conflicts in Spain, China and Abyssinia, however, that aerial attack would be inevitable if war occurred. Distinctive from the air both during the day and by moonlight it was an easy target for airborne bombers. Spread along sixty-nine miles of tideway, the Port was extremely difficult to defend. The following years were to become some of the most dramatic and challenging in the long history of the Port of London.

The PLA had some time earlier developed a defensive plan at the government's request that was adopted for all ports. A River Emergency Service had been formed, able to aid and advise the Navy with local expertise. Thames lightermen and barge-owners formed the Lighterage Emergency Executive (later superseded by the London Tug & Barge Control), making themselves available to the Port Emergency Committee. Shelters were provided for workers, pillboxes constructed, first-aid stations established and some buildings strengthened. Steel pylons were erected as lookout posts. A wartime nerve centre was created at the PLA headquarters although aspects of its work moved to a safer location at Thames Ditton. Naval ships were stationed at the sea entry to the Thames. From September 1941 they were replaced by Maunsell Sea Forts, constructed in the Surrey Docks and towed downriver from there. Gun batteries were installed on each bank of the lower river. Locks and other key points were guarded by military police. The Navy requisitioned a number of Thames tugs to act as guardships, forming the Thames & Medway Examination Service, with several based at the Naval Control Centre at Southend. Conscription into the forces began in April 1939 but Port workers were included on the Schedule of Reserved Occupations and were thus exempt.

There was an initial period known as the 'phony war' when the British people prepared themselves for the worst. Women and children were evacuated to the countryside, leaving Port workers separated from their families. Yet during the first year there was no significant harm done to London and some of those evacuated drifted back to their homes. During that period more than 6,000 port workers were trained in various aspects of defence.

By the end of 1939 magnetic mines were being dropped into the Thames Estuary by German aircraft, sinking a number of merchant vessels. Each morning thereafter minesweepers left Gravesend and Sheerness to clear the shipping channels. It took several months for the Navy to introduce the 'degaussing' method that neutralized a ship's magnetism and thus made them resistant to the devices. In the meantime, the PLA's jurisdiction for the salvaging of ships was extended to a greater area. Groups of dockers were formed into units of the Royal Engineers, of which there were twelve by the end of the war, and they assisted in the British Expeditionary Force mission in September 1939 and their retreat in 1940. Operations took place in coastal areas as far as the Arctic Circle, North Africa and Burma.

From the summer of 1940 Germany took occupation of the Netherlands, Belgium and France and for the following four years their forces were only a short distance from shipping entering and leaving the Estuary. Allied troops were suddenly forced to depart for the Continent and 'Operation Dynamo' was launched to undertake the evacuation. A bizarre fleet of small vessels of all shapes and sizes, some having not been designed to go out to sea, were assembled to rescue troops from the beaches of Dunkirk, including thirty Thames tugs. Much of the fleet was assembled, provisioned and crewed at Tilbury Docks. Some, including at least eight Thames sailing barges, failed to return. At that time a German invasion seemed inevitable and two booms were laid across the Estuary, the outer one from Shoeburyness in Essex to Minster in Kent and the inner boom from Canvey Island to St Mary's Bay. Gaps were kept open during the day, guarded by the Navy, but they were closed at night. Merchant ships began sailing in convoys, which assembled at the Naval Control Service station at Southend Pier. Shipmasters received their orders in the pier's dance hall.

Scattered German air raids started to take place along the east coast. For London, the phony war ended in late August 1940 with a raid on north and east London followed by another on the City the next day. In the following year air-raid sirens were a familiar sound to Londoners and gave warning to take shelter. A bomb partially destroyed a boatyard at Tilbury on 1 September. The Estuary fuel depot of Thameshaven was targeted by German bomber planes on 5 September, creating a conflagration that burnt for several days and could be seen far out to sea. Then, at around 5pm on the sunny Saturday afternoon of 7 September 1940, 348 bombers, supported by 617 fighter planes, flew in perfect formation along the Thames, with the Port as the main target. Warehouses, docks, factories and homes between Woolwich and Tower Bridge were immediately destroyed by high explosives or set alight by incendiary bombs. Most areas of the Port suffered, as well as Woolwich Arsenal and Beckton Gasworks. Timber at the Surrey Commercial Docks began to burn, as it did at the West India and Royal Victoria Docks. A bomb hit the entrance lock of the King George V Dock as a ship was passing through. Fires burnt at the great flour mills at the Royal Victoria Docks. Several ships took hits in the West India and Royal Victoria Docks. Firefighters were so occupied with major blazes that smaller ones had to be left to burn themselves out. Damage throughout the Port was so great that some buildings were subsequently demolished and left as open ground for decades. Huge clouds blackened the sky as warehouses full of inflammable goods and nearby houses were set alight. Sixty craft were sunk or destroyed and blazing barges set adrift floated down the river.

Incendiaries were perhaps a bigger threat to the Port than high explosive bombs. Fires were still burning from the afternoon raid when, shortly after sunset, the next wave of bombers arrived, with enemy aircraft guided by the light of the flames. The Surrey Commercial Docks, still lit by burning timber from the earlier raids, suffered most severely during the first weekend. Forty-two major fires took place, spread over 250 acres, along three miles of the south bank of the river. They were tackled by firefighters from as far as Bristol and Rugby. Containers of fuel oil, dropped from aircraft, as well as delayed-action bombs and years of accumulated woodchips, ensured the continuation of the conflagration for several days. Daylight revealed a landscape of gutted warehouses, sunken ships and human bodies. Rum barrels exploded in the Royal Docks; and paint, pepper and flour burned in various docks and wharves. Burning rubber was particularly difficult to tackle. The heat was so intense that paint blistered and peeled on vessels moored some distance away. The Woolwich ferry worked all night to evacuate residents of Silvertown and their belongings. In the first night alone 430 civilians died in London including a number of dock workers. In the first 12 hours 120 major incidents were reported in the Port, with over 60 craft sunk or destroyed.

Bombs inevitably failed to hit their intended targets and hit others. For example, on that first afternoon many of the residences in Stebondale Street in Cubitt Town, at the southern end of the Isle of Dogs, were destroyed. Yet the bombers failed to put out of action the anti-aircraft battery at nearby Mudchute and almost all the nearby wharves were left untouched. The residential area north of Mudchute, between Manchester Road and the Millwall Inner Dock, was devastated during the course of the war, whereas the adjacent Millwall Docks were left relatively unscathed.

One hundred and seventy one bombers returned for nine and a half hours the following night, leaving 400 dead and more destruction. The basins of the St Katharine Docks became a cauldron of flames when a fire in E Warehouse spread to others filled with flammable goods. Burning coconut oil and paraffin wax spread out across the water, blazing for several days and laying waste to some of the warehouses. The Rum Quay at Millwall docks burned out, destroying one and a quarter million gallons of the spirit. The dockmaster and his assistants worked continuously for forty-eight hours to move imperilled barges as blazing rum flowed across the water, puncheons exploded and fiery rivers of glutinous sugar crept from burning warehouses. The PLA headquarters on Tower Hill took a direct hit that night, completely destroying the central rotunda and causing extensive damage to other parts of the building. Incredibly there were no major injuries and staff within the building continued their work. The bombers returned again and again, every night for seventy-six nights, except on one when there was bad weather, until mid-May 1941 when a final 500-bomber onslaught was unleashed on the capital.

In the first few days, Anti-Aircraft Command were ill prepared. Guns had mainly been located at downriver sites. Within a week warning systems, communications, searchlights and anti-aircraft guns were relocated to suitable places, as well as mobile guns mounted onto lorries. Those measures ensured that bombers had to fly at greater altitudes with subsequent lack of accuracy. Barrage balloons could be raised to a height of almost a mile and their steel mounting cables acted as a deterrent to enemy pilots. On Sunday, 15 September alone, fifty-six Luftwaffe bombers were brought down by RAF fighters. As well as high explosive bombs, incendiaries and oil bombs, the enemy also dropped time bombs that unexpectedly exploded later, plus parachute bombs that detonated above roof level and thus caused a wider area of destruction.

As damage occurred to roads and bridges, some riverside communities around the docks became cut off from neighbouring districts. After the first week the Isle of Dogs was looking quite derelict and many residents had moved away. By mid-September the dock bridges had been withdrawn for protection and the foot tunnel to Greenwich closed due to bomb damage, making it very difficult to leave the Island. Residents of Wapping were evacuated on a flotilla of boats and a similar evacuation took place at the LCC Hospital at Rotherhithe. Some brave souls remained even after being bombed out of their homes several times. Despite the destruction around them, and in some cases the loss of their homes, workers continued to keep the Port operating.

There were many tragic stories. One took place at Bullivant's Wharf rope and wire factory at Millwall on the Isle of Dogs in March 1941. With specially reinforced concrete floors to support heavy machinery, it appeared to be particularly safe and was thus used as a public night-shelter during bombing raids. Sadly, when the building was hit, the heavy floors collapsed, killing around 40 and injuring a further 40 people sheltering below.

The coming and going of vessels still had to continue according to the tides, despite the bombing raids. A blackout was imposed at night so navigation and dockside work was required to be undertaken in darkness. Many regular tasks, such as pulling a tail of laden barges under Thames bridges or passing a ship through a lock, became extremely difficult and dangerous when undertaken in complete darkness. Despite the great damage being inflicted, a diminished staff and the need to continue its normal operations, PLA staff also took on the civil defence of the docks and river. That included the provision of first-aid stations, firefighting, salvage and wreck-raising. Along the length of the tidal river volunteers kept watch each night, reporting anything falling into the water to the Flag Officer In Charge at the PLA headquarters, from where mine-sweeping and clearance activities were coordinated. Ordinary dock workers extinguished incendiary bombs, which often fell in awkward places such as on roofs, in order to protect the contents of warehouses. Fires that took hold in private wharves, often in cramped conditions and with limited staff, were particularly difficult to extinguish. Tugs and lighters continued their journeys during raids, their crews often kicking incendiary bombs overboard. Most Thames tugs, operating as the River Tug Fire Patrol, were equipped with powerful pumps that could be used for firefighting. Between 1940 and 1950 the PLA had to deal with eight shipwrecks caused by the conflict and raise 35 ships and 600 small craft from the river. Staff kept the port operational despite the difficult and dangerous conditions, although trade had been reduced to a quarter of its pre-war levels.

From early 1941 the enemy began dropping parachute magnetic bombs as far upstream as Hammersmith. These could lie dormant on the bed of the river or dock until triggered by a passing vessel. A dramatic example occurred in April 1941 when the oil tanker *Lunula*, having arrived at Thameshaven from Halifax in Canada, detonated a mine dropped the previous night. The resulting fire blazed for ninety-seven hours.

As the war progressed the authorities became more prepared, with air-raid early-warning and anti-aircraft guns in place and better defence provided by the Royal Air Force. Despite the constant destruction, the Port somehow managed to continue operating, although at a reduced level. The river had to be closed on some occasions to sweep for mines. With diminishing returns, and other fronts on which to fight, the Germans had largely given up their efforts to destroy the

Port by the middle of 1941. From the second half of April the Luftwaffe instead concentrated on other British ports such as Belfast, Plymouth, Portsmouth, Merseyside, Tyneside and Glasgow. Despite the respite from bombing, the Port remained under a state of siege as the enemy continued dropping mines and maintaining U-Boat operations in the approaches. In June 1941 Winston Churchill reported in a secret session of the House of Commons: 'The Port of London has now been reduced to one-quarter ... and the English Channel, like the North Sea, is under close air attack of the enemy.'

Patterns within the Port dramatically changed. Some ships familiar in London were requisitioned by the Navy. Others that worked particular trades became general carriers and berthed in different docks than previously. Unfamiliar ships arrived in London. Most long-distance trade was diverted to less vulnerable ports such as the Clyde, to where some London port staff, sea-pilots, equipment such as cranes, locomotives, tugs, lighters and a floating crane, had been transferred. From there London's imported food supplies arrived by rail or coaster into storage facilities at the Royal and West India Docks. Reserve buffer depots were organized in safe places around the country. An exception was flour, which had to be kept within easy reach but in safe places. The solution was to store it on barges that were dispersed along the river between Teddington and the Pool. Most cargo was carried by smaller coasters, which were less vulnerable to attack than larger vessels. During the course of the war a million tons of rubble from demolished homes and factories was sent around the coast, much of it on sailing barges, to be used as hardcore for the construction of airfields on the east coast. There was an acute shortage of young workers as they were diverted to other ports or into the services. Those who remained were nearly all over fifty years of age.

It remained necessary for colliers to continue supplying London's Thames-side power and bunkering stations with coal. During the course of the conflict there were many losses as they travelled back and forth around the coast. They were constantly threatened by submarines, E-boats and mines. Although immune from magnetic mines, wooden-hulled Thames sailing barges, which were unable to travel in convoy, were a sitting duck for enemy aircraft and only a small number survived the conflict.

At the outset, twenty Thames ship-repair yards came under Naval control in order that priorities could be set. For several years London once again became Britain's main ship-repair port, handling over 23,000 vessels. Yards installed armaments, adapted craft for wartime duties and repaired damaged vessels.

Work continued uninterrupted throughout the war, despite a number of direct hits on the yards.

W.S. Morrison, Minister of Food, pointed out that the transportation of food by ship was putting the lives of seamen at unnecessary risk. Lessons had been learnt from the Great War and the navy organized escorted convoys from the start of the conflict. Nevertheless, there was a great loss of shipping and lives from enemy action, particularly from German and Italian submarines. Over 2,700 British merchant navy ships, or the equivalent of over fifty per cent of British merchant navy tonnage at the start of the war, was sunk during the course of the conflict, with the loss of over 30,000 lives. Many of the total of over 1,350 Royal Navy ships that were sunk were on escort duty.

With food being rationed, and in some cases homes obliterated Lord Woolton, who took over as Minister for Food in April 1940 commented: 'With my right honourable friend Mr Bevin, I entered some months ago into a joint campaign to increase the provision of works canteens. We took very seriously the old idea that you should feed your troops well.' Most dockers ate and drank in pubs close to where they worked but establishments had been damaged, or simply shut up shop during the Blitz. The government passed the Docks (Provision of Canteens) Act that compelled the PLA, along with other ports, to provide canteens for all the workers. The first works canteens were vans, donated by well-wishers from British colonies and operated by the Women's Legion, but they were later supplemented with twenty-seven permanent premises. 'With regard to dockside canteens,' said the Minister, 'I take a very special interest in this problem, because I was well acquainted with the docks in Liverpool … We have now erected a large number of new canteens … They are capable of feeding people by day and by night. I have seen the canteens, and I have been among the dock labourers, and men whom I know have told me of the very great advantage that they are getting as a result of the excellent meals which are being served to them at what are really very low prices.' The provision of canteens continued after the war and at the end of the decade were providing 6,000 meals each day in the Port.

By 1942, after the end of the first wave of bombing, there was a different rhythm in the Port and some shipping returned. American-built 'Liberty' ships – low-cost, mass-produced cargo vessels – were arriving. The British war emphasis moved from defence to attack. Up and down the river, craft were being built or modified at existing yards and other suitable sites ready for a future offensive or for mine-sweeping duties. Many were constructed of wood due to the dangers of magnetic mines.

In retaliation for Allied air raids on Germany, in January 1943 Luftwaffe bombers returned to the London skies in what was named the 'Baby Blitz'. By then British defences were far more effective than in earlier years and considerably less damage occurred. One casualty however was the Tilbury Hotel that was burnt to the ground by incendiary bombs. It had stood on the riverside since 1882 and had been until then a landmark for passengers and crews passing along the river.

As the bombs rained down on their homes during the Second World War, casual workers, who were not obligated to work set hours or days, were able to take time off to clear damaged properties. This absenteeism occasionally left the Port undermanned and distribution of food and military supplies disrupted at a crucial time for the nation. As wartime Minister of Labour, it was Ernest Bevin's responsibility to solve this problem. The National Dock Labour Corporation was created as a statutory body in March 1942 to oversee the availability of workers in British ports and ensure there was the correct amount of manpower available wherever and whenever it was required. Workers were incentivized to arrive each morning for the call-on, with an 'attendance pay' for those who came, even if work was not available, and provided with paid holidays. Rather than the previous chaotic situation of men crowding outside London's dock gates, new meeting halls were erected where they assembled until assigned their tasks. In November 1944 the stevedores at Surrey Commercial Docks walked out in protest at the necessity to meet in their hall. As the backlog of unloaded ships grew, the dock management were forced to acquiesce and allow the men to continue gathering at the dock gates for the selection. The same occurred when meeting halls were erected at the Royal Docks in early 1945, with a mass walkout organized by the stevedores and the Transport & General Workers Union. When the government this time refused to give way, the strike spread to Tilbury and only ended after a week when the government promised an enquiry.

During the spring of 1944 large quantities of supplies were being stockpiled in the Port in readiness for 'Operation Overlord', the military return to the Continent. Troop and supply ships moored in the Tilbury, Royal and West India Docks. The American 14th Army Transportation Corps based themselves at the Royal Albert Dock. From the Royal Victoria Dock, General Montgomery addressed an audience of over 16,000 London dock workers throughout the Port, relayed by telephone wires and speakers, telling them that their efforts in the following months would help determine the outcome of the war. To ensure that everything ran smoothly there was a general overhaul of lock gates, cranes and other equipment, and new bridges were constructed. Temporary huts and facilities were put in place to accommodate the large number of awaiting military personnel. All this activity took place while the Port continued with its normal business.

Marshalling of vessels for the D-Day Landings took place in London on 27 May 1944 and the following day at Tilbury Docks. The next week the armada gathered in the Thames Estuary off Southend and departed on 6 June. Three hundred and seven ships sailed from the Port, carrying 50,000 soldiers, 9,000 vehicles and 80,000 tons of supplies. London's pilots worked around the clock, often in darkness, and commercial work at Tilbury ceased for a period in order to accommodate the British Liberation Army.

The forces that arrived on those beaches were immediately followed from Tilbury by six 30-foot-diameter, 250-ton floating '*HMS Conundrum*' bobbins. Around each drum was wound seventy miles of 'Pluto' pipeline that was unrolled to lie on the bed of the English Channel, supplying the advancing troops with fuel pumped from England. The system had originally been devised and tested two years earlier, with pipes from a Thames-based submarine cable manufacturer. Over eight miles of concrete caissons, weighing up to 6,000 tons, were then floated across the Channel and sunk on the Continental coast to form prefabricated 'Mulberry' harbours. Two-thirds of these caissons had been constructed in the Port of London during the winter of 1943–44 from the rubble of destroyed buildings. Some were made in dry docks. To create other manufacturing sites, the East India Import Dock and parts of the Surrey Commercial Docks had been drained and later refilled in order to float the completed caissons.

After the initial landings, London continued to operate as the principle supply base for the British Army of Liberation as it moved across the Continent. Special arrangements were put in place for the rapid turnaround of supply ships. During the year between D-Day and the end of the war in Europe 2,760,000 tons of military stores, including over 200,000 tanks and vehicles, left the Port.

D-Day was not the end of the war for London and its Port however. Just a few weeks later, in June 1944, the enemy began launching 'Vergeltungswaffen' or 'retaliatory weapons', unmanned flying rockets. Fired at London from occupied Europe they simply fell when their fuel supply was exhausted, hitting random targets. They had a very distinctive sound when in the air and became known as 'doodlebugs'. On 30 June 1944 the Millwall Docks river entrance lock took hits from two rockets, having already been damaged by high explosive bombs early in the Blitz. After the war it was decided that repair could not be justified due to the high cost and the lock was permanently dammed with concrete in 1955. The only entrance thereafter was via the West India Docks.

Despite flying at about 400 miles per hour the rockets eventually became vulnerable to air defences. In September 1944 Germany began launching a more effective ballistic missile known as the Vergeltungswaffe 2. Carrying a one-ton warhead, V-2s were fired high into the earth's atmosphere before turning and descending on their targets at 2,000 miles per hour, a speed that was too fast to be hit by a human-operated anti-aircraft gun. Poplar and West Ham, around the docks, were particularly badly hit. The only serious harm to the Port itself was at the important Exchange railway sidings of the Royal Victoria Dock and on the bascule bridge over the entrance to the King George V Dock, the latter temporarily closing the dock entrance. The last V2 to land in London fell in Stepney, killing 131 people in March 1945.

During the course of the war London had come under bombardment for almost 2,400 hours. Approximately 1,500 high-explosive bombs, 800 Vergeltungswaffen rockets and 350 parachute mines had fallen on the Port's riverside boroughs, as well as countless thousands of incendiary bombs. The many casualties among port workers and seamen included sixteen London ships' pilots who lost their lives.

The aftermath of the Second World War

The conflict in Europe finally ended in May 1945 but London was never to be the same again. The Port area had been one of the most intensively bombed areas of Britain. Civilian deaths on the Isle of Dogs had been three times the average for London as a whole. Bombs and incendiaries had destroyed a third of the PLA's warehousing and transit sheds and half of its storage facilities, some never to be replaced, as well as much of the equipment. At the Surrey Commercial Docks alone 176 sheds had been destroyed and a further 57 had to be demolished. Up to eighty per cent of storage space at the West India Docks was lost. Where necessary, prefabricated huts were erected as temporary storage. Gaps were left where wharves and riverside factories had formerly stood along the river. Of 900 riverside premises in the County and City of London, nearly 300 had received anything from minor damage to complete destruction. Many in the City such as

Brewer, Chester and Galley Quays would be given over to new uses such as office buildings. During the course of the war many of the Port's services and much of its equipment had been transferred elsewhere for safety or to aid the military campaign. What was left was old and in need of repair. The river had gone six years with little dredging. Tilbury Docks, identified by the Germans for their use in the event of a successful invasion, had been largely spared. The country was bankrupt so the PLA and wharf-owners faced the massive task of rebuilding and reviving trade without the possibility of state aid or priority over other recovery projects. During the following decade they often had to make do with temporary accommodation and second-hand equipment. The last replacement crane was finally delivered to the PLA in 1955. At least reconstruction eventually provided the opportunity to modernize.

Manufacturing industry experienced a boom during the First World War as London's many factories were kept busy producing military equipment and other wartime requirements. As German bombers targeted London's industry and infrastructure, the reverse was true during the Second World War. For centuries London had been Britain's leading manufacturing city but in just five years businesses were forced to move away if they could in order to survive the onslaught. Many that relocated before or during the war did not return and, with much of the infrastructure obliterated, industry continued to migrate from London in the 1950s. In the following forty years factories and warehouses were gradually abandoned throughout the capital. It began in the inner East End and spread throughout the other manufacturing centres, at West Ham, Park Royal, the Lea Valley and elsewhere. In the post-war planning, many sites that had previously been used for industry were reclassified as residential zones. With less manufacturing and a switch to road transport there was less requirement for goods trains. Railway lines used specifically for that purpose were taken away, notably at King's Cross, Stratford and New Cross. As coal gas went out of use in favour of that from the North Sea, large gasworks at Beckton (closed in 1969) and Greenwich Peninsula (production ending in 1976) were decommissioned as were electricity-generating stations. Industry began to expand after the war in the more suburban areas and in the South-East in general, albeit at a slower rate than in the country as a whole where chemical and vehicle production were booming. Within the London area there was a shift westwards and away from the East End, encouraged by the growth of Heathrow Airport. All these factors had a long-term negative affect on the Port of London.

Around East London many homes had gone, displacing families and changing forever the uniformity and neatness of the terraced streets. The borough of Stepney, where the St Katharine and London Docks were located, had lost almost 11,000 houses, a third of its total. It was a similar story in Poplar, the borough that included the West India, East India and Millwall Docks. Fifteen per cent of Southwark, which included the Surrey Commercial Docks, had been devastated. A priority of the government, the London County Council and local borough councils was to rehouse those who had been displaced by bombing. Initially, temporary prefabricated ('prefab') homes were produced and erected while longer-term solutions were considered. In many cases the permanent answer was for the LCC to take over devastated areas and create new, modern estates of social housing designed by its architects.

In 1943 the LCC's architect, J.H. Forshaw, together with Patrick Abercrombie, professor of town planning at University College, produced the *County of London Plan*, followed in 1944 by Abercrombie's *Greater London Plan*, and some parts of these two documents formed the basis of planning in post-war London for the next thirty years. Following their ideas, new satellite towns were proposed between 20 and 30 miles from the centre of London, with the Green Belt separating the main city from the satellites. During the period of 1947–48 the new towns of Stevenage, Crawley, Hemel Hempstead, Harlow, Hatfield, Welwyn Garden City, Basildon and Bracknell began to be built or expanded. Despite the best intentions of the planners and architects, the result of the new housing estates and satellite towns was to disperse East End communities far and wide.

Many of those who worked in the docks moved out of their traditional areas in the East End and around Rotherhithe, breaking links that had existed for generations. In some cases they were demobbed servicemen who preferred to find a new career. Others continued to work in the Port but found family accommodation away from the East End, perhaps in Essex or north Kent, taking advantage of the availability of motor cars and motorbikes.

Chapter Seven

The Closure of the Upper Port and the Development of Docklands

The decade following the Second World War was a good period for British shipping. Older vessels lost during the war were replaced by more efficient and competitive ships. There was also a general lack of competition from those of other nations and rates could be kept high. In 1957 Britain still had one of the world's largest merchant fleets. Conditions for seamen improved during that period but in 1966 there was a major strike for better pay and a 40-hour week that dealt a blow to the industry. At the end of the 1950s a third of the British maritime fleet consisted of tramp ships, small cargo vessels owned by private companies with four ships or less. They were itinerant around the coast and worked from job to job, usually obtaining their work at the Baltic Exchange in London. However they were ill-equipped for the revolution in cargo-handling that was to take place in the last quarter of the twentieth century. The number of British cargo vessels gradually declined but the amount they were capable of carrying increased as ships grew larger. Yet they still carried a declining share of the world's tonnage as the fleets of other nations increased at a faster rate. In order to be competitive in the international market, shipowners registered their vessels under flags of convenience to nations with lower registration standards, taxes and rates of pay. By the start of the twenty-first century there were less than 400 UK-registered cargo ships.

As the British merchant fleet reduced in size, so did shipbuilding, which had long since departed the Thames in favour of the North East of England, the Clyde and Belfast. In the late 1920s the shipbuilders Harland & Wolff employed 35,000 men in the United Kingdom, with a major operation at the entrance to London's Royal Docks. At the beginning of the twentieth century over 60 per cent of the world's merchant ships were built in Britain but by its end that had fallen to less than 1 per cent, partly due to under-investment and a failure to modernize. In 1997 Japan and South Korea were building 80 per cent.

Nevertheless, trade in the Port of London continued to flourish and once again reached a peak in the early 1960s. Tower Bridge continued to open for ships entering the Upper Pool, rows of lighters lined the river, and the riverside wharves were still functioning. The most important of London's docks were by that time the three Royal docks, where the quays were lined with an impressive 211 cranes. Tobacco, fruit, vegetables, as well as beef from South America, arrived at the Royal Victoria. Frozen meat and bananas were the specialities at the Royal Albert. Tilbury was capable of handling most of the largest vessels of the time, up to 30,000 tons, and with substantial passenger traffic. Grain arrived at the India, Millwall, Surrey and Victoria Docks. Sugar and rum continued to be stored at the West India and the London Docks. Tea, wool, brandy and numerous other commodities were inspected and sorted by the PLA's expert staff at the London and the St Katharine Docks, lightered there after having been unloaded from ships in one of the downstream docks. The Surrey Commercial Docks were the centre of London's softwood trade. A vast wealth of goods, including Oriental carpets, cigars, fine wines and vintage port and sherry, were stored over fifteen acres of floorspace at the PLA's fortress-like Cutler Street warehouse close to Liverpool Street station.

Yet the writing was on the wall. The 1960s were the swansong for most of London's docks. In the middle of the twentieth century cargo-handling in the Port was undertaken much as it had been for centuries before, although by then with the aid of mechanical cranes. Each item was lifted, carried and put down multiple times by a number of men between the ship and leaving the dock or warehouse, with risk of damage, theft and injury. While items were waiting to be loaded or unloaded they had to be stored on the dock-side. A 15,000-ton cargo ship, filled with individual items, took several days to discharge. Labour was still relatively cheap, plentiful and readily available so there was little incentive for change. Continental ports that had been completely devastated in the latter part of the war were in a better position to rebuild according to modern standards and requirements, aided by American capital. The port was ill-prepared and the old docks and riverside wharves were incapable of being converted for the changes that were to revolutionize shipping and cargo-handling in the 1970s. In North America more efficient new methods of collecting and delivering goods meant that dockside warehouses were no longer necessary. The number of men required to load and discharge vessels was minimized. Those efficiencies quickly spread around the world, including ports on the near-Continent such as Rotterdam, which was handling three times as much as London.

The end of the call-on

A bewildering array of arrangements and agreements were in place for the loading and discharging of cargoes that varied between different types of commodity, docks and wharves. Much teamwork was involved, with strong working and community bonds. Generation after generation worked in the port, with children following their fathers and grandfathers, leading to great camaraderie. On the other hand, it produced something of a closed shop, which was difficult to break into without the necessary connections, and created a lack of diversity in the workforce.

Labour requirements in the Port had greatly changed since the unpredictable arrivals of sailing ships; work was more regular, yet there had been little difference in employment practice since the mid-nineteenth century. Those referred to as 'Perms' were permanently employed at the docks or wharves, a prized position that would usually be handed down from father to son. When additional work was available it would be given to preferred workers – 'prefs' – who were known to the foremen. Finally, if further workers were required, 'casuals' (or 'nonners', meaning not preferred) would be hired.

Despite militancy shown by the unions, with continuous agitation for higher wages for fewer hours, there was little push from their side to end the casual system. Men continued to assemble at the many dock and wharf gates each morning at half past seven in the hope of being chosen as casuals by the foremen. It was a leftover from the Victorian era and seemed somewhat out of place in the mid-twentieth century. On the employers' side Joseph Broodbank gave the opinion in the 1920s that: '… labour leaders have hitherto been so apathetic when the question of casual labour has been discussed. Permanent labour might be too satisfied and prefer to deal direct with the employer. To keep the labourer in the union fold, the leader has, therefore, to preach the doctrine of aloofness between employer and employed.'

In 1947 the National Dock Labour Corporation, created during wartime, was superseded by the National Dock Labour Board, which consisted of equal numbers of representatives for the employers and workers. A compulsory registration scheme for all dock workers, the National Dock Labour Scheme, was introduced. The Board had responsibility for allocation of workers to the employers, weekly payment of wages, training and medical care. Each employer paid the Board, who in turn paid the employee. Initially workers were allocated on a half-day basis, from 8 am until midday and 1 pm until 5 pm.

Following the Devlin Committee report of 1965, casualization was finally discontinued in 1967 and workers were from then allocated to employers on a five-day basis, with shifts from 7 am until 2 pm and from 2 pm until 9 pm at any location from London to Sheerness. From the early 1970s, with the abolition of the Temporarily Unattached Register, everyone working in the Port did so for a permanent employer. A new system of workplace representation was created, although it largely failed to create harmony between employers and workers and the number and frequency of strikes increased. Some, such as Ernest Bevin, had fought for years for the 'de-casualization' of the workers. Yet there were many docker families that had spent all their working lives as casual labourers, as had their fathers, grandfathers and great-grandfathers. The freedom of seeking work when they chose was entrenched in their way of life. The idea of being permanent staff and the necessity of working set hours every week, and losing the freedom to work as they wished, seemed alien. To them, working time meant whatever time it took to unload a cargo. Many found it difficult to settle down to the rigid routine of set hours and they resented it.

Mechanization and containerization

The first moves towards mechanization had come as early as the nineteenth century with the introduction of steam power to operate pumps and mechanical lifting devices, followed by hydraulically-driven equipment. The earliest electric conveyors in the port were installed in 1908 at the transit sheds at Tilbury, followed by an overhead runway for carrying beef carcasses at the Royal Albert Dock in 1910. There were minor innovations in the 1920s but little progress in the 30s. It took the Second World War to bring about further change. In 1948 Leslie Ford was appointed general manager of the PLA and one of his priorities was to find new efficiencies through mechanical handling. A modern new riverside grain terminal, one of the most efficient in the world, capable of unloading at 2,000 tons per hour into silos, barges or coasters, was opened at Tilbury at a cost of £6 million. New silos could store 100,000 tons of grain and after Britain's entry into the Common Market it was possible to make exports from there to the Continent. Three privately-owned flour mills were built beside the terminal. As early as 1949 sugar was arriving in bulk for the Tate & Lyle refinery instead of in sacks as it was previously.

The transportation of wine quickly evolved after the Second World War. For hundreds of years it had been brought from the Continent in various forms of casks but large tanks were introduced, holding 550 gallons, that could be lifted on and off ships. Next came ships with built-in tanks and then purpose-built wine tanker vessels. In 1959 the PLA built bulk wine tanks at the London Docks to hold 800,000 gallons but before long even greater capacity was required. Within a decade, tanks of 980,000 gallons had been created at the Millwall and IndiaDocks.

The dock contractor Scruttons first experimented with prototype forklift trucks in Liverpool in 1945, which were not at that time generally being used in Britain. American forces used London's docks as a base during the Second World War and when they departed in 1946 they left behind some forklift trucks, mobile cranes and tractors. These were inherited by Colonel Oram of the PLA's Mechanical Equipment Committee, who in 1951 initiated tests in how they could best be used at a specially modified berth at the West India Docks. Export cargo was unloaded from trucks and railway wagons onto pallets, stacked and stored, then transferred to a ship's hold. The time taken to load a ship was reduced by twenty per cent. Goods stored on a pallet could easily be moved and then stacked to greater heights within a transit facility, allowing the shed to hold more than three times of that non-palletized. Previously, large gangs could handle only 50 tons per day compared with 300 tons by smaller gangs with mobile cranes and forklifts. The unit size of goods shifted from what one man could carry to that of a pallet. Bigger pallets could be created for bulkier goods such as timber and lifted and moved around within the docks by mobile straddle carriers. A new quay was constructed on the south side of the West India Import Dock with two large brick and concrete sheds that allowed access for mobile cranes and forklift trucks. A modern warehouse was built at Canary Wharf, at the west end of the West India South Quay, for the discharge of fruit from the Canary Islands. In the two decades after the war the movement and stacking of timber at the Surrey Commercial Docks was largely mechanized, with storage sheds adapted accordingly.

These simple innovations, whereby goods were no longer restricted to the size and weight that a man could carry, opened the door to new ways of thinking throughout the Port. It was also found that using mobile cranes was not only more efficient in the speed at which a barge could be discharged but also allowed the equipment to be taken to the vessel rather than having to manoeuver the vessel to a fixed point in a dock. During the 1950s mobile cranes were therefore introduced at all five of the London dock groups. At the beginning of the next decade the PLA owned over 100 forklifts. Storage facilities were modified, with doorways to allow entry by forklift truck and ceilings high enough for palletized stacking. Facilities such as the timber sheds at Quebec Dock, destroyed in the war, were rebuilt to new standards, with concrete floors, higher ceilings for higher stacking and wide aisles to allow mobile cranes to circulate. By the 1960s electrically-driven cranes of various sizes and capacities, large-capacity floating cranes, gantry-cranes, grain suction machines, floating grain elevators, trimmers to 'sweep' bulk sugar, ship-to-shore telephones, diesel-electric railway locomotives and diesel tugs were in use at the relevant berths and sidings. It was by then necessary for many of the staff working in the port to be skilled in the use of the new equipment.

It was yet another American military method used in the Second World War that was ultimately to lead to the closure of all the upriver docks and most of the wharves in the port. The roll-on/roll-off (or 'ro-ro') concept had started with tank-landing craft. It led to the idea of loading goods onto a trailer pulled by a truck and forming an articulated lorry. The trailer was towed from where it was loaded to a port. There it was rolled into a ferry for a short sea crossing, leaving the cab to be attached to an incoming trailer. At the receiving country, the outgoing trailer was rolled off, attached to a new truck and driven to its final destination. Once packed at the source, the goods did not need to be unpacked again until they reached their destination, cutting time at each transfer. The port had a minimal involvement in the goods on the trailer. Loading time, as well as the turnaround for the vessel, was minimized. Goods could be transported from a warehouse in Britain to another on the Continent in under two days instead of a week or more. The UK's first ro-ro service, to Hamburg for British forces, began at Tilbury in 1946. Commercial services to Antwerp were initiated in 1957 and to Rotterdam in 1960.

During the 1960s and 1970s there were a number of other types of ship built in attempts to streamline the movement of cargo. There were, for example, American-designed LASH (lighter aboard ship) vessels into which specially-built push-barges could be lifted directly into the ship's hold. These had the advantage of both saving time normally taken in transferring a cargo from lighters to the ship and in being able to load and discharge on an open river without the need of a dock or quay. LASH ships operated at Sheerness on the Thames Estuary for a short time. Ships of another American variation of this system, known as SEABEE, visited Gravesend.

The ro-ro concept needed a large amount of open space to park the trailers as they waited to board, yet minimal manpower. What London's docks offered was exactly the opposite: acres of warehousing, minimal open space and a large amount of manpower. The new method did not prevail overnight because new ships had to be built to accommodate the trailers but from the 1960s London's upper docks and wharves began to find themselves bypassed by other ports with suitable facilities. In Britain those routes were on the East Coast sailing to Denmark, and the West Coast to Ireland service.

At the same time, as this revolution was occurring within the ports, Britain's road network was being quickly upgraded, with new bypasses to take traffic around towns instead of through them and with the introduction of German-style high-speed motorways. Manufacturing plants and warehouses could therefore be located wherever a road could be laid out instead of needing to be beside a less flexible railway or canal as in the past. Goods were increasingly carried by truck instead of train, river or canal. A 1973 study by the Greater London Council noted that only 14 per cent of exports were transported by rail in 1960 compared with 41 per cent before the Second World War. It was no longer necessary for industry to be located along the riverside.

Ro-ro transportation required the goods to be moved throughout its journey on a trailer. The idea then came about that if they were loaded into a standard-sized container it could be lifted on and off a trailer or goods train and craned into a ship without the need for the trailer accompanying it. The basic idea was not new and had for decades been used elsewhere, such as on barges on Britain's canal network. Within Britain, agreement had been reached between railway companies in the 1920s to create a standard size of container that could be transferred between rolling stock. In 1965 international agreement was reached by shippers in the US, Canada and Denmark that such containers would be of a standard size, being 8 feet wide by 8 feet high but could vary in length between 10 to 40 feet, and ships were built to accommodate those containers. The standard measurement of a ship's capacity became 'twenty foot equivalent units' or TEUs. Standardized containers saved space within the ship, allowing a greater amount of cargo per vessel; providing protection against the elements when being transported or stored; and security from theft of the contents during transportation. The early container ships could carry 1,500 twenty-foot-long containers but ships have grown much larger over the decades, rising to capacities of over 18,000 TEUs by 2014.

A container service began in 1960 from No.4 berth at the Royal Victoria in 1960, with the creation of the largest transit shed in the docks. In 1964 PLA general manager Dudley Perkins visited New York's Port Elizabeth and witnessed for himself how containerization was revolutionizing cargo-handling. Major upgrading work was taking place in London but Perkins immediately sent back a telegram to put that on hold. His new ideas were not popular with the more conservative dock managers but he knew London's docks had to adapt to roll-on/roll-off and containerization if they were to survive into the future. By the middle of 1965 the PLA's board agreed to the necessary changes.

A serious issue that Perkins had to tackle was that goods were no longer stored in dockside warehouses and transit sheds. Instead they simply arrived by truck at the dock gates, causing long tailbacks of traffic. 'The dockers can be slack for four days and then have to work furiously to load a ship because people find it convenient to send goods at the last moment. The men don't like it,' he is reported as saying in January 1965. 'We are expected to deal with hundreds of tons one day and thousands the next.' His solution was a proposal for a computerized booking-in and clearing-house system.

A container berth could handle 10 times the amount of cargo compared with a conventional berth and the ship turned around in 36 hours rather than the previous 10 to 14 days. Without the requirement for large numbers of workers, the port could operate 24 hours each day, 7 days a week and ships could be unloaded and loaded simultaneously. During the 1960s cargo terminals around the world were adapted to the containerization method but most of the old docks and wharves in the Port of London were not able to be altered and the container ships were too large and deep to reach them. The exception was Tilbury where from 1963 the PLA began to upgrade the facilities to handle palletized storage, roll-on/roll-off trailers, and containers and packaged timber using specially-designed cranes and straddle carriers. Within three years of the first service, Tilbury was handling 150,000 containers annually. The first ever transatlantic container ship arrived there in June 1968.

The new methods were a major threat to the workforce, the majority of whom were no longer required. Trailers or containers merely needed to be received, parked or stacked for a short time and then dispatched. A relatively small number of skilled men were needed for all the tasks involved in carrying out that process within the docks. The goods were packed and stripped, and even customs duties paid, outside the port. The unions refused to man the new container berths and in order to open them the PLA had to provide the workers with a new deal. Some companies took advantage of the methods to avoid the militant unionized dock labour by setting up packing and stripping warehouses relatively close to the docks, employing cheaper unregistered workers. Those locations were picketed by the unions.

The ports that specialized in these new methods were quite different from those of the past. There were no crowds of dockers waiting at the gates for work, spending their time and money in nearby pubs. Ships quickly came and went so there was no need for a multitude of guest houses where seamen would rent a room while waiting for the return voyage. Multi-ethnic 'sailor-towns' that existed in Liverpool, Cardiff and London's East End became things of the past.

A period of change at the Port of London Authority

It was not only shipping methods and work within the docks and wharves that underwent change in the latter twentieth century. The PLA itself underwent modernization and efficiencies within its own organization. Thomas Wiles, grain merchant and politician, served as chairman of the PLA during most of the war years. He was succeeded in 1946 by John Anderson, a scientist by training who became an outstanding civil servant. A Minister of Shipping during the Great War, Anderson survived an assassination attempt while serving in colonial India, later becoming Lord Privy Seal, Home Secretary, Chancellor of the Exchequer and a member of Winston Churchill's War Cabinet. He is perhaps best-known today for giving his name to the 'Anderson' shelters during the war. He was elevated to the House of Lords in 1952 as Viscount Waverley and served as chairman until his death in 1956. He was succeeded by Lord Simon.

Flights were still an expensive novelty for the average person in the 1950s and passenger liners were the main form of transport to overseas destinations. The 1930 passenger landing stage at Tilbury was still in use when, in 1957, a modern new passenger terminal was constructed at a cost of £1,590,000. It included a large covered car park for 700 vehicles and a rail link to St Pancras. The terminal included a magnificent reception hall decorated with black and white murals and a statue of St Christopher. At the end of that decade liners of 35,000 tons were berthing, with a quarter of a million travellers passing through each year. With hindsight, the timing was ill-judged. Holidaying abroad was starting to become more affordable for the British public but they wanted to travel to and from their destination in the shortest possible time. London Airport had opened close to the village of Heathrow to the west of

London in 1946 on a former wartime military transport base. By 1960, 6 million passengers were flying from there each year. Gatwick Airport opened as a commercial airport in 1958, followed by Stanstead and Luton in the following decade. As a result, by the 1970s the passenger facilities at Tilbury had become redundant.

Leslie Ford was appointed general manager in 1948 (and later director general), having already had a long career in railway and dock management with the Great Western Railway, as had his father before him. He took over at a time when London's docks were still recovering from the extensive wartime damage. When Ford retired in the early 1960s he was succeeded by Dudley Perkins. It became clear during his tenure that the upper docks were in terminal decline and the first of the dock closures took place. Large numbers of dockers began to be laid off either through voluntary redundancy or retirement. Tilbury was becoming more important for freight than previously however. It gained a further advantage from 1963 when the nearby Dartford to Purfleet tunnel was opened, providing a road link across the river. The docks were significantly expanded between 1963 and 1966 with the addition of a large fourth basin, almost a mile long. The tidal basin was at that time closed and filled in.

Despite regular industrial action, trade in the port continued to increase, rising from just 33 million tons in 1947 to a post-war record of 61 million tons in 1964, which equalled nearly a third of all UK trade. With so many ships passing through there was congestion, with vessels queuing to enter the docks.

Lord Aldington, the former Conservative MP Toby Lowe, became the new chairman of the PLA in 1971. From that same year, John Lunch, previously the chief accountant, held the post of director general. The organization had been losing money for several years and needed streamlining. Head office staff in all departments was reduced from 800 down to 100 and many jobs devolved out to locations such as Tilbury and other docks. Needing to economize, and with the PLA having a diminishing role, the grand headquarters building on Tower Hill was sold in 1971 and the reduced staff moved into one floor of the new World Trade Centre building at St Katharine Docks. Those remaining dealt with policy and strategy and unused property was sold off. During that time a number of subsidiary companies were acquired dealing with cargo handling. John Lunch and other managers travelled around the world, including to China, Japan and North America, selling the benefits of the Port of London. After five years of losses, starting in 1966, the PLA once again began to generate increasing profits from 1971. It was a period of intense industrial unrest, with workers being laid off due to dock closures and containerization. In 1972 Aldington and the Transport & General Workers Union leader Jack Jones jointly chaired a committee to deal with industrial action in order to keep the port operating, with some success. The Port of London thereafter underwent dramatic changes that created enormous challenges for the PLA. During that intense period Lord Aldington was followed as chairman by three men in turn with a record of commercial success: Lord Cuckney (1977–79), Victor Paige (1980–84) and Sir Brian Kellett (1984–92).

As the old docks closed, the sale of assets became a major priority in a rollercoaster property market in order to fund the costs of redundancies and losses. In 1990 the organization was divided into three divisions – Tilbury, River, and Property, each with its own chief executive. The headquarters moved downriver to Gravesend, adjacent to Royal Terrace Pier, to be with the Thames Navigation Service and marine services divisions.

Industrial action led by militant leaders

As men went off to fight in the Second World War it created a shortage of labour in Britain's ports and factories, which played into the hands of socialists on the shop floor to increase the influence, membership and bargaining position of the trade unions. Despite much rebuilding and mechanization in the decades after the war, dockers often continued to work in the same primitive and dangerous conditions as their Victorian predecessors well into the 1960s. It was hard, physical labour, with little protection or safety equipment, so accident rates were high. Workers and unions strived to put pressure on the PLA and wharfingers to modernize their sites and introduce safer working practices.

Significant parts of Britain's basic industries had been taken into public ownership under the Atlee Labour government in the immediate post-war years and it was the belief of some amongst the workforce that docks should also be nationalized. To them, in the first decades after the war, industrial action was as much about ending capitalism as bringing immediate benefits to the workers. The Port of London found itself caught between the opposing extremes of capitalism and communism. Another factor was the National Dock Labour Scheme that had been introduced after the war. Casual workers were assigned to employers, with neither the worker nor employer choosing the place of work and thus loosening any bond or loyalty between the two parties.

In London's docks, one of the key militants was Jack Dash. He was already a committed socialist and member of the Communist Party before he began working in the Royal Docks in 1945. Four years later he was suspended from holding office by his own union, the TGWU, for leading unofficial industrial action by fellow workers in support of striking Canadian seamen. As an outsider to the main dock workers' union, Dash instead became part of the London Docks Liaison Committee, which organized dock-gate meetings, and in 1958 became its chairman. A natural orator, he would address these gatherings, usually outside the Connaught pub at the northern end of the bridge between the Royal Victoria and Royal Albert docks, with his catchphrase: 'Good morning, brothers!' A number of unofficial walkouts were organized and in 1966 Dash was singled out by Prime Minister Harold Wilson in the House of Commons as a communist who was spreading industrial unrest in the country. Despite his standing outside of the main union bodies, in 1965 he was called to give evidence to Lord Devlin for the report that was to recommend 'decasualization', adopted in 1967. Perversely, and true to his communist leaning, Dash and the militants claimed the move was to protect the profits of employers by reducing the workforce. As an alternative they called for the full nationalization of the entire port. An unofficial strike was called that lasted eight weeks.

New handling methods led to much frustration with union action that was crippling the port. In 1962 Leslie Ford, general manager at the PLA, was reported as saying: 'There has been a deliberate policy by a small segment of labour of creating disruption in the transport world. There is no doubt in my mind of the Communist influence behind this. The Communists don't want a general strike. In a large strike, national leaders would negotiate a long peace. Instead, it is only minor labour incidents that blow up with irritating regularity.' Most wildcat strikes were individual walkouts by gangs of dockers regarding safety issues that lasted only an hour or two.

If bringing the partly privately-owned Port of London to a standstill was the target, it was having some effect. In the decade from 1945, thirty-seven major strikes and many minor stoppages took place. This encouraged shipowners to direct their cargoes away from London to ports such as Felixstowe, Harwich, Dover and Southampton. Massive delays were caused by a weekend overtime ban in 1964; the port was closed from May to July 1966 during the period of the seaman's strike; and there was a nine-week unofficial strike at the Royal Docks the following year. In the two years between 1964 and 1966 there were ninety-three stoppages. Strikes were certainly not the main reason for the closure of London's Upper Port but they probably hastened the demise. When roll-on/ roll-off began to be introduced, and later containerization, without the need for a large workforce, union action began to be taken to preserve the jobs of the dockers. Yet disputes over decasualization, with Tilbury 'blacked' in 1969, caused most general cargo to and from Australia to be lost to Antwerp. The Port was also closed for six weeks in July the following year due to a national dock strike, the first since 1926.

The work of loading and unloading containers moved out of the port, to depots where shippers were not subject to the high costs and militancy of the dockers. In 1972 shop stewards from the docks closed one such location, Chobham Farm at Stratford in East London, for three weeks. It was one of the disputes where the militant dockers found themselves at odds with lorry-driver members of the TGWU. The picketing ended with the imprisonment of the leaders of the shop stewards, including Vic Turner, London docker, chairman of the National Dock Shop Stewards Committee, and a colleague of Jack Dash. They became known as the 'Pentonville Five' and a national dock strike followed in protest at their incarceration after a peace formula from Jack Jones of the TGWU and Lord Aldington of the PLA was rejected.

A further dispute between dockers and lorry drivers closed the port for six weeks in 1975. Another, regarding payments for abnormally-stowed cargoes, caused an unofficial strike in 1977. Further strikes were held in 1978 resulting in 100 ships moving elsewhere. There was congestion in the Port during a lorry drivers' strike in 1979; a two-week strike over dock pay in 1980 and a seaman's strike in 1980. A national dock strike in 1984 ended after three weeks due to patchy support from workers, strengthening the political hand of Prime Minister Margaret Thatcher. The number of dockers employed in the Port peaked in 1955 at 32,000 but by 1985 had shrunk to just three thousand.

After the 1960s the volume passing through the Port of London declined dramatically as it became increasingly uncompetitive. The PLA and wharfingers continued to be burdened by the National Dock Labour Scheme, paying wages to thousands of underemployed workers. Instead of goods arriving in London from around the world and being trans-shipped to the Continent, the reverse was happening. By then ships were directed to modern and efficient ports without labour problems, such as Rotterdam or Ostend, and goods moved from there to Felixstowe. Britain's trade with the world had also changed, towards the Continent instead of the Commonwealth.

With a declining business and the burden of paying registered dockers for whom there was not enough work, or paying them off with a very generous redundancy scheme, the PLA was effectively insolvent by 1977. The Mersey Docks & Harbour Board, in a similar position, declared itself bankrupt. Yet the government were unable to reform the Labour Scheme due to the threat of a national strike that would cripple the entire country. Significant changes to trade union legislation took place in the 1980s under the Conservative government of Thatcher that finally allowed the scheme to be abolished in 1989.

The closure of the upper docks and wharves

After the war, despite the great destruction, the Port of London began to function again and by the early 1950s had already surpassed pre-war tonnage, aided by more efficient goods-handling. During that decade 8,000 lighters were in use in the Port and more than 250 tugs, most privately-owned. An all-time peak was reached in the early '60s when 1,000 ships were entering or leaving every week. Employment peaked in 1955, when there were over 31,000 registered dock workers. Forty-six per cent of shipping entering the port was berthing in the enclosed docks, 14 per cent at PLA-operated wharves and 40 per cent either overside onto lighters or at privately-operated wharves. In 1960 over two and three quarter billion pounds of cargo passed through the Port and a record amount of tonnage was achieved in the years 1962 to 1964. A decade later the Port handled over 21 per cent of the nation's exports and over 17 per cent of imports. Yet the post-war cargo boom was to be short-lived.

From the late 1940s the Port of London Authority began to find itself in much the same position as the private dock companies that preceded it at the end of the nineteenth century. Trade was again increasing as the world's economies improved following the disruption of the war. Yet ocean-going transcontinental ships became ever bigger and by the 1950s were too large to navigate up the Thames to reach the upper docks and wharves. At the same time, new forms of cargo-handling were being introduced for which many of the old docks and wharves were not suitable. The greater part of new investment by the PLA was directed ever further downriver and from the 1960s that was at Tilbury. Despite a great deal of modernization over many decades, much cargo in the Port was still being handled as it had done for centuries.

Recognizing that many of Britain's ports were outdated, at a time of regular industrial action, and concerned about the slow speed of handling goods, the government set up a committee in 1961 chaired by Lord Rochdale to consider the adequacy and future of Britain's major ports. Following the report, the National Ports Council was created to coordinate national planning, investment and development. As far as London was concerned it concluded that:

'… we think that port activity should be moved away from the centre of London and there is, on the face of things, land at these docks which could be valuable for redevelopment. We are aware that at present the docks perform a useful and to some extent specialised function, but we think it at least possible that the traffic could be catered for elsewhere in the port, especially if pressure can be eased by development at Tilbury.

'As for the potential use of the land, it may be doubted whether it is suitable for development for industry or housing, but the docks themselves might be filled in and at least or otherwise developed for storage purposes and the warehouses might be sold or let to private enterprise; it could be that capital derived from such arrangements could be put to very good use by the authorities elsewhere, for example at Tilbury.'

Thus, the upper port was under sentence of death for the next few years while consideration was taking place.

Each of England's major ports was losing money by the end of the 1960s, hampered by loss of trade to the Continent, regular strike action and the burdens imposed on them by the National Dock Labour Scheme. In the 1969–70 financial year London lost almost £2 million. Bristol and Liverpool were in a similar predicament. Yet the PLA, with 5,000 acres of property, owned a massive amount of underused land that could be sold off for redevelopment while at the same time it needed finance to modernize the profitable and viable docks downriver.

The East India Docks, small and isolated from the other dock groups, were the first to completely close. The Export Dock finished in 1946 and was filled in. Between 1947 and 1956 the Brunswick Wharf Power Station was built over it for the British Electricity Authority. (It was in use until 1984 after which it was decommissioned and demolished). During the 1960s only smaller coastal and short-voyage vessels were berthing at the East India Import Dock but it was no longer financially viable and was closed in 1967 and filled in. Workers were offered a transfer to the West India or Millwall Docks.

For some years the neighbouring St Katharine and London Docks (together with the PLA's Cutler Street and Commercial Road warehouses) had acted merely as warehouses and showrooms for exotic goods that had been discharged downriver and brought up by lighter. Between the two docks there was nearly 5 million square feet of storage. At the London Docks a new bulk wine berth had been installed in 1963 and was profitable, yet overall the two sets of docks together were running at an annual loss of over £1 million per year. They were closed during 1968 and 1969 with the loss of 1,300 jobs. Most of the magnificent Georgian warehouses of the London Dock were demolished in the 1970s without much protest.

All the wharves in the Upper Port closed between 1967 and 1971 with the loss of many traditional skills built up over generations. In the 1950s the Hay's Wharf complex on the south bank of the Pool of London was handling over 1,700,000 tons of produce each year. Since then trade had gradually declined and the last shipowners deserted the wharves in 1969 during walkouts by the staff. Hay's Wharf closed between June and November 1969 with the loss of 1,000 jobs. Others quickly followed. New Fresh Wharf on the north bank in the City closed in May 1970, Free Trade Wharf at Ratcliff in January 1971, Butler's Wharf, across the river from the entrance to St Katharine Docks in March 1972.

In the early 1960s the Port of London was handling about a quarter of the country's imports of softwood, half of its hardwood and two thirds of its plywood, much of it passing through the Surrey Commercial Docks. Yet ships carrying timber in packed quantities dwarfed those of earlier decades that had brought loose planks. The newer vessels were far too large to reach so far up the river. The London timber trade moved downstream to Tilbury, with its No.34 berth specially adapted and opened in 1966, and two more berths the following year. The last timber ship to depart the 372-acre complex at Rotherhithe left in December 1970 and with it a century and a half of skills in handling timber. Thereafter wood arrived packaged and palletized at Tilbury or elsewhere. The Surrey Docks were no longer profitable so, despite protests from the unions, they closed in 1970.

Following the closure of the East India, St Katharine, London and Surrey Commercial Docks the PLA hoped that the remaining Royal, West India and Millwall Docks would be adequate for the reduced amount of trade and there were no further dock closures for several years. Yet London's share of UK imports and exports fell from a third to just twelve per cent between 1964 and

1975, overtaken by airports such as Heathrow and Gatwick. The PLA's results plummeted from £500,000 profit in 1974 to a loss of £5 million the following year. Further closures became inevitable as berths lay idle. The West India and Millwall Docks closed in 1980. The deeper Royal Docks continued for another year with the help of government subsidy but their losses were too great to sustain. The three giant flour mills at the Royal Victoria were shut down. The last ship to depart the Royal Docks left in October 1981, with the scrap metal business transferring to Tilbury two years later.

The Port of London was bound by the restraints and inefficiencies of the National Dock Labour Scheme, making it uncompetitive with other ports in Britain and the near-Continent that worked outside the scheme. Militant dockers continued to strike. Shipowners were taking their business elsewhere, falling from 60 million tons in 1967 to 42 million in 1982. The amount of cargo was increasing at Tilbury, which was the only dock in the Port of London capable of handling the new methods of freight handling. Yet those new methods required far less manual labour than the old ways. Businesses throughout the port closed down with the loss of 10,000 jobs between 1967 and 1976. As services essential to the operation of the Port went out of business, the PLA were obliged to take them on. By 1967 there were 3,000 registered dockers surplus to requirements in the Port who could not be laid off and still had to be paid each week. As other companies closed, an ever-greater wage burden fell upon those that remained, particularly the PLA. In 1966 a voluntary redundancy scheme was introduced but it was generous of necessity and therefore costly. Between 1966 and 1989 the number of registered dockers fell from 24,000 to 9,000.

The decline of East London

Many businesses that left London before or during the war did not return and with much of the infrastructure obliterated, industry continued to migrate in the 1950s. Factories and warehouses were gradually abandoned throughout the capital. In the post-war planning, many sites that had previously been used for industry were reclassified as residential zones. It was also the government's policy from the 1950s until the mid-1970s to encourage decentralization and for businesses to move away from London.

East London, on both sides of the river, was badly hit during the war. They had been the slowest areas to rebuild and the decline of the docks had a knock-on effect for industries such as warehousing, transport and food across that whole part of the capital. Large numbers of residents moved out to Essex and the new towns while some bomb sites remained undeveloped for decades. In the early 1980s most of the upper docks lay empty and derelict with the loss of 25,000 direct jobs. The parts of London from Wapping to East Ham, including the Isle of Dogs, as well as along the south bank around Bermondsey and Rotherhithe, had relied on the Port for their employment. The riverside factories, warehouses and power stations had depended on easy access to the arrival of raw materials as well as the convenience of being able to transport their manufactured goods by ship or rail to the far corners of the world. Around the docks, wharves and factories, rows of terraced houses had been developed to accommodate the workers who toiled in those many enterprises. Service industries had grown up around all of them, ranging from ship-repair yards and chandlers to gas and electricity generating plants. Without dockers and sailors, numerous pubs lost their trade.

The closure of the Upper Port was in the end perhaps predictable but what was surprising was its suddenness. What the Great Fire of London was to the City of London in the seventeenth century, the closure of the docks and wharves was to East London in the twentieth century. As business declined so too did the entire East End, as well as on the south side of the river. During the period of the earliest dock closures, from 1966 until 1976, 150,000 jobs were lost in those districts, around twenty per cent of the total, and thereafter the decline continued. A decade later the once bustling East End was one of the most depressed areas in the country. As the upper docks closed, their sale by the PLA was delayed as studies took place to determine a new use, while London's property market boomed. Yet by the latter end of the 1970s the economy was in a state of depression and property prices low. For a time, many of the docks lay closed off and disused, with great basins of empty water. Former dockers had largely moved away and taken up new employment elsewhere, leaving behind an ageing population.

The redevelopment of the Upper Port

While the Second World War was still in progress the planners at the London County Council were considering how the metropolis could be rebuilt after the conflict. Much as Sir Christopher Wren and his contemporaries were proposing utopian ideas to create the perfectly-planned urban area following the Great Fire of 1666, so the men at the London County Council were seeing the opportunity to create a better city out of the ashes of wartime London. The LCC planners envisaged a time when the docks might become redundant. In proposals drawn up in 1943 and 1944, J.H. Forshaw of the LCC and Patrick Abercrombie, professor of town planning at University College proposed that a public tree-lined riverside walkway be created from the Tower of London to the King Edward VII Park at Shadwell. Should the St Katharine Docks become redundant they envisaged replacing it with a public park from Tower Hill and down past the Tower of London.

As the docks closed, much of the PLA's large portfolio of land was sold off, with proceeds used to fund the wages of underemployed dockers. Little was done to save magnificent and historic buildings, such as those at the London Docks, that we can now only admire in old black and white photographs. Initially many of the solid riverside warehouses, such those at Wapping and Shad Thames, were rented as low-cost loft apartments or artist studios. In 1969 the St Katharine Docks were sold to the Greater London Council for a mere £1,500,000, less than the original cost in 1828, for which the PLA was much criticized. The GLC in turn invited tenders for the redevelopment of the docks, setting out requirements that had been agreed with Tower Hamlets Borough Council. The winners of the St Katharine's tender were the developers Taylor Woodrow who in 1969 were granted a 125-year lease to create a marina, hotel, shopping and apartment complex. The only buildings to survive from the original docks are the Ivory House warehouse facing into the central basin and the lockside dockmaster's house.

During the following years, individual developers began proposing numerous plans for the districts vacated by the docks. Rather than allow piecemeal schemes, the GLC commissioned reports as to how the area could best be redeveloped and regenerated. A Docklands Joint Committee was formed, including the five London boroughs affected: Tower Hamlets, Newham, Southwark, Lewisham and Greenwich. With so many different proposals being presented, in 1971 Peter Walker, Secretary of State for the Environment, together with the GLC, commissioned a report from the planners Travis Morgan & Partners. During the period of their deliberations all planning applications were put on hold. An inter-disciplinary team was formed, led by Alfred Goldstein, and their report was submitted in January 1973. Five different schemes were proposed, all of which assumed the commercial activities of the upper docks would end, and each combining a mixture of residential and commercial use. It introduced ideas that were to come to fruition eventually.

Published during the GLC elections, the Travis Morgan report became a political issue and was heavily criticized for its lack of consultation with local authorities. With that in mind, Walker's successor at the Department for the Environment, Geoffrey Rippon, established the Docklands Joint Committee, formed of the GLC, local boroughs and leading business and finance people. Its remit was to decide a strategic plan, under the chairmanship of Sir Reg Goodwin. Unlike the Travis Morgan report it required consultation with all the various parties affected: authorities, residents and employers. Their London Docklands Strategic Plan was published in July 1976. With so many varying opinions, it is not surprising therefore that the report was quite conservative in its conclusions, with the participants wanting to keep the status quo rather than any radical change. It called for a large amount of public investment and, while welcoming the report, Peter Shore, Rippon's successor, warned of 'present financial stringencies'. Much of the land around the former docks was owned by the PLA, local authorities or energy companies and there was no clear consensus between them as to how the area should be redeveloped. Some small infrastructure work was carried out but this largely involved the filling-in of docks, with little regard for their amenity value. The PLA, who desperately needed the income, were enthusiastic regarding the decommissioning and sale of unused docks. The Docklands Joint Committee possibly also had the motive of preventing further private-enterprise marina-style developments such as that being created at the former St Katharine Docks. Little widespread regeneration took place in the following period, although several small developments proceeded, creating between 1976 and 1980 some warehousing, housing and road schemes at Beckton and on the Greenwich Peninsula.

There were too many self-interested participants in the regeneration process. In the meantime, jobs in the area were disappearing, the population was diminishing and an increasing amount of land lay derelict. Clearly, by the end of the decade none of the key targets set out in the London Docklands Strategic Plan regarding housing and jobs were going to be met. In July 1981 therefore, Michael Heseltine, Peter Shore's successor, created the London Docklands Development Corporation to regenerate the riverside from London Bridge to Beckton, within the boroughs of Tower Hamlets, Newham and Beckton. He later wrote in his memoirs of taking a flight in a small plane across the area and of his 'indignation' at seeing '6000 acres of forgotten wasteland'. The LDDC was based on the earlier model used to create new towns around the South East, giving control of the scheme to a board of experienced businessmen and independent of the local authorities. In effect, it had powers similar to a local authority, including that of compulsory land acquisition, although its remit did not cover local services such as housing, education and health, which remained with the local boroughs. It was given an initial budget from Government of over £60 million per annum. From the outset, the LDDC made the decision to attract private finance to the area to create new business enterprises; provide land, currently then held by public bodies, on which to do so; and to improve the poor transport infrastructure.

In 1982 most of the Isle of Dogs became an Enterprise Zone, with tax and other incentives to attract investment, seventy per cent of which came from abroad. That same year Billingsgate Fish Market moved from its traditional home beside the Thames in the City to a new site at the North Quay of the West India Docks. It was considered somewhat of a coup for the LDDC when a new TV company decided to site their studios at the West India Docks, with a former dock building refashioned by the renowned architect Terry Farrell. Many notable TV programmes were recorded in subsequent years at Limehouse Studios, including the Spitting Image series. The newspaper publisher Rupert Murdoch's News International, controversially opened offices and a printing works at the London Docks in 1986. With limited retail facilities in the area, a Kuwaiti investment company acquired part of the former tobacco warehouses of the London Docks and converted them into a small shopping centre. Unfortunately, the timing was too early and the enterprise failed, with the building currently used as the Tobacco Dock events space. Perhaps another example of being ahead of its time was the London Arena. It opened as a sports and concert venue in 1989 at Crossharbour, to the east of Millwall Docks on the Isle of Dogs, seating an audience of up to 15,000. Its location was considered too isolated and it struggled financially. When the Millennium Dome opened at Greenwich, offering similar facilities, its American owners called it a day in 2005. It was demolished the following year and the land reused as a residential area. In 1987 London City Airport opened at the former Royal Albert and King George V docks and the central quay that separated the two basins was converted into a single runway.

During their working life, the quays and areas between the docks had been accessed by several drawbridges and swing bridges. When the docks closed, their maintenance ceased and they regularly stopped working, leaving the small amount of traffic with circuitous routes to access the area. Consequently the Isle of Dogs became even more remote from the rest of London than it had been previously. In order to create better access and attract investment, the LDDC began building new roads through the area.

The former docks had been linked with the City by railways. The GLC and LDDC decided to utilize the lines to create a modern, privately-operated rail network, known as the Docklands Light Railway. Seven and a half miles of track ran on the disused London & Blackwall railway, built mostly on viaducts. The first sections, from Tower Gateway to Stratford, with a branch to Island Gardens on the Isle of Dogs, began operation in August 1987 with fifteen stations. In 1991 a line was created at the western end that forked to off to Bank, a tunnelled section that cost twice as much as the entire previous route. A branch was opened from Poplar to Beckton via Canning Town in 1994 and another from Poplar to Lewisham via Greenwich in 1999. In 2009 the network was extended once again to Woolwich via the Royal Docks and London City Airport. It is now an extensive network throughout East London.

While the Docklands district was becoming more easily accessible from other parts of London by rail, it still took a considerable length of time to reach there from the City by road. A better road connection was required with the City, so the seven-mile-long Docklands Highway was created. It was completed in May 1993 with the opening of the mile-long Limehouse Link tunnel that bypassed the busy East India Dock Road.

After years of consideration, it was finally decided in 1990 to link the Docklands and the West End with an extension of the Jubilee line from Green Park via Westminster and Waterloo, Southwark, and Canning Town, before terminating at Stratford. Along the way, a number of modern station designs were created, including Europe's largest underground station at North Greenwich. After much delay, and double the original budget, the line finally opened in November 1999.

The timing of the development of Docklands coincided with changes in banking. In 1985 the Bank of England relaxed the ruling that bank headquarters were obliged to be located in the City of London. The New York Stock Exchange had been deregulated several years earlier and its less rigorous rules allowed it to gain business from London. The Thatcher government's response was to discontinue the regulations that separated different kinds of financial institutions in Britain, allowing them the possibility to offer a full range of services to their clients from October 1986. The event was known as the 'Big Bang' and it firmly re-established London as one of the world's most significant financial centres.

With the simultaneous technology revolution that allowed financiers to work from computer screens, the style of operations within financial institutions changed. From then on most staff could work in large open-plan trading floors within their businesses, yet most City buildings were either from the Edwardian era or functional but uninspiring post-war offices. The American property developer G. Ware Travelstead of First Boston Real Estate was the first to have the idea of a new business district in London of the kind that was commonplace in North America, consisting of high-rise offices with large open-plan floors. A consortium of American property developers was brought together in 1985 to build a centrepiece building on what had been the quayside of the West India Docks. The location had been known as Canary Wharf since the 1930s when the shipping company Fruit Lines had been landing fruit from the Canary Islands. Unfortunately the plans required the demolition of the relatively new Limehouse TV studios. As the scheme escalated it became necessary for it to be handled by a company with greater financial resources, so two years later it passed to the Canadian Olympia & York company who brought in a new architect, the Argentinian César Pelli. The final building, at 250 metres was more than twice the height of St Paul's Cathedral and at the time Europe's tallest building. Construction began in 1987 and it was given the address No.1 Canada Square when opened in 1991, but is more generally known as simply 'Canary Wharf'. It was joined by other high-rise buildings, creating a cluster of skyscrapers around the former basins of the West India Docks.

The south bank between London Bridge and Tower Bridge, occupied by Hay's Wharf, was acquired in the 1980s by the State of Kuwait, through their St Martin's Property Corporation. Supported by the LDDC, the section downstream from London Bridge was given the name 'London Bridge City' and redeveloped as offices, the Hay's Galleria tourist attraction, the London Bridge Hospital, Southwark Crown Court, and housing. Several of the former warehouse buildings were retained and converted for new uses. The preserved former Second World War battle cruiser HMS *Belfast* has been moored there as a museum since 1971. In 1998 St Martin's sold the remaining stretch down to Tower Bridge, where City Hall, successor to County Hall, and the More London office complex, were built.

Much of the change on the Rotherhithe Peninsula resulted in residential development. The many docks were filled in, with the exception of Greenland and South Docks, Surrey Basin (renamed Surrey Water) and parts of Canada Dock and Lavender Dock. The centre of the peninsula, including the historic St Mary's church and the small Brunel Museum, was largely preserved. The

Surrey Quays shopping centre was opened in 1988 as was the nearby Canada Water station on the Jubilee line. The handsome, former nineteenth century headquarters building of the Surrey Commercial Docks on Surrey Quays Road remains and is a listed building.

Butler's Wharf, downstream of Tower Bridge, ceased to be used for receiving goods in 1972 and was thereafter occupied as art studios. The designer and restaurant-owner Terence Conran successfully put forward a plan that was accepted by the LDDC to redevelop the complex for apartments and restaurants. In addition, the 'Boilerhouse Project' at the Victoria & Albert Museum was given a new home there as the Design Museum. A school for chefs that opened in 1996 was the last grant provided to a project by the LDDC.

The warehouses on the north quay of the West India Import Dock remained in place, one of which now houses the Museum of Docklands. The basins themselves have been kept largely intact around the new developments and are today managed by the Canal & River Trust, the successor to the British Waterways Board. There are frequent visits by super-yachts, cruise ships and the occasional naval vessel. During the 1990s a large new exhibition centre known as Excel opened on the former North Quay of the Royal Victoria Dock. A large, dome-shaped riverside event venue was built at Greenwich Peninsula on the site of the former East Greenwich Gas Works and Blackwall Point Power Station. Designed by Richard Rogers, it was opened in time for the year 2000 Millennium celebrations and is currently called the O2 Arena. Further stimulus to the development of East London came with the decision to locate the 2012 London Olympics at Stratford.

The 'Air Line' cable-car link between the Greenwich Peninsula and Royal Victoria Dock opened in 2012 but is so far underused, largely due to its particular location. At the time of writing there are several options being considered for rail, road and foot bridges, and tunnels. One of these is a foot and bicycle bascule bridge between Rotherhithe and Canary Wharf.

In 1998 the London Docklands Development Corporation was disbanded and control of the area was given back to the relevant local authorities. By then, 2,700 businesses were trading in the Docklands area, over 24,000 new homes had been built and 144 kilometres of roads had been laid out or upgraded. The work of the LDDC, Olympic organizers, the many developers and local boroughs has transformed almost beyond recognition the East of London around the former docks. Yet the thousands of new jobs that were created were primarily for those with different skills to the dockers and other workers who had lived in the area prior to the 1980s.

Chapter Eight

The Modern Port of London

Despite the growth of air transport, the United Kingdom still relies on the sea for ninety-five per cent of its imports, and much of its exports. The volume of goods passing through the major British ports has increased in recent decades. In the 1990s that trade passed 500 million tonnes per year, with three quarters being oil derivatives or other bulk cargoes. Seventy-five per cent of the total amount passed through 15 ports, including London. Since a downturn in trade after the global financial crisis of 2008 there has been overcapacity in the global shipping of dry bulk cargoes such as iron ore and coal, and containers, leading to rock-bottom rates, bankruptcies and restructuring in those businesses. British ports have been competing with each other to better serve supply chains. On the Thames there is the new London Gateway terminal, the number of berths has increased at Felixstowe and Southampton, a new terminal is being built at Liverpool, and Tilbury has been investing in new facilities.

A hundred years ago the largest portion of London's overseas trade was with the British Empire, with wool, cheese, butter, wine and canned fruits arriving from Australia, lamb from New Zealand, tea from Ceylon, tea and tobacco from Africa, as well as sugar and bananas from the West Indies. That changed even before Britain's entry into the Common Market in 1973 as the former colonies gained independence and patterns of world trade also refocused. Today the biggest portion of UK trade is with the European Union. While the docks and wharves of the Upper Port were closing between the late 1960s and early 1980s, the terminals further downriver, which could handle larger vessels and were more easily adaptable, continued to flourish. New ones opened and others evolved with the continually-changing requirements of UK trade and methods of cargo-handling. Oil and aggregates, more suited to sites away from the city, increased in importance.

Today London is the second-largest UK port by tonnage handled. There are almost sixty active commercial docks, wharves and terminals along the tidal river, from Wandsworth downriver to Canvey Island. The main concentrations are in the boroughs of Thurrock and Barking & Dagenham. Between them these sites handle a great range of consignments, from more than eighty countries. Other than bulk cargoes, a multitude of general goods arrive at Tilbury and London Gateway in containers or on roll-on/roll-off trailers. The majority of individual terminals along the river however handle particular types of specialized shipments and processes. Many of them deal in imports of construction materials and bulk liquids. As would be expected, almost three quarters are sited on the deeper, wider river below the Thames Barrier. Fifteen per cent of London's waste is taken by barge down to Cory Environmental's facility at Belvedere, where it is used to generate electricity and produce ash-aggregates for road building.

Petroleum has been arriving along the Essex coast of the Estuary since the late nineteenth century when Standard Oil (Esso) opened a terminal at Purfleet, which is still in operation. Until the Second World War it was normally shipped in its crude form. Following the 1951 seizure and nationalization of the Abadan refinery in Iran, owned by the Anglo-Iranian Oil Company (later renamed British Petroleum), refining has mostly taken place in consumer nations. By the 1960s oil accounted for forty per cent by value of cargo entering the Port. The section of tideway downriver from Purfleet continues to be a major storage and refining centre, particularly at Coryton and Canvey Island. Shell closed its major and long-established refinery at Shell Haven in 2000 however, but continues to import aviation fuel at nearby Stanford-le-Hope, the largest such facility in the UK. NuStar Terminals has two jetties at Grays to receive hydrocarbons. At Canvey Island, Calor Gas deals in liquefied petroleum gas and Oikos Storage pumps aviation fuels and other petroleum products directly into government and commercial pipelines. Navigator Terminals (formerly Vopak) receives, stores and processes petroleum products further upriver at West Thurrock.

Motor vehicles and parts are an important contributor to trade. The Ford Motor Company has been located on the riverside at Dagenham since 1931 where it now manufactures around one million engines each year. The majority are shipped to Continental Europe from the company's jetty, with two ship arrivals each day. Ford imports over a quarter of a million vehicles each year, with a relatively small number exported. Another major location for cars is C Ro Ports at its ro-ro terminal close to the Dartford Bridge and a large number arrive at Tilbury.

The discharging and distribution of marine-dredged aggregates, used in London's buoyant construction industry, is a major industry on the river. Much of it comes from approved sites in the English Channel and is received at various wharves. These include Tarmac, with several terminals between Charlton and the Queen Elizabeth II Bridge at Dartford. Aggregate Industries at Northfleet operates its own ships and is a major manufacturer of concrete. It moves bulk materials along the river with its company-owned tugs and barges. CEMEX has terminals and cement and paving-stone manufacturing facilities at Northfleet, Dagenham, Greenwich and Fulham, as well as within the Port of Tilbury, moving aggregates and materials between them by barge. Several trains leave Brett's terminal at Cliffe on the North Kent coast each day, one of several of the company's facilities along the Thames and Kent coast, loaded with aggregates dredged from the North Sea. Hanson has facilities at Wandsworth, Dagenham, Greenwich and West Thurrock for concrete and asphalt. Rail connections link their riverside terminals with other company plants around the London area.

Downriver of the QEII Bridge, Seacon Terminals handles around half a million tonnes of steel and forest products a year, operating its own ships from its all-weather covered berth at Northfleet. Industrial Chemicals has an 80-acre site on the former West Thurrock Power Station where it employs 300 people and handles a million tonnes of materials annually. As we have seen in an earlier chapter, a long-established name on the river is Tate & Lyle and forty ships arrive each year at the company's two Silvertown jetties. The adjoining refinery, now owned by American Sugar Holdings although still operating under the Tate & Lyle brand, is one of the world's largest such operations, producing up to forty per cent of the UK's refined sugars as well as a range of products sold to food and drink manufacturers. Raw sugar arrives in bulk from Africa, the Caribbean, Central and South America and the Pacific. Sugar products are also exported by ship.

The Port of London Authority

The Port of London Authority continues as the guardian of the tidal Thames. It is one of over a hundred Trust Ports in the UK, each answerable to the Department of Transport and governed by its individual regulations. Its legal status was most recently defined by the Port of London Act 1968. Unlike others, such as Dover, while it no longer operates docks and wharves directly, it continues to be responsible for navigation, safety and environmental matters, and economic sustainability. Its remit covers 95 miles of river downstream from Teddington Lock, increased by 22 miles to Margate and Clacton in 1964. To carry out these responsibilities, a wide variety of disciplines and skills are involved, from planning to pilotage, engineering, environmental and regulation. The tidal river is Britain's busiest inland waterway and, as well as commercial activities, almost 10 million passengers use it each year, including tourists and commuters. The PLA works together with twenty-two local boroughs along the length of the river, as well as Kent and Essex County Councils and the Greater London Authority. There are also numerous other partners, ranging from the Royal National Lifeboat Institution, the Royal Society for the Protection of Birds, to numerous sports and community organizations. Since 1992 the PLA has been based at London River House at Gravesend, beside its Port Control Centre.

The PLA is self-funding in a competitive environment, with high capital costs. Since the closing of the Shell Haven refinery in 2000, the loss of a major source of income, there has been much focus on being a lean and cost-effective service provider. In 2015 it made an operating profit of over £7 million. In that year 34 per cent of the PLA's income came from pilotage, 31 per cent from fees from vessels entering and leaving the port, 19 per cent from rents and licensing and 16 per cent from marine services and licensing.

For much of the twentieth century, when it was the operator of the dock complexes, the PLA employed over 13,000 workers. Now, when commercial activity is dealt with by private and public companies and some tasks are contracted out, the PLA employs less than 400 managerial and specialist staff. It no longer keeps dock tugs and floating cranes as it had done in the past but a fleet of forty PLA vessels is maintained at Denton Wharf at Gravesend where a redevelopment was completed in 2006.

The PLA has been responsible for pilotage in and out of the port since it took over from Trinity House in 1988. Pilots board or disembark ships at the pilotage stations at either Harwich or Ramsgate, depending on their route in and out of the Estuary. Ninety pilots are employed, including 15 'river pilots' with specialist knowledge of bridges and piers between London Bridge and Putney. It takes four to five years before a pilot obtains the necessary qualifications. Pilots are trained on the PLA's own advanced simulator and when an unusually large vessel, such as a cruise ship, is due to enter the river they practice its arrival using this facility. The PLA's Thames Navigation

Service was established in 1959 at Gravesend to provide ships' crews and pilots with up-to-the-minute information via VHF radio regarding conditions and obstructions on the river. It also enables wharfingers to know the timing of incoming vessels. On the river itself there are PLA control centres located at Gravesend, covering the lower river, and near the Thames Barrier covering the tidal river upstream of Coldharbour Point (approximately the eastern border of Greater London). All commercial vessels using the river are required to carry transponders so their location can be tracked. The PLA's control centres oversee the movement of 230,000 commercial and leisure vessels each year, more than 10,000 of which are large ships such as container, cruise ships, or tankers, over an area of 600 square miles. The post of Chief Harbour Master is currently held by Rear Admiral David Snelson who is responsible for navigation safety. The organization operates patrol boats between Teddington and Southend and is also responsible for buoys, beacons and bridge lights on the tideway. It was involved in the implementation of new safety regulations following the sinking of the *Marchioness* pleasure boat near Cannon Street railway bridge in the summer of 1989.

Oversight of the dredging of the river in order to maintain navigation channels is a continuous task for the PLA (although the actual dredging has been contracted out since 1991). It operates sophisticated underwater equipment to monitor the shifting riverbed over 400 square miles. The new hydrographic vessel *Maplin* was introduced in 2015 allowing for higher speeds of underwater survey. The PLA also has a team of divers and salvage experts.

The Port of Tilbury

Tilbury remained as the sole survivor of the old Port of London Authority's enclosed docks when all of the upriver ones were closed. It was not only very extensive but also distant from an urban area and had never been boxed-in by warehouses. It therefore had space to expand and adapt to new methods of cargo-handling, and far enough downriver to be reached by larger, modern cargo vessels. As ships carrying timber increased in size in the 1960s, and began to carry packaged cargoes, that trade moved to Tilbury from the Surrey Commercial Docks. During the same decade the PLA began leasing berths and land to tenants who then erected buildings and supplied their own equipment. In its first hundred years or so Tilbury Docks had almost doubled in land area. By the mid-1970s over half of London's container traffic was passing through

Tilbury and it continued to evolve to handle more general cargoes, containers and bulk grains. A new rail terminal opened in 1970, as well as what was the world's largest refrigerated container storage in 1978.

The PLA were, however, burdened by the requirements and costs of the National Dock Labour Scheme. As with other wharves along the river, Tilbury was hampered by industrial disputes, so new container facilities that opened in 1967 could not be fully utilized until several years later. With such a disadvantage, it was overtaken in volume by some other ports on the Continent and in Britain, especially Felixstowe, that were able to operate outside the scheme. With the abolition of the National Dock Labour Scheme by the Thatcher government in 1989, Tilbury went from loss to profit in one year to the next.

In 1990 Tilbury Docks were separated within the PLA from the river management and property divisions. It was by then the only publicly-owned freight facility on the Thames. It needed massive investment that the PLA was unable to provide if it was to compete with other major ports. The decision was therefore taken to privatize the docks and a Parliamentary Bill was passed in 1991. A management buy-out was undertaken, led by Alan Ravenscroft and John McNab, and Tilbury parted from the PLA in March 1992. Three years later it was resold to Forth Ports, which also operates a number of ports in Scotland.

In 2016 the main Port of Tilbury covered 850 acres including 180 acres of dock water, with seven and a half kilometres of quayside and more than 500,000 square metres of warehousing. The entrance lock is 32 metres wide and deep enough for vessels with a draught of 10.5 metres. The three pairs of gates, with a top, middle and bottom set, which cater for both smaller and larger vessels, will be replaced during 2017 and 2018 to provide enhanced flood protection. Tilbury is now served by three rail terminals. It has the advantage of being located close to the M25 motorway and QEII river crossing and supports the idea of a second bridge further downriver in order to provide road access from both east and west to ease traffic congestion. Within the complex, 9,000 road traffic movements take place each day along the port's seven miles of roads. Four on-site wind turbines provide up to 60% of the electricity requirements.

Tilbury handles 16 million tonnes of cargo each year, with a value of nearly 9 billion pounds. These include grain, paper, construction materials, scrap metals and waste, cars, animal feed from South America, wine, and chilled food for supermarkets. Around 60 per cent of traffic is to and from Europe, anywhere from the Baltics to the Mediterranean Sea. Some of the largest vessels arriving at Tilbury are owned by the Grimaldi line, carrying timber from South America and returning via Nigeria with general goods. Their ships are too big to pass through the entrance lock so berth on a riverside quay.

One hundred and twenty companies work within the complex. The Port of Tilbury directly manages some of the enterprises, while others are independently operated by tenants. The Allied and ADM flour mills, EMR scrap metals and Travis Perkins building materials are some of the largest, operating their own independent berths within the docks. Three thousand seven hundred workers are employed in the Port, of which over 700 are directly employed by the Port of Tilbury. An on-site academy provides training for 70,000 people each year to both work within the Port and in the wider logistics industry. As in the days of the PLA, security continues to be provided by Tilbury's own police force of 14 officers. They have jurisdiction up to one mile from the boundary of the Port, with the same powers as other police forces.

Tilbury is the UK's third largest container port after Felixstowe and Southampton. In 2012 the Port took full ownership of Tilbury Container Services, previously a joint-venture with Associated British Ports and P&O Ports. They renamed it the London Container Terminal and combined it with their own short-sea container operation that handled cargo from the near-Continent. Much of it is perishable foodstuffs arriving in 'reefer' (refrigerated) containers. To an extent, Tilbury now competes for container business with the new London Gateway operation further downriver. Perry Glading, Chief Operating Officer for the Port of Tilbury, responded to this point, saying: 'Tilbury's uniqueness is the diversity of its business base. We have a large container business but it only represents about 5 to 6% of our overall turnover and tonnage.' P&O Ferries' roll-on/roll-off service to Zeebrugge is a major route, with 24 sailings each week carrying 200,000 trailers per year. Hyundai imports 90,000 cars annually from Korea and the Czech Republic. A new sorting and fulfillment centre is being created in the London Distribution Park, covering over 70 acres, where cargo will arrive in containers and trailers, to be offloaded, sorted and distributed around the UK. The site will contain the UK's largest warehouse of over 200,000 square metres as a logistics centre for Amazon.

Another important cargo is animal feed and Tilbury is the UK's leading port for both the importation of forest products and grain. It is also the UK's largest waste export facility. A substantial volume passing through is scrap steel, with around a million tonnes exported each year. A recent development is that prices to put general rubbish into landfill sites have increased substantially following the EU Landfill Directive of 1999. 'Waste has now become a valuable commodity,' explains Glading. 'Once cleaned and tidied up it can be baled and incinerated to create electricity. What we're seeing here is all forms of waste, whether that be general household waste, office waste, wood waste, being shredded, cleaned and exported all around the world but primarily to Scandinavia for district heating systems.' About 80% arrives at Tilbury by truck but an increasing amount is coming by water. 'It's early days but there is a focus on using the river better for the movement of waste,' states Glading. Ireland's Electricity Supply Board is currently constructing an energy-from-waste facility in the Port that will produce 300 gigawatts per year from waste wood, enough to power 70,000 homes.

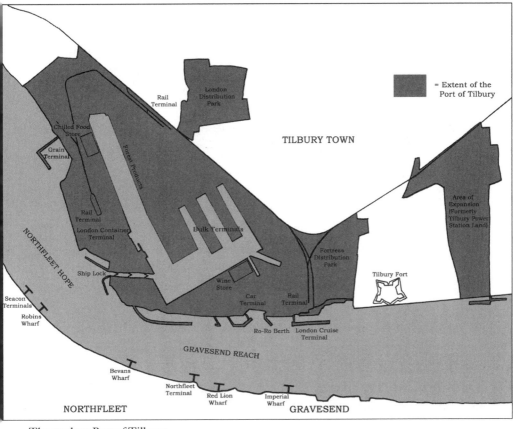

The modern Port of Tilbury.

Tilbury's moth-balled 1930s passenger terminal was reopened in 1995 as cruise-ship holidays became increasingly popular. Now renamed as the London Cruise Terminal it primarily acts as an embarkation point for British holidaymakers taking cruises around the Baltic area, serving 55 sailings and over 100,000 passengers per year. Based on existing bookings, Tilbury will be handling 70 sailings and 140,000 passengers in 2018. Ships berth against the 348-metre-long floating quayside that rises and falls together with the vessel by about six metres on each tide. With the potential for further traffic, the Port of Tilbury is investing and upgrading the facilities.

DP World London Gateway

In the early 1970s the PLA, still then an operator of berthing facilities, proposed a new deep-water container port and oil terminal further downriver at Maplin Sands. It was to be created in partnership with Shell and the construction company Mowlem but they were frustrated by the government's plans for a third London airport in the Estuary. The airport scheme was eventually abandoned and the PLA had anyway decided to concentrate resources at Tilbury. In the meantime – and despite improvements at Tilbury – cargo vessels grew to a size that made it difficult for them to pass into enclosed docks and too large to berth at London. Large, long-distance container ships have in recent years often unloaded at Continental ports such as Rotterdam, Hamburg or Antwerp and the parts of their cargoes bound for Britain then transshipped across the North Sea.

The solution came with the proposal by P&O Ports to open a new deep-water container terminal on the former oil refinery site at Shell Haven, vacated by Shell in 2000. It is located on the Essex coast of the Thames Estuary, near Stanford-le-Hope, thirty miles from Central London. The planning application process was lengthy and approved in May 2007. In the meantime P&O Ports had been acquired by the Dubai-based DP World, which operates sixty-five ports around the world. Having decided to continue with the scheme, DP World London Gateway opened its first riverside berths in November 2013, allowing the world's largest container ships to be unloaded and loaded. The first ship to arrive was the 58,000-tonne *Caledon*, carrying fruit and wine from South Africa. By 2015 the terminal was handling vessels of over 18,000 TEUs, the largest ever to navigate the Thames. That was previously only possible in the south of England at Felixstowe or Southampton, from where containers were normally trucked to logistics parks in the Midlands for redistribution of goods around the country. London Gateway is directly connected to the rail network, with services operated by DB Schenker Rail. It includes a 230-acre logistics park from where cargoes can be broken down, repacked, stored and distributed. The target is to eventually handle 3,500,000 containers each year and to be Europe's largest such operation.

The total area of the complex is twice that of the City of London. It began with two berths but six are planned in the long-term, which would provide a total of 2,700 metres of quay, with a depth of 17 metres, and 24 cranes. The third berth became operational in the second half of 2016. London Gateway was built 400 metres out into the river, requiring 30 million tonnes of silt to be dredged to create the new land. A nature reserve had to be created to accommodate wildlife that was disturbed. The cost of creating the terminal is expected to be £1.5 billion during the first 15 years.

The cranes that load and unload ships at London Gateway are the tallest in the world, rising to 138 metres. They can reach across 25 containers and lift 80 tonnes. Constructed in Shanghai, they were shipped fully assembled from there. Loading and unloading of containers is computerized and pre-planned in advance, although the cranes are manually operated. Unlike those at Felixstowe and Southampton they are weather-resistant, allowing London Gateway to operate around the clock in almost all conditions.

The future of the Port

Trade passing through the Port of London remains at only around two-thirds of the volume achieved in the heady days of the 1960s. By then London had already been overtaken by Rotterdam, which was passed by Singapore in 1992. Currently the world's leading port is Shanghai. The Port of London competes against Grimsby & Immingham (currently Britain's leading port by volume), the oil and chemical port of Tees & Hartlepool, as well as Felixstowe and Southampton in the container business, and a new deep-sea port development at Liverpool. Traffic in the Port of London recently peaked in 2008 at 53 million tonnes and since then has averaged 45 million tonnes, much reduced from the peaks of the late 1930s and early 1960s. Container and ro-ro traffic steadily increased during the decade until 2015. With London Gateway – the most significant expansion in the Port since the opening of the King George V Dock in the 1920s, as well as a rapid expansion and adaption at

Tilbury to an ever-changing market – perhaps London can once again rise to become Britain's premier port. Although London itself is far from being the manufacturing centre it was until the 1960s, the downriver Port is still well-placed for the traffic of goods and commodities. Fifty per cent of the UK's manufacturing and trading activity is located within a two-hour drive of the Port's main terminals. The PLA are currently forecasting further growth to 60 million tonnes or more by 2036. There are now over 43,000 people employed in the Port, of which about 27,000 are involved in port operations and the remainder in supply-chain activities.

In comparison with some ports, London has the advantage of handling a diversified range of products. Over a third is general merchandise that passes through in containers and ro-ro trailers. Almost a quarter is oil and nearly the same in aggregates and cement. The remainder includes vehicles and engines, paper and forest products, fertilizers and animal feeds, chemicals, steel and scrap metal, and food and wine. Britain imports more goods than it exports and currently eighty-four per cent of goods passing through the Port are imports. For every ten containers that arrive with merchandise at Tilbury, about four leave empty.

Forth Ports has a 15 to 20-year plan to double the amount of cargo being handled at Tilbury, to over 30 million tonnes per year. It has been acquiring adjacent land that will increase the size of the estate to around 1,100 acres. This includes half of the adjacent Tilbury Power Station to the east of Tilbury Fort, with its river frontage and a deep-water jetty, in order to increase facilities by a quarter. One area of expansion is in building-related traffic. A Port of Tilbury-owned business, London Construction Links, works together with construction companies to consolidate materials and equipment before onward passage by river to London sites.

With the opening of London Gateway, the Port of London offers a wider range of opportunities to shipowners. Tilbury and London Gateway compete in the container business but according to Perry Glading, 'Tilbury is more short-sea European and smaller niche services, whereas London Gateway is more about the very large Far East to the UK vessels, so we're talking about different economies of size when it comes to vessels.'

Tilbury won the contract to ship building materials upriver to the site when Canary Wharf was being developed in the 1980s. Since then spoil and building components related to major London infrastructure projects have become a significant traffic on the river. With a continuous stream of new projects in London, that is likely to remain the case for the foreseeable future. The rebuilding of Blackfriars Station and the tunnelling of Crossrail are the latest projects to be completed, with the 25-kilometre-long Thames Tideway Tunnel, the largest single project on the tidal river in over a century, now also underway. In 2016 the PLA acquired Peruvian Wharf at Silvertown, to the south of the former Royal Docks. The intention is to lease it for the creation of a building materials terminal, which should be operational in 2017.

The Thames is too small for the biggest cruise ships, which instead head for Southampton. London is becoming a popular destination for cruise vessels of up to 48,000 tons however, and their large structures can now regularly be seen moored at Tilbury, Greenwich, the West India Docks and the Upper Pool of London. A new 230-metre berth will be privately developed at Enderby Wharf at Greenwich. Passenger numbers at Tilbury's London Cruise Terminal, reopened in 1995, reached 100,000 in 2015 and are expected to continue rising. Despite being relatively small amongst cruise ships, the *Viking Star* and *Viking Sea* were the largest ships to squeeze through the Thames Barrier in 2015 and 2016. Passenger numbers along the river, such as on trip boats and river buses, exceeded 10 million for the first time in 2015. The current target set by the Mayor of London is to reach 12 million. Various new piers and pier extensions have been planned accordingly.

Significant investment is being made in the Port infrastructure by private enterprise and the PLA, with around one billion pounds planned in the five years to 2020, notably at Tilbury and London Gateway. These include facilities to handle bulk liquids, in passenger piers, for cruise ships, and for new vessels. In 2015 the £7 million multi-purpose mooring maintenance vessel *London Titan* was launched, the largest single investment by the PLA in two decades. The PLA are encouraging the opening of new independent wharves in order to achieve their goal. With a shortage of land for residential use in the South East of England, and the attractiveness of riverside locations, there is the temptation for private wharf-owners to sell off their sites. In order to preserve the Port and reduce road traffic, the PLA have worked with the mayors of London and the government to secure those sites for continuing commercial and passenger use under planning regulations. A report in 2005 listed 25 wharves upstream of the Thames Barrier and a further 25 below it, from Fulham to Erith, requiring protection.

The City of London has long been dominant in global maritime finance and insurance. Many of the contracts that match ships and cargoes around the world are brokered in the City. In addition to its well-established facilities and institutions, London has the advantage of being in a convenient time zone between East and West and of a globally-spoken business language. Yet these maritime businesses have in recent years been in danger of moving abroad, most notably to Singapore, which has offered attractive tax breaks. In November 2016 the City's Baltic Exchange, where shipping contracts have been agreed since the mid-eighteenth century, was acquired by the Singapore Exchange. In May 2016 the British electorate voted in a national referendum to leave the European Union, a process dubbed as 'Brexit'. No doubt there will be challenges and opportunities as a result. The possibility of offering globally competitive tax breaks and reducing excessive bureaucracy are examples of the opportunities that may exist in a future outside the European Union. I asked Perry Glading of the Port of Tilbury whether Brexit will have any major effect on his trade. 'About 60% of our business [at Tilbury] is with Europe,' he pointed out. 'Will Brexit change that? There's the million dollar question. It will have a change of some description. I think the core of our business is likely to remain with Europe. Whether that becomes 55% as opposed to 60%, I don't know. When I look forward, as to how we trade, I would say that will not materially change in the foreseeable future, Brexit or not.'

If you want to see ocean-going cargo ships on the Thames today, they are best viewed passing Gravesend on their way into Tilbury and the other nearby wharves. The larger vessels may not be as charming as those of the past but they are still an impressive sight. All the old docks and wharves of the Upper Port have long since closed. The massive cranes that lined them have been dismantled. You will no longer hear the sounds of ships' horns in the East End. Large ocean-going cargo vessels do not venture further upstream than Tate & Lyle at Silvertown. There is no longer waterside industry between Deptford and London Bridge and commercial riverside activity now begins downstream from around Greenwich. Is it possible that, despite the efforts of the PLA, urban London will in the future continue to expand eastwards, driving maritime industry off the Thames altogether?

Visit the tidal Thames today and look closely. You can still spot a few clues to the existence of what was there in the past: traces of former dock entrance locks and old dock warehouses; some old wharves around Wapping, Limehouse, Bermondsey and Rotherhithe that have been converted into apartments; parts of the West India Docks as a water feature surrounding the gleaming skyscrapers of Canary Wharf; St Katharine's and Regent's Canal Docks as yacht marinas; and London City Airport in the former Royal Albert and King George V Docks. The river police still operate from the same base at Wapping Stairs as they have done for 200 years. Many of the stations on the Docklands Light Railway remind us of London's maritime heritage, notably West India Quay, Canary Wharf, East India, Royal Victoria, Royal Docks, Royal Albert, and King George V. The river is more open and accessible than in its commercial heyday; there are gaps between buildings and the banks less densely crowded. Where the public were previously forbidden they are now welcome and can enjoy the views from riverside paths.

A century ago, as Sir Joseph Broodbank was writing his book *History of the Port of London*, a major expansion of the Port was taking place. The King George V Dock was then being constructed as an extension of the Royal Albert. Broodbank had previously been the Secretary of the London & India Docks Company and a founder board member of the Port of London Authority. He was therefore very familiar with the vast and bustling docks and wharves that stretched from London Bridge to North Woolwich and further down the tideway at Tilbury. He understood that the earlier dock operators before him could not possibly have foreseen the transition ahead of them, especially from wood and sail to iron and steam vessels, which progressively revolutionized the Port. Broodbank looked back on 1,900 years of history and stated with confidence: 'The future of the Port of London is as secure as the future of any human institution can be.' But he was not able to predict the great change ahead of him, from sacks, crates and barrels, to containers and bulk carrying, that would kill the Upper Port he knew so well. Nor could he have known that during the following century air transport would have such a big effect on both passenger travel and the movement of cargo. Our generation can only take a guess at the changes in the next hundred years. One wonders what new science, technology and engineering, as well as shifts in economies and politics, lie ahead that may bring fundamental differences to shipping and the world's ports.

Selective Bibliography

The following printed works have been consulted to varying degrees:

Barber, Peter, *London: A History in Maps*, 2012

Barron, Caroline M., *London in the Later Middle Ages, Government and People 1200–1500*, 2004

Bates, L.M., *The Thames on Fire*, 1985

Bell, Beresford, *The French in London and their Woad and Wine Business 1200–1500*, Royal Holloway College

Bird, James, *The Geography of the Port of London*, 1957

Bolton, J.L., *The Medieval Economy 1150–1500*, 1985

Broodbank, Sir Joseph, *History of the Port of London*, 1921

Brooke, Christopher, *London 800–1216: The Shaping of a City*, 1975

Bryant, Arthur, *Liquid History*, 1960

Canny, Nicholas (ed.), *The Oxford History of the British Empire – the Origins of Empire*, 1998

Carus-Wilson, E.M., *Medieval Merchant Venturers*, 1954, 1967

Cobb, H.S. (ed.), *The Overseas Trade of London: Exchequer Customs Accounts 1480–1*, 1990

Cooper, Michael, *Robert Hooke and the Rebuilding of London*, 2003

Cowie, L.W., 'The Steelyard of London', *History Today*, November 1975

Cowie, Robert, Lyn Blackmore etc., *Lundenwic – Excavations in Middle Saxon London 1987–2000*, 2012

Crawford, Anne, *A History of the Vintners' Company*, 1977

Croft, Pauline (ed.), *The Spanish Company*, London Record Society, 1973

Cunningham, Peter, *Handbook of London*, 1850

Defoe, Daniel, *A Tour Through the Whole Island of Great Britain*, 1724–1726

Dickens, Charles, *The Uncommercial Traveller*, 1861

Dietz, Brian (ed.), *The Port and Trade of Early Elizabethan London*, London Record Society, 1972

Dyson, Tony, 'Two Saxon Land Grants for Queenhithe', 1978

Ellmers, Chris and Werner, Alex, *London's Lost Riverscape*, 1988

Epstein, M. *The Early History of the Levant Company*, 1908

Essex-Lopresti, Michael, *Exploring the Regent's Canal*, 1987–1994

Friel, Ian, *Maritime History of Britain and Ireland*, 2003

Gairdner, James (ed.), *Gregory's Chronicle: 1427–1434, The Historical Collections of a Citizen of London in the Fifteenth Century*, 1876

Godden, Malcolm, and Simon Keynes (eds.), *Anglo-Saxon England*, Vol. 34, Cambridge, 2005

Gray, Robert, *Cardinal Manning*, 1985

Harding, Vanessa and Laura Wright (eds.), *London Bridge: Selected Accounts and Rentals, 1381–1538*, London Record Society, 1995

Harris, C.G., *The Trinity House of Deptford 1516–1660*, 1969

Hobhouse, Hermione (ed.), *The Survey of London*, Volumes 43 and 44, 1994

Huelin, Gordon, *Vanished Churches of the City of London*, 1996

Humphrey, Stephen, *The Story of Rotherhithe*, 1980

James, Margery Kirkbride (ed. Elspeth M. Veale), *Studies in the Medieval Wine Trade*, 1971

Keane, Derek, Arthur Burns and Andrew Saint (eds.), *St Paul's, The Cathedral Church of England 604–2004*, 2004

Keay, John, *A History of India*, 2000

Kim, Keechang, *Aliens in Medieval Law*, 2000

Lemmerman, Mick, *The Isle of Dogs During World War II*

Llewellyn Smith, H, and Nash, Vaughn, *The Story of the Dockers' Strike*, 1889

Lloyd, T.H., *England and the German Hanse 1157–1611*, 1991

Lloyd, T.H., *The English Wool Trade in the Middle Ages*, 1977

Marsden, Peter, *Ships of the Port of London, First to Eleventh centuries AD*, 1994

Marsden, Peter, *Ships of the Port of London, Twelfth to Seventeenth centuries AD*, 1996

Marshall, Geoff, *London's Docklands, An Illustrated Guide*, 2008

Mayhew, Henry, *London Labour and the London Poor*, 1851

Edward Miller, Edward and Hatcher, John, *Medieval England: Towns, Commerce and Crafts 1086–1348*, 1995

Milne, Gustav, *The Port of Medieval London*, 2003

Milne, Gustav, *The Port of Roman London*, 1985

Morris, John, *Londinium - London in the Roman Empire*, 1982

Norman, Philip, *Notes on the Later History of the Steelyard in London*, 1909

Owen, D.J., *The Port of London – Yesterday and Today*, 1927

Pepys, Samuel, *The Diary of Samuel Pepys, 1660–1669* (Penguin Classics Edition)

Picard, Liza, *Elizabeth's London*, 2003

Picard, Liza, *Restoration London*, 1997

Porter, Roy, *London: A Social History*, 1998

Price, John Edward, *Reminiscences of the Steelyard Formerly in Upper Thames Street*, Middlesex Archaeological Society, 1856

Pudney, John, *London's Docks*, 1975

Richardson, John, *The Annals of London*, 2000

Riley, Henry Thomas (ed.), *Chronicles of the Mayors and Sheriffs of London 1188–1274*, 1863

Riley, Henry Thomas (ed.), *Munimenta Gildhallae Londoniensis*, 1859–1862

Robins, Nick, *The Corporation That Changed the World*, 2012

Rose, Millicent, *The East End of London*, 1951

Rule, Fiona, *London's Docklands, A History of a Lost Quarter*, 2009

Schofield, John, *London 1100–1600*, 2011

Sellers, Maud (ed.), *The Acts and Ordinances of the Eastland Company*, 1906

Shane, Leslie, *Henry Edward Manning: His Life and Labours*, 1885

Stowe, John, *A Survey of London*, 1598

Summerson, John, *Georgian London*, 1945, 2003

Thornbury, Walter, *Old and New London*, 1897

Thrupp, Sylvia, *The Merchant Class of Medieval London 1300–1500*, 1948

Tinniswood, Adrian, *By Permission of Heaven*, 2003

Vallance, Edward, *The Glorious Revolution*, 2006

Waller, Maureen, *1700 – Scenes from a London Life*, 2000

Ward, Robert, *The Man Who Buried Nelson*, 2007

Watson, Nigel, *A Century of Service 1909–2009 – The Port of London Authority*, 2009

Webb, Simon, *Life in Roman London*, 2011

Welch, Charles (with J. Wolfe Barry), *History of the Tower Bridge*, 1894

West, Christopher, *The Story of St. Katharine's*, 2014

West, Richard, *Daniel Defoe – The Life and Strange, Surprising Adventures*, 1998

Wheatley, Henry Benjamin, *London Past and Present: Its History, Associations and Traditions*, 1891

White, Jerry, *London in the 18th Century*, 2012

White, Jerry, *London in the 19th Century*, 2008

White, Jerry, *London in the 20th Century*, 2001

Williams, Montagu, *Down East and Up West*, 1894

Williams, Roger, *London's Lost Global Giant*, 2015

Also:

A Map of Tudor London 1520, Historic Towns Trust, 2008

Liber Albus, compiled by John Carpenter, 1419, translated by Henry Thomas Riley, 1861

PLA 16 – Port of London Authority Handbook 2016, Compass Publications, 2016

The Origin and Early History of the Muscovy Company, 1830

The Port of London – Official Handbook of the PLA, 1963

The Thames Police History, Dicky Paterson 1996, John Joslin 2011

The Works of the Right Honourable Joseph Addison Vol. III, 1811

Index